AF825692

India: A Pocket Book of Data Series

India

A Pocket Book of Data Series

2012

EPW Research Foundation

ACADEMIC FOUNDATION
NEW DELHI

www.academicfoundation.com

First published in 2012
by

ACADEMIC FOUNDATION
4772-73 / 23 Bharat Ram Road, (23 Ansari Road),
Darya Ganj, New Delhi - 110 002 (India).
Tel : +91-11-23245001 / 02 / 03 / 04.
Fax : +91-11-23245005.
E-mail : books@academicfoundation.com
www. academicfoundation.com

in association with

EPW Research Foundation
(Unit of Sameeksha Trust)
E-mail: epwrf@vsnl.com

Cataloging in Publication Data--DK
Courtesy: D.K. Agencies (P) Ltd. <docinfo@dkagencies.com>

India : a pocket book of data series, 2012 / EPW Research Foundation.
p. cm.
ISBN 13: 9788171889334
ISBN 10: 8171889336

1. India--Economic conditions--1947- --Statistics. 2. India--Social conditions--1947- --Statistics. I. Economic and Political Weekly Research Foundation.

DDC 330.954 23

Design and typesetting : Italics India, New Delhi.
Printed and bound in India.

10 9 8 7 6 5 4 3 2 1

Contents

Money & Banking

Regional Rural Banks

Capital Market

Corporate Statistics

Price Trends / Inflation

Government Finance - Centre

Government Finance - State

Government Finance - Centre and State

External Sector

II. Social Sector

Demography

Population

Vital Rates

Health & Family Welfare

Housing

Living Standard

Education

Law & Order

Trade Union

Mass Media

Insurance

Employment

I. Infrastructure

Land Use Pattern

Mineral

Electricity

IV. Profile of States

Population

Vital Rates

Education

Employment

Standard of Living

Health Infrastructure

Housing and Amenities

V. International Comparisons

People

Foreword

EPW Research Foundation (EPWRF), set up in January 1993, as a sister unit of Economic & Political Weekly under the Sameeksha Trust has been engaged in research on financial and macroeconomic issues in India. Over the years, the EPWRF has in particular been focussing upon systematic compilation and dissemination of current and long-term data series pertaining to several critical macro and sectoral dimensions of the Indian economy. These data sets are being disseminated along with underlying concepts and methods and procedure of data compilation. The foundation has so far either published or put on its website about 30 sets of long-term data series.

Building upon the strength and expertise on data base studies, EPWRF has decided to come out with a handy pocket book of data series with the objective of providing a ready reference for critical socioeconomic data series on India. The pocket book contains a comprehensive set of tables conveniently divided into five parts: I. Macro-economy, II. Social Sector, III. Infrastructure, IV. Profile of States and V. International Comparison. Attempt has been made to provide data at convenient intervals between 1950-1951 to 2000-01 and on annual basis thereafter.

The data series have been mainly drawn from official sources meticulously compiled from scattered publications of various ministries and websites. For international comparison, data were sourced from the publications/ websites of multilateral institutions such as the International Monetary Fund, World Bank and Food and Agriculture Organization.

The feedback received for the maiden issue of the publication for 2010-11 showed overwhelming response from academics and official circles. The current (Second) issue is an updated version for 2012 which takes into account some suggestions made for its improvement and comes out with a simplified design and at a more affordable price. The release date has been advanced by several months to maintain timeliness. We hope that the publication would continue to be found useful by academics, executives, students and researchers and public at large.

I record my wholehearted commendation to R. Krishnaswamy who worked on this publication with a single-minded devotion, ably supported by Rema K. Nair, Rajesh Ambadaskar, Pravin S. Jadhav, Shruti J. Pandey and K. Srinivasan. I also acknowledge with grateful thanks the suggestions and the continued support received from the trustees of the Sameeksha Trust.

K. Kanagasabapathy
Director, EPW Research Foundation

I. MACRO ECONOMY

- National Income
- Agriculture
- Horticulture and Allied Activities
- Industry
- Money & Banking
- Regional Rural Banks
- Capital Market
- Corporate Statistics
- Price Trends / Inflation
- Government Finance - Centre
- Government Finance - State
- Government Finance - Centre and State
- External Sector

1 : Gross Domestic Product (GDP) at Factor Cost

	GDP (Rs. crore)	Decadal/Annual Growth (%)	Per Capita (Rs.)	GDP (Rs. crore)	Decadal/Annual Growth (%)	Per Capita (Rs.)
Series with Base Year 1999-2000		(At 1999-2000 Prices)			(At Current Prices)	
1950-51*	224786		6261	9719		271
1960-61*	329825	3.9	7600	16512	5.7	380
1970-71*	474131	3.8	8764	42981	10.2	794
1980-81*	641921	3.2	9454	132520	12.1	1952
1990-91*	1083572	5.4	12915	515032	14.6	6139
2000-01*	1864300	5.6	18296	1925017	14.1	18891
2004-05	2388768	7.4	21935	2877701	13.4	26425
New Series with Base Year 2004-05		(At 2004-05 Prices)			(At Current Prices)	
2004-05	2971464		27286	2971464		27286
2005-06	3254216	9.5	29423	3389621	14.1	30648
2006-07	3566011	9.6	31783	3952241	16.6	35225
2007-08	3898958	9.3	34261	4581422	15.9	40259
2008-09	4162509	6.8	36070	5282086	15.3	45772
2009-10 QE	4493743	8.0	38408	6133230	16.1	52421
2010-11 RE	4877842	8.5	41129	7306990	19.1	61610

Note : * : Growth for rows from 1950-51 to 2000-01 is compounded annual growth rate over the decade. Growth for subsequent yearly periods is annual growth rates.

RE : Revised Estimates.

QE : Quick Estimates.

Source : Central Statistical Office.

2 : Gross Domestic Product (GDP) at Market Prices

(Rs. crore)

	GDP (Rs. crore)	Decadal/Annual Growth (%)	Per Capita (Rs.)	GDP (Rs. crore)	Decadal/Annual Growth (%)	Per Capita (Rs.)
Series with Base Year 1999-2000		(At 1999-2000 Prices)			(At Current Prices)	
1950-51*	236067		6576	10085		281
1960-61*	350117	4.0	8067	17407	9.5	401
1970-71*	517148	4.0	9559	46249	10.4	855
1980-81*	695361	3.1	10241	145370	11.3	2141
1990-91*	1193650	5.6	14227	569624	14.7	6789
2000-01*	2030711	5.5	19928	2102314	14.0	20631
2004-05	2602065	8.3	23894	3149407	14.3	28920
New Series with Base Year 2004-05		(At 2004-05 Prices)			(At Current Prices)	
2004-05	3242209		29772	3242209		29772
2005-06	3544348	9.3	32047	3692485	13.9	33386
2006-07	3872974	9.3	34518	4293672	16.3	38268
2007-08	4253184	9.8	37374	4986426	16.1	43817
2008-09	4462967	4.9	38674	5582623	12.0	48376
2009-10QE	4869317	9.1	41618	6550271	17.3	55985
2010-11RE	5298129	8.5	44672	7875627	20.2	66405

Note: * : Growth for rows from 1950-51 to 2000-01 is compounded annual growth rate over the decade. Growth for subsequent yearly periods is annual growth rates.
RE : Revised Estimates.
QE : Quick Estimates.

Source: Central Statistical Office.

3 : GDP by Economic Activity (Constant Prices)

	Agriculture, Forestry & Fishing		Industry		Services	
	Rs. crore	% to GDP	Rs. crore	% to GDP	Rs. crore	% to GDP
Series with 1999-2000 as Base Year						
1950-51*	123884	55.3	33796	15.1	66417	29.6
1960-61*	166954	50.8	61620	18.8	99992	30.4
1970-71*	209843	44.3	104661	22.1	159088	33.6
1980-81*	243421	37.9	154340	24.0	244159	38.0
1990-91*	339893	31.4	280882	25.9	462797	42.7
2000-01*	445403	23.9	480961	25.8	937937	50.3
2004-05	482910	20.2	626663	26.2	1279195	53.5
New Series with 2004-05 as Base Year						
2004-05	565426	19.0	829783	27.9	1576255	53.0
2005-06	594487	18.3	910397	28.0	1749332	53.8
2006-07	619190	17.4	1021170	28.6	1925651	54.0
2007-08	655080	16.8	1119863	28.7	2124015	54.5
2008-09	654118	15.7	1168920	28.1	2339471	56.2
2009-10QE	656975	14.6	1261999	28.1	2574769	57.3
2010-11RE	700390	14.4	1361263	28.0	2816190	57.9

Note : * : Growth for rows from 1950-51 to 2000-01 is compounded annual growth rate over the decade. Growth for subsequent yearly periods is annual growth rates.
Industry includes mining and quarrying, manufacturing, electricity and construction.
Services includes trade, hotels and communication, financing, insurance, real estate and business service and community, social & personal services.
RE : Revised Estimates.
QE : Quick Estimates.

Source : Central Statistical Organisation.

4 : GDP by Economic Activity (Current Prices)

	Agriculture, Forestry & Fishing		Industry		Services	
	Rs. crore	% to GDP	Rs. crore	% to GDP	Rs. crore	% to GDP
Series with 1999-2000 as Base Year						
1950-51*	5080	52.6	1403	14.5	3181	32.9
1960-61*	7090	42.9	3242	19.6	6214	37.6
1970-71*	18192	42.4	8935	20.8	15777	36.8
1980-81*	47312	35.7	32716	24.7	52491	39.6
1990-91*	150800	29.3	138459	26.9	225773	43.8
2000-01*	449565	23.4	504137	26.2	971315	50.5
2004-05	552422	19.2	811078	28.2	1514201	52.6
New Series with 2004-05 as Base Year						
2004-05	565426	19.0	829783	27.9	1576255	53.0
2005-06	637772	18.8	953872	28.1	1797977	53.0
2006-07	722984	18.3	1140197	28.8	2089060	52.9
2007-08	836518	18.3	1330276	29.0	2414628	52.7
2008-09	928943	17.6	1490444	28.2	2862699	54.2
2009-10QE	1089297	17.8	1653870	27.0	3390063	55.3
2010-11RE	1386882	19.0	1920751	26.1	3999357	54.9

Note: * : Growth for rows from 1950-51 to 2000-01 is compounded annual growth rate over the decade. Growth for subsequent yearly periods is annual growth rates.
Industry includes mining and quarrying, manufacturing, electricity and construction.
Services includes trade, hotels and communication, financing, insurance, real estate and business service and community, social & personal services.
RE : Revised Estimates.
QE : Quick Estimates.

Source: Central Statistical Office.

5 : Private Final Consumption Expenditure (PFCE) by Object

	PFCE (Rs. crore)	Decadal/ Annual Growth (%)	Percentage Share in PFCE				
			Food	Clothing	Rent, Fuel and Transport	Medical Expenses	Education
			PFCE at Current Prices				
Series with 1999-2000 as Base Year							
1950-51*	9643		61.0	3.4	25.9	1.1	0.6
1960-61*	16312	(5.6)	51.3	4.6	29.7	1.5	0.9
1970-71*	39493	(9.4)	55.9	4.8	23.5	1.8	1.0
1980-81*	120094	(12.0)	52.2	6.1	21.6	2.9	1.3
1990-91*	392142	(12.6)	47.7	5.7	25.0	2.0	1.6
2000-01*	1345583	(14.3)	41.3	5.3	26.9	4.8	2.0
2004-05	1848110	8.5	36.4	4.5	29.3	5.4	2.3
New Series with 2004-05 as Base Year							
2004-05	1925592		33.8	5.6	33.1	5.0	1.7
2005-06	2159434	12.1	33.1	5.9	32.6	4.9	1.7
2006-07	2488410	15.2	31.7	6.5	32.2	4.7	1.6
2007-08	2850088	14.5	31.4	5.9	31.2	4.5	1.6
2008-09PE	3266461	14.6	30.1	5.6	31.3	4.3	1.6
2009-10QE	3795901	16.2	29.7	5.3	31.8	4.1	1.6

Note : * : Growth for rows from 1950-51 to 2000-01 is compounded annual growth rate over the decade. Growth for subsequent yearly periods is annual growth rates.
PE : Provisional Estimates.
QE : Quick Estimates.
AE : Advance Estimates.

Source : Central Statistical Office.

6 : Gross Domestic Saving (GDS) at Current Prices: Aggregate and by Type of Institution

	GDS (Rs. crore)	Rate (% to GDP)	*of which:* Household Sector (Rs. crore)	Household Sector Rate	Private Sector (Rs. crore)	Private Sector Rate	Public Sector (Rs. crore)	Public Sector Rate
Series with 1999-2000 as Base Year								
1950-51	871	8.6	578	5.7	93	1.0	200	2.0
1960-61	1952	11.2	1136	6.5	281	1.6	535	3.1
1970-71	6571	14.2	4371	9.5	672	1.5	1528	3.3
1980-81	26881	18.5	18724	12.9	2339	1.6	5818	4.0
1990-91	130010	22.8	104789	18.4	15164	2.7	10057	1.8
2000-01	499033	23.7	454853	21.6	81062	3.9	(36882)	(1.8)
2004-05	997874	31.7	716875	22.8	212048	6.7	68951	2.2
New Series with 2004-05 as Base Year								
2004-05	1050703	35.4	763685	25.7	212519	7.2	74499	2.5
2005-06	1235288	36.4	869176	25.6	277157	8.2	88955	2.6
2006-07	1486044	37.6	994631	25.2	338484	8.6	152929	3.9
2007-08	1837498	40.1	1119829	24.4	468707	10.2	248962	5.4
2008-09PE	1798347	34.0	1331033	25.2	438376	8.3	28938	0.5
2009-10QE	2207423	36.0	1536071	25.0	531403	8.7	139949	2.3

Source : Central Statistical Office.

7 : Gross Domestic Saving (GDS): Share of Household Sector

	GDS (Rs. crore)	Household Sector Saving		of which: Financial Savings		Physical Assets	
		(Rs. crore)	(% to GDP)	(Rs. crore)	Share in Household Sector Savings (%)	(Rs. crore)	Share in Household Sector Savings (%)
Series with 1999-2000 as Base Year							
1950-51	871	578	5.7	62	10.7	516	89.3
1960-61	1952	1136	6.5	456	40.1	680	59.9
1970-71	6571	4371	9.5	1371	31.4	3000	68.6
1980-81	26881	18724	12.9	8610	46.1	10114	54.0
1990-91	130010	104789	18.4	49640	47.4	55149	52.6
2000-01	499033	454853	21.6	215219	47.3	239634	52.7
2004-05	997874	716875	22.8	317547	44.3	399328	55.7
New Series with 2004-05 as Base Year							
2004-05	1050703	763685	25.7	327956	42.9	435729	57.1
2005-06	1235288	869176	25.6	438331	50.4	430845	49.6
2006-07	1486044	994631	25.2	484303	48.7	510328	51.3
2007-08	1837498	1119829	24.4	581935	52.0	537894	48.0
2008-09PE	1798347	1331033	25.2	600141	45.1	730892	54.9
2009-10QE	2207423	1536071	25.0	771527	50.2	764544	49.8

Source: Central Statistical Office.

8 : Gross Capital Formation (Unadjusted) at Current Prices

(Rs. crore)

	Total Capital Formation by Industry of Use	Rate (% to GDP)	Agriculture	Rate (% to GDP)	Manufacturing (Registered)	Rate (% to GDP)	Infrastructure	Rate (% to GDP)
Series with 1999-2000 as Base Year								
1950-51	1037	10.3	178 **17.1**	1.8	215 **20.7**	2.1	203 **19.5**	2.0
1960-61	2511	14.4	296 **11.8**	1.7	768 **30.6**	4.4	582 **23.2**	3.3
1970-71	7211	15.6	1109 **15.4**	2.4	1810 **25.1**	3.9	1771 **24.6**	3.8
1980-81	26964	18.5	4146 **15.4**	2.9	4008 **14.9**	2.8	8384 **31.1**	5.8
1990-91	137598	24.2	14596 **10.6**	2.6	30295 **22.0**	5.3	39550 **28.7**	6.9
2000-01	493285	23.5	40048 **8.1**	1.9	86647 **17.6**	4.1	136236 **27.6**	6.5
2004-05	955046	30.3	61285 **6.4**	1.9	256350 **26.8**	8.1	219690 **23.0**	7.0

contd...

...contd...

	Total Capital Formation by Industry of Use	Rate (% to GDP)	Agriculture	Rate (% to GDP)	Manufacturing (Registered)	Rate (% to GDP)	Infrastructure	Rate (% to GDP)
New Series with 2004-05 as Base Year								
2004-05	1011178	31.2	69148	2.1	245984	7.6	212681	6.6
			6.8		**24.3**		**21.0**	
2005-06	1224853	33.2	81895	2.2	352996	9.6	265801	7.2
			6.7		**28.8**		**21.7**	
2006-07	1491040	34.7	90400	2.1	408453	9.5	335549	7.8
			6.1		**27.4**		**22.5**	
2007-08	1842971	37.0	112356	2.3	583837	11.7	413101	8.3
			6.1		**31.7**		**22.4**	
2008-09	1901322	34.1	150452	2.7	445492	8.0	445328	8.0
			7.9		**23.4**		**23.4**	
2009-10	2230805	34.1	170230	2.6	580381	8.9	541163	8.3
			7.6		**26.0**		**24.3**	

Note : Infrastructure investment is the summation of the investment in mining & quarrying, electricity, gas & water supply, construction and transport and equipments. Figures in bold below each line are percentages to total GCF.

Source : Central Statistical Office.

9 : Net Capital Stock

(Rs. crore)

End-March	Net Capital Stock	Public Sector	Private Sector		Average Capital Output Ratio* (ACOR)** Net Capital Stock to Output			Incremental Capital Output Ratio (ICOR)	
			Private Corporate Sector	Household Sector	Total	Public Sector	Private Sector	NDCF to Output*	NFCF to Output***
Series with 2004-05 as Base Year Constant Prices									
2005	9325629	3394064	2234370	3697195					
2006	10162674	3564427	2596273	4001974	3.05	5.77	2.42	2.70	3.07
2007	11158662	3771783	3043563	4343316	3.06	5.59	2.47	2.88	3.33
2008	12323856	4031621	3625599	4666636	3.07	5.56	2.51	2.97	3.48
2009	13514747	4328000	4092271	5094476	3.23	5.33	2.72	5.79	6.32
2010	14700599	4645250	4547811	5507538	3.24	4.99	2.79	2.93	3.41

contd...

...contd...

End-March	Net Capital Stock	Public Sector	Private Sector		Average Capital Output Ratio* (ACOR)** Net Capital Stock to Output			Incremental Capital Output Ratio	
			Private Corporate Sector	Household Sector	Total	Public Sector	Private Sector	NDCF to Output*	NFCF to Output***
Series with 1999-2000 as Base Year Current Prices									
2005	9325629	3394064	2234370	3697195					
2006	10529765	3708043	2677933	4143789	2.98	5.82	2.35	1.86	2.12
2007	12256314	4166344	3283475	4806495	2.94	5.73	2.34	1.69	1.96
2008	14338731	4706109	4092393	5540229	2.95	5.77	2.37	1.85	2.17
2009	16958893	5450275	4932622	6575996	3.12	5.57	2.57	2.37	2.59
2010	19402011	6307830	5639214	7454967	3.08	5.31	2.57	1.55	1.80

Note : * : Average of beginning and year-end capital stock as ratio of the year's NDP at factor cost.
** : ACOR data for 1981 pertains to 1981-82, for 1991 it is 1990-91 and for 2001 it is 2000-01 and so on.
*** : Based on increase in NDP at Factor Cost.

Source : Central Statistical Office.

10 : Increases in Financial Assets and Liabilities of Household Sector

Year	Changes in Financial Assets (Gross Savings) (Rs. crore)	Currency		Bank Deposits		LIC, PF, Pension & Claims on Govt.		Others		Changes in Financial Liabilities (Rs. crore)	Net Savings (Rs. crore)
		(Rs. crore)	Share in %	(Rs. crore)	Share in %	(Rs. crore)	Share in %	(Rs. crore)	Share in %		
1970-71	2110	355	16.8	754	35.7	802	38.0	199	9.4	591	1519
1980-81	12118	1625	13.4	5550	45.8	3749	30.9	1194	9.9	3508	8610
1990-91	58908	6251	10.6	18777	31.9	24587	41.7	9243	15.7	9267	49641
2000-01	247475	15632	6.3	94709	38.3	123731	50.0	13401	5.4	31779	216614
2010-11	1043978	139344	13.3	463992	44.4	416031	39.9	24610	2.4	281334	762644

Note: Others include Non-Banking Deposits, Shares & Debentures, Unit of UTI and Trade Debt.
Source : Reserve Bank of India.

11 : All-India Area, Production and Yield: Food Grains

Year	Area (million hectares)	Production (million tonnes)	Yield (kg/ hectare)	Per cent Area under Irrigation
1950-51	97.3	50.8	522	18.1
1960-61	115.6	82.0	710	19.1
1970-71	124.3	108.4	872	24.1
1980-81	126.7	129.6	1023	29.7
1990-91	127.8	176.4	1380	35.1
2000-01	121.1	196.8	1626	43.4
2001-02	122.8	212.9	1734	43.0
2002-03	113.9	174.8	1535	42.8
2003-04	123.5	213.2	1727	42.2
2004-05	120.0	198.4	1652	44.2
2005-06	121.6	208.6	1715	45.5
2006-07	123.7	217.3	1756	46.3
2007-08	124.1	230.8	1860	46.8
2008-09	122.8	234.5	1909	na
2009-10	121.4	218.1	1798	na
2010-11$	na	241.6	na	na

Note: $: Fourth Advance Estimates as on 10-07-2011.
na : not available.

Source : Ministry of Agriculture.

12 : All-India Area, Production and Yield: Rice

Year	Area (million hectares)	Production (million tonnes)	Yield (kg/ hectare)	Per cent Area under Irrigation
1950-51	30.8	20.6	668	31.7
1960-61	34.1	34.6	1013	36.8
1970-71	37.6	42.2	1123	38.4
1980-81	40.1	53.6	1336	40.7
1990-91	42.7	74.3	1740	45.5
2000-01	44.7	85.0	1901	53.6
2001-02	44.9	93.3	2079	53.2
2002-03	41.2	71.8	1744	50.2
2003-04	42.6	88.5	2077	52.6
2004-05	41.9	83.1	1984	54.7
2005-06	43.7	91.8	2102	56.0
2006-07	43.8	93.4	2131	56.7
2007-08	43.9	96.7	2202	56.9
2008-09	45.4	99.2	2178	na
2009-10	41.9	89.1	2130	na
2010-11$	na	95.3	na	na

Note: $: Fourth Advance Estimates as on 10-07-2011.
na : not available.

Source : Ministry of Agriculture.

13 : All-India Area, Production and Yield: Wheat

Year	Area (million hectares)	Production (million tonnes)	Yield (kg/ hectare)	Per cent Area under Irrigation
1950-51	9.8	6.5	663	34.0
1960-61	12.9	11.0	851	32.7
1970-71	18.2	23.8	1307	54.3
1980-81	22.3	36.3	1630	76.5
1990-91	24.2	55.1	2281	81.1
2000-01	25.7	69.7	2708	88.1
2001-02	26.3	72.8	2762	87.4
2002-03	25.2	65.8	2610	88.0
2003-04	26.6	72.2	2713	88.4
2004-05	26.4	68.6	2602	89.4
2005-06	26.5	69.4	2619	89.6
2006-07	28.0	75.8	2708	90.2
2007-08	28.0	78.6	2802	90.9
2008-09	27.8	80.7	2907	na
2009-10	28.5	80.8	2830	na
2010-11$	na	85.9	na	na

Note : $: Fourth Advance Estimates as on 10-07-2011.
na : not available.

Source : Ministry of Agriculture.

14 : All-India Area, Production and Yield: Coarse Cereals

Year	Area (million hectares)	Production (million tonnes)	Yield (kg/ hectare)	Per cent Area under Irrigation
1950-51	37.7	15.4	408	7.9
1960-61	45.0	23.7	528	7.7
1970-71	46.0	30.6	665	8.3
1980-81	41.8	29.0	695	9.2
1990-91	36.3	32.7	900	9.0
2000-01	30.3	31.1	1027	12.5
2001-02	29.5	33.4	1131	11.3
2002-03	27.0	26.1	966	11.0
2003-04	30.8	37.6	1221	6.6
2004-05	29.0	33.5	1153	6.6
2005-06	29.0	34.1	1172	13.0
2006-07	28.7	33.9	1182	13.4
2007-08	28.5	40.8	1431	14.2
2008-09	27.5	40.0	1459	na
2009-10	27.6	33.6	1222	na
2010-11	na	42.2	na	na

Note : Coarse cereals includes *jowar*, *bajra*, maize, *ragi*, small millets and barley.
$: Fourth Advance Estimates as on 10-07-2011.
na : not available.

Source : Ministry of Agriculture.

15 : All-India Area, Production and Yield: Pulses

Year	Area (million hectares)	Production (million tonnes)	Yield (kg/ hectare)	Per cent Area under Irrigation
1950-51	19.1	8.4	441	9.4
1960-61	23.6	12.7	539	8.0
1970-71	22.6	11.8	524	8.8
1980-81	22.5	10.6	473	9.0
1990-91	24.7	14.3	578	10.5
2000-01	20.4	11.1	544	12.5
2001-02	22.0	13.4	607	13.3
2002-03	20.5	11.1	543	14.4
2003-04	23.5	14.9	635	13.6
2004-05	22.8	13.1	577	13.9
2005-06	22.4	13.4	598	15.0
2006-07	23.2	14.2	612	15.4
2007-08	23.6	14.8	625	16.2
2008-09	22.1	14.6	659	na
2009-10	23.4	14.7	625	na
2010-11$	na	18.1	na	na

Note : Pulses includes gram, *arhar, urad* and *moong.*
$: Fourth Advance Estimates as on 10-07-2011.
na : not available.
Source : Ministry of Agriculture.

16 : All-India Area, Production and Yield: Oilseeds

Year	Area (million hectares)	Production (million tonnes)	Yield (kg/ hectare)	Per cent Area under Irrigation
1950-51	10.7	5.2	481	na
1960-61	13.8	7.0	507	3.3
1970-71	16.6	9.6	579	7.4
1980-81	17.6	9.4	532	14.5
1990-91	24.1	18.6	771	22.9
2000-01	22.8	18.4	810	23.0
2001-02	22.6	20.7	913	24.3
2002-03	21.5	14.8	691	22.7
2003-04	23.7	25.2	1064	24.5
2004-05	27.5	24.4	885	26.6
2005-06	27.9	28.0	1004	28.0
2006-07	26.5	24.3	916	28.3
2007-08	26.7	29.8	1115	27.1
2008-09	27.6	27.7	1006	na
2009-10	26.1	24.9	955	na
2010-11$	na	31.1	na	na

Note : Oilseeds includes groundnut, rapeseed & mustard, castor seed, sesamum, nigerseed, linseed, safflower, sunflower and soyabean.
$: Fourth Advance Estimates as on 10-07-2011.
na : not available.
Source : Ministry of Agriculture.

17 : All-India Area, Production and Yield: Cotton

Year	Area (million hectares)	Production (million tonnes)	Yield (kg/ hectare)	Per cent Area under Irrigation
1950-51	5.9	3.0	88	8.2
1960-61	7.6	5.6	125	12.7
1970-71	7.6	4.8	106	17.3
1980-81	7.8	7.0	152	27.3
1990-91	7.4	9.8	225	32.9
2000-01	8.5	9.5	190	34.3
2001-02	9.1	10.0	186	34.0
2002-03	7.7	8.6	191	33.1
2003-04	7.6	13.7	307	27.1
2004-05	8.8	16.4	318	36.9
2005-06	8.7	18.5	362	36.1
2006-07	9.1	22.6	421	35.0
2007-08	9.4	25.9	467	35.1
2008-09	9.4	22.3	403	na
2009-10	10.3	24.2	395	na
2010-11	11.0	33.4	518	na

Note : $: Fourth Advance Estimates as on 10-07-2011.
na : not available.
Source : Ministry of Agriculture.

18 : All-India Area, Production and Yield: Sugarcane

Year	Area (million hectares)	Production (million tonnes)	Yield (kg/ hectare)	Per cent Area under Irrigation
1950-51	1.7	57.1	33	67.3
1960-61	2.4	110.0	46	69.3
1970-71	2.6	126.4	48	72.4
1980-81	2.7	154.2	58	81.3
1990-91	3.7	241.0	65	86.9
2000-01	4.3	296.0	69	92.1
2001-02	4.4	297.2	67	91.6
2002-03	4.5	287.4	64	91.3
2003-04	3.9	233.9	59	90.7
2004-05	3.7	237.1	65	91.2
2005-06	4.2	281.2	67	92.5
2006-07	5.2	355.5	69	93.2
2007-08	5.1	348.2	69	93.5
2008-09	4.4	285.0	65	na
2009-10	4..2	292.3	66	na
2010-11$	4.9	339.2	67	na

Note : $: Fourth Advance Estimates as on 10-07-2011.
na : not available.
Source : Ministry of Agriculture.

19 : Availability of Cereals and Pulses

Year	Net Quantity Available (million tonnes)		Per Capita Per Day (grams)		
	Cereals	Pulses	Cereals	Pulses	Food Grains
1950-51	44.8	8.0	334.2	60.7	394.9
1960-61	64.6	11.1	399.7	69.0	468.7
1970-71	84.0	10.3	417.6	51.2	468.8
1980-81	104.8	9.4	417.3	37.5	454.8
1990-01	145.7	12.9	468.5	41.6	510.1
2000-01	145.6	11.3	386.2	30.0	416.2
2001-02	175.9	13.6	458.7	35.4	494.1
2002-03	159.3	11.3	408.5	29.1	437.6
2003-04	169.1	14.2	426.9	35.8	462.7
2004-05	157.3	12.7	390.9	31.5	422.4
2005-06	168.8	13.3	412.8	32.5	445.3
2006-07	169.0	14.7	407.4	35.5	442.8
2007-08	165.9	17.6	394.2	41.8	436.0
2008-09*	173.7	15.8	407.0	37.0	444.0

Note: * : Provisional.

Net availability of food grains is estimated to be gross production (-) seed, wastage and feed (-) exports (+) imports, (+/-) change in stock.

Net availability is 82.5% of total production. The balance 12.5% provided for feed & seed requirements, plus imports minus exports and net changes in stocks.

Net availabilty divided by population and by 365 days gives net availability in terms of grams per day.

Source: Directorate of Economics & Statistics, Department of Agriculture and Cooperation & *Economic Survey 2010-11.*

20 : Availability, Procurement and Public Distribution of Food Grains

Year	Availability	Procurement		Public Distribution	
	(million tonnes)	(million tonnes)	Share (%)	(million tonnes)	Share (%)
1950-51	52.4	3.8	7.9	8.0	15.3
1960-61	75.7	0.5	0.7	4.0	5.3
1970-71	94.3	8.9	9.3	7.8	8.3
1980-81	114.3	13.0	11.4	11.4	10.0
1990-01	158.6	19.6	12.7	20.8	13.1
2000-01	156.9	42.6	24.7	13.2	8.4
2001-02	189.5	40.3	21.7	18.2	9.6
2002-03	170.6	34.5	22.6	23.2	13.2
2003-04	183.3	41.1	22.0	28.3	15.5
2004-05	170.0	41.5	23.9	31.0	18.2
2005-06	181.9	37.0	20.3	31.8	17.5
2006-07	183.7	35.8	18.8	32.8	17.8
2007-08	183.5	54.2	25.8	34.7	18.9
2008-09*	189.5	60.5	29.5	41.3	21.8

Note: * : Provisional.

Figures for procurement and distribution referes to respective calender years. and its share is with respect to total production of food grains.

Source: *Economic Survey 2010-11.*

21 : Per Capita Availability of Important Articles of Consumption

Year	Edible Oils (net) Kg	Sugar (kg)	Cloth (metres)	Tea (gram)	Coffee (gram)
1955-56	2.5	5.0	na	362.0	67.0
1960-61	3.2	4.8	15.0	296.0	80.0
1970-71	3.5	7.4	15.6	401.0	65.0
1980-81	3.8	7.3	17.3	511.0	79.0
1990-01	5.5	12.7	24.1	612.0	59.0
2000-01	8.2	15.8	30.7	631.0	58.0
2001-02	8.8	16.0	32.0	650.0	67.0
2002-03	7.2	16.3	31.4	623.0	67.0
2003-04	9.9	16.1	31.0	662.0	70.0
2004-05	10.2	15.5	33.5	663.0	72.0
2005-06	10.6	16.3	36.1	687.0	75.0
2006-07	11.1	16.8	39.6	687.0	77.0
2007-08	11.4	17.8	41.9	na	80.0
2008-09	12.7	18.8	39.0	na	82.0
2009-10*	13.1	18.6	43.1	na	85.0

Note: * : Provisional.

Tea and coffee data upto 1971-72 refer to coffee season, thereafter on calendar years. Sugar data are based on November-October season.

Source: *Economic Survey 2010-11.*

22 : Consumption of Fertilisers

Year	(Thousand Tonnes of Nutrients)			
	Nitrogenous	Phosphatic	Potassic	All
1950-51	59	7	0	66
1960-61	210	53	29	292
1970-71	1487	462	228	2177
1980-81	3678	1214	624	5516
1990-01	7997	3221	1328	12546
2000-01	10920	4215	1567	19702
2001-02	11310	4382	1667	17360
2002-03	10474	4019	1601	16094
2003-04	11076	4124	1598	16798
2004-05	11714	4624	2060	18398
2005-06	12723	5204	2413	20340
2006-07	13773	5543	2335	21652
2007-08	14419	5515	2636	22570
2008-09	15090	6506	3313	24909
2009-10	15580	7274	3632	26486

Source: *Economic Survey 2010-11.*

23 : Agriculture Subsidies

(Rs. crore)

Year	Food	Fertiliser	Electricity	Irrigation	Others
1999-00	9434	13244	6033	11196	3118
2000-01	12060	13800	8919	13465	2733
2001-02	17499	12595	10410	13009	3234
2002-03	24176	11015	8521	12794	3173
2003-04	25181	11847	14544	10921	4132
2004-05	25798	15879	17977	12290	3640
2005-06	23077	18460	19431	14280	5647
2006-07	24014	26222	19729	16978	4764
2007-08	31328	32490	20661	19457	15100
2008-09	43751	76603	27489	23665	33160
2009-10	58443	61264			
2010-11RE	60600	54976			
2011-12BE	60573	49998			

Note: BE: Budget Estimates, RE: Revised Estimates.

1. Others include subsidies given to marginal farmers.
2. Electricity subsidy to electricity boards, separate estimates for agriculture are not available.
3. The rates for supply of water to farmers are kept low as a matter of policy, resulting in losses to the government irrigation system. The excess of operating costs over the gross revenue is treated as imputed irrigation subsidy.

Source : Ministry of Agriculture.

24 : Distribution of Operational Holdings: All-India

Category of Holdings	No. of Operational Holdings ('000 number)		Area Operated ('000 hectares)		Average Size of Operational Holdings (hectares)	
	1995-96	2000-01	1995-96	2000-01	1995-96	2000-01
Marginal	71179	75408	28121	29814	0.40	0.40
(< 1 hectare)	**61.6**	**62.3**	**17.2**	**18.7**		
Small	21643	22695	30722	32139	1.42	1.42
(1.0 to 2.0 hectares)	**18.7**	**19.0**	**18.8**	**20.2**		
Semi-Medium	14261	14021	38953	38193	2.73	2.72
(2.0 to 4.0 hectares)	**12.3**	**11.8**	**23.8**	**24.0**		
Medium	7092	6577	41398	38217	5.84	5.81
(4.0 to 10.0 hectares)	**6.1**	**5.5**	**25.3**	**24.0**		
Large	1404	1230	24163	21072	17.21	17.12
(=> 10 hectares)	**1.2**	**1.0**	**14.8**	**13.2**		
All Holdings	115580	119931	163357	159436	1.41	1.33

Note : Figures in bold refer to per cent of total area.

Source : Agricultural Census Division, Ministry of Agriculture, New Delhi.

25 : Indian Horticulture: Area, Production and Yield

	Area (in '000 ha)	Production (in '000 tonnes)	Productivity (tonne/ha)
1991-92	12770	96562	7.56
1992-93	12903	107399	8.32
1993-94	13033	114661	8.80
1994-95	13080	118394	9.05
1995-96	13723	125483	9.14
1996-97	14362	128482	8.95
1997-98	14754	128611	8.72
1998-99	15103	146200	9.68
1999-00	15247	149224	9.79
2000-01	15694	150197	9.57
2001-02	16592	145785	8.79
2002-03	16270	144380	8.87
2003-04	19449	157835	8.12
2004-05	18445	166938	9.05
2005-06	19327	185207	9.58
2006-07	19389	191813	9.89
2007-08	20207	211235	10.45
2008-09	20662	214716	10.39
2009-10	20876	223089	10.69

Note : Horticulture includes fruits, vegetables, plantation crops, spices, flowers, nuts, honey, mushroom and aromatic & medicinal plants.

Source : Indian Horticulture Data Base 2010.

26 : Production of Selected Horticultural Crops

(in '000 tonnes)

	Fruits	Vegetables	Flowers (loose)	Nuts	Plantation Crops	Spices
1991-92	28632	58532			7498	1900
1992-93	32955	63806	233		8347	2291
1993-94	37255	65787	261		8866	2515
1994-95	38603	67286	334		9767	2477
1995-96	41507	71594	366		9630	2410
1996-97	40458	75074	366		9730	2805
1997-98	43263	72683	386		9449	2801
1998-99	44042	87536	419		11063	3091
1999-00	45496	90831	509	111	9278	3023
2000-01	43138	93850	556	122	9458	3023
2001-02	43001	88622	535	114	9697	3765
2002-03	45203	84815	735	114	9697	3765
2003-04	45645	93165	580	121	13161	5113
2004-05	50867	101246	659	121	9835	4001
2005-06	58740	109050	694	134	11263	5108
2006-07	59563	114993	880	150	12007	3953
2007-08	65587	128449	868	177	11300	4357
2008-09	68466	129077	987	173	11336	4145
2009-10	71516	133738	1021	193	11928	4016

Note : Fruits include banana, mango, orange, *mosambi*, lime, grapes, guava, litchi, papaya, pineapple, apple, pomegranate, sapota etc.

Vegetables include potato, onion, tomato, brinjal, cabbage, cauliflower, okra, peas, sweet potato, tapioca etc.

Spices include black pepper, chillies, ginger, turmeric, garlic etc.

Source : Indian Horticulture Data Base 2010.

27 : Production of Selected Fruits

(in '000 tonnes)

	Banana	Mango	Citrus Fruits	Others
1991-92	7790	8716	2822	9305
1992-93	10460	9223	2979	10293
1993-94	11901	10113	3912	11329
1994-95	13168	10993	3701	10741
1995-96	13095	10811	3798	13803
1996-97	12440	9981	4456	13581
1997-98	13340	10234	4311	15379
1998-99	15073	9782	4575	14613
1999-00	16814	10504	4651	13528
2000-01	14137	10057	4386	14558
2001-02	14210	10020	4789	13982
2002-03	13304	12733	5677	13488
2003-04	13857	11490	5787	14512
2004-05	16328	11830	5933	16776
2005-06	18702	12538	6326	21174
2006-07	20998	13734	7145	17686
2007-08	23823	13997	8015	19752
2008-09	26217	12750	8623	20876
2009-10	26470	15027	9638	20381

Note : Citrus fruits include lime, *mosambi*, orange.
Others include grapes, guava, litchi, papaya, pineapple, pomegranate, sapota, apple etc.

Source : Indian Horticulture Data Base 2010.

28 : Production of Selected Vegetables

(in '000 tonnes)

	Potato	Onion	Tomato	Brinjal	Others
1991-92	18195	4706	4243		31388
1992-93	18479	5705	4550		35073
1993-94	17392	4006	4934	4612	34842
1994-95	17401	4036	5261	6232	34355
1995-96	18843	4080	5442	6443	36786
1996-97	24216	4180	5788	6586	34305
1997-98	17652	3140	6184	7735	37972
1998-99	22495	5467	8272	7882	43421
1999-00	25000	4900	7427	8117	45387
2000-01	22243	4721	7242	7652	51992
2001-02	24456	5252	7462	8348	43104
2002-03	23161	4210	7617	8001	41826
2003-04	27926	6268	8126	8477	42369
2004-05	28788	7761	8825	8601	47272
2005-06	29094	9248	9362	9136	52210
2006-07	28600	10847	10055	9453	56038
2007-08	34658	13900	10303	9678	59910
2008-09	34391	13565	11149	10378	59594
2009-10	36577	12159	12433	10563	62006

Note : Others include cabbage, cauliflower, okra, peas, sweet potato, tapioca etc.

Source : Ministry of Agriculture.

29 : Production of Selected Livestock Products

	Milk (million tonnes)	Eggs (million numbers)	Fish ('000 tonnes)
1950-01	17.0	1832	752
1960-01	20.0	2881	1160
1970-01	22.0	6172	1756
1980-01	31.6	10060	2442
1990-01	53.9	21101	3836
2000-01	80.6	36632	5656
2001-02	84.4	38729	5956
2002-03	86.2	39823	6200
2003-04	88.1	40403	6399
2004-05	90.7	45201	6304
2005-06	97.1	46231	6572
2006-07	100.9	50653	6869
2007-08	104.8	53532	7127
2008-09	108.5	55638	7608
2009-10	112.5	59800	7850

Source : Department of Animal Husbandry and Dairying.

30 : Production of Selected Plantation Crops

	Tea* (million kg)	Coffee ('000 tonnes)	Natural Rubber ('000 tonnes)
1950-51	285		
1960-61	354		
1970-71	435		
1980-81	560		
1990-01	704	170	330
2000-01	847	301	630
2001-02	854	301	631
2002-03	846	275	649
2003-04	878	271	712
2004-05	907	276	750
2005-06	949	300	800
2006-07	973	300	900
2007-08	987	300	900
2008-09	973	300	900
2009-10	1000	300	800

Note: * : Calender year data for year ending December 1950 and so on.

Source : Tea, Coffee and Rubber Boards.

31 : Production of Selected Condiments and Spices

(in '000 tonnes)

	Black Pepper	Chillies	Dry Ginger	Turmeric
1990-01	48	719	154	342
2000-01	64	984	288	714
2001-02	62	1069	322	563
2002-03	64	897	280	574
2003-04	73	1235	302	565
2004-05	73	1186	359	718
2005-06	na	1015	391	852
2006-07	69	1015	377	836
2007-08	47	1294	390	794
2008-09	47	1270	380	821
2009-10	51	1203	385	793

Source: Ministry of Agriculture.

32 : India's Position in World Fruit & Vegetable Production

	2008-09			
	World (million tonnes)	India (million tonnes)	Share in World Production (%)	Rank
Fruits	*579.9*	*71.5*	*12.3*	*2*
Banana	93.4	26.5	28.4	1
Mango	34.9	17.6	50.4	1
Papaya	10.1	3.9	38.6	1
Pine Apple	19.3	1.4	7.3	6
Apple	69.8	1.8	2.6	8
Vegetables	*931.9*	*133.7*	*14.3*	*2*
Brinjal	34.0	10.2	30.0	2
Cabbage	69.7	7.3	10.5	2
Cauliflower	18.8	6.4	34.0	2
Okra	6.4	4.8	75.0	1
Onion	72.3	12.2	16.9	2
Potato	325.6	36.5	11.2	2
Tomato	136.2	12.4	9.1	3

Source: India Horticulture Data Base 2010.

33 : Index of Industrial Production: (Base 2004=100): Sector-wise and Use-Based Classification

Year	General Index	Industry: Sector-wise			Use-Based Classification of Industries					
		Mining & Quarrying	Manufacturing	Electricity	Basic Industries	Capital Goods Industries	Intermediate Goods Industries	Consumer Goods Industries	Consumer Durables	Consumer Non-Durables
Weight	100.0	14.2	75.5	10.3	45.7	8.8	15.7	29.8	8.5	21.3
Indices										
2005-06	108.6	102.3	110.3	105.2	106.1	118.1	106.6	110.7	116.2	108.6
2006-07	122.6	107.5	126.8	112.8	115.6	145.6	118.8	128.6	145.6	121.9
2007-08	141.7	112.5	150.1	120.0	125.9	216.2	127.5	151.2	193.8	134.3
2008-09	145.2	115.4	153.8	123.3	128.1	240.6	127.6	152.6	215.4	127.7
2009-10	152.9	124.5	161.3	130.8	134.1	243.0	135.3	164.3	252.0	129.5
2010-11	165.4	131.0	175.6	138.0	142.1	279.5	145.1	177.9	287.4	134.5

contd...

...contd...

Year	General Index	Industry: Sector-wise			Use-Based Classification of Industries					
		Mining & Quarrying	Manufacturing	Electricity	Basic Industries	Capital Goods Industries	Intermediate Goods Industries	Consumer Goods Industries	Consumer Durables	Consumer Non-Durables
Growth Rates (year-on-year)										
2005-06	8.6	2.3	10.3	5.2	6.1	18.1	6.6	10.7	16.2	8.6
2006-07	12.9	5.1	15.0	7.2	8.9	23.3	11.4	16.2	25.4	12.2
2007-08	15.6	4.7	18.4	6.4	8.9	48.5	7.3	17.6	33.1	10.2
2008-09	2.5	2.6	2.5	2.8	1.7	11.3	0.1	0.9	11.1	(5.0)
2009-10	5.3	7.9	4.9	6.1	4.8	1.0	6.0	7.7	17.0	1.4
2010-11	8.2	5.2	8.9	5.5	6.0	15.0	7.2	8.3	14.1	3.9

Note : IIP with new base 2004-05=100 introduced with effect from June 10, 2011.
Source : Central Statistical Office.

34 : Electronic Goods Production

(Rs. crore)

Year	Consumer Electronics	Industrial Electronics	Computers	Commercial Broadcasting & Equipments	Strategic Electronics	Components	Total Electronic Production	Software Production		Exports: Electronic Hardware
								for Exports	for Domestic	
Production in Rs. crore										
2000-01	11950	4000	3400	4500	1750	5500	31100	28350	9400	4788
2004-05	16800	8300	8800	4800	3000	8800	50500	80180	21740	8000
2005-06	18000	8800	10800	7000	3200	8800	56600	104100	29600	9625
2006-07	20000	10400	12800	9500	4500	8800	66000	141000	37000	12500
2007-08	22600	11910	15870	18700	5700	9630	84410	164400	47010	13200
2008-09	25550	12740	13490	26000	6840	12040	97260	216190	59000	31230
2009-10	30150	13630	14430	31390	6980	13360	109940	235080	66200	31250

contd...

...contd...

Year	Consumer Electronics	Industrial Electronics	Computers	Commercial Broadcasting & Equipments	Strategic Electronics	Components	Total Electronic Production	Software Production		Exports: Electronic Hardware
								for Exports	for Domestic	
Growth Rate (year-on-year)										
2005-06	7.1	6.0	22.7	45.8	6.7	0.0	12.1	29.8	36.2	20.3
2006-07	11.1	18.2	18.5	35.7	40.6	0.0	16.6	35.4	25.0	29.9
2007-08	13.0	14.5	24.0	96.8	26.7	9.4	27.9	16.6	27.1	5.6
2008-09	13.1	7.0	(15.0)	39.0	20.0	25.0	15.2	31.5	25.5	136.6
2009-10	18.0	7.0	7.0	20.7	2.0	11.0	13.0	8.7	12.2	0.1

Source : Department of Information Technology.

35 : Index of Industrial Production: Sector-wise and Use-Based Classification

Year	Base Period	General Index	Industry: Sector-wise (Growth %)			Use-Based Classification of Industries (Growth %)					
			Mining & Quarrying	Manufacturing	Electricity	Basic Industries	Capital Goods Industries	Intermediate Goods Industries	Consumer Goods Industries	Consumer Durables	Consumer Non-Durables
1956-60	1956=100	7.4	7.2	6.9	14.5	..	..	..	..	..	..
1961-70	1960=100	5.8	4.1	5.4	11.8	7.6	7.9	4.7	4.4	..	..
1971-80	1970=100	4.2	3.8	3.9	7.1	5.2	5.4	3.5	3.2	5.0	3.0
1981-90	1980-81=100	7.4	8.4	7.1	8.8	8.0	11.0	6.1	6.7	14.2	5.4
1991-00	1993-94=100	6.3	3.4	6.5	7.0	6.3	5.4	7.5	5.8	8.9	5.0
2000-10	1993-94=100	7.0	4.3	7.5	4.8	5.6	11.5	5.8	8.0	10.0	7.5

Note : Growth rate worked out by using calender year averages for the years 1956 to 1970 and then fiscal year averages.

Source : Central Statistical Office.

36 : Principal Characteristics of Factories (All-India)

Year	Number of Factories	Fixed Capital (Rs. crore)	Number of Employees ('000)	Value of Output (Rs. crore)	Gross Value Added (Rs. crore)	Gross Capital Formation (Rs. crore)
1970-71	64565	8752	5216	13768	3753	
1980-81	96503	29900	7715	61084	13846	7920
Growth (%)*	5.1	15.1	5.0	18.4	16.6	0.0
1990-91	110179	133648	8163	270564	61578	32559
Growth (%)*	1.4	14.9	0.6	16.1	15.3	14.7
2000-01	131268	399604	7918	926902	178350	61415
Growth (%)*	(0.2)	(0.6)	(2.8)	3.2	(5.4)	(5.0)
2005-06	140160	606940	9039	1908355	364697	171567
Growth (%)*	2.8	18.3	7.8	14.1	17.8	55.9
2006-07	144710	715131	10252	2408548	460180	199330
Growth (%)*	3.2	17.8	13.4	26.2	26.2	16.2
2007-08	146385	845132	10378	2775709	552756	262299
Growth (%)*	1.2	18.2	1.2	15.2	20.1	31.6
2008-09	155321	1055966	11253	3272798	611312	261585
Growth (%)*	6.1	24.9	8.4	17.9	10.6	(0.3)

Note: Figures in brackets represents negative value.

* : Values upto 2000-01 denote average annual growth rate for the decade; thereafter yearly rate.

Source: *Annual Survey of Industries* (Factory Sector).

37 : Performance of Micro, Small and Medium Enterprises (MSMEs)

	Number of MSMEs (in lakh)	Fixed Investment (Rs. crore)	Production (Rs. crore)	Employment (number in lakh)	Export (Rs. crore)
2000-01	101	146845	261297	239	69797
Growth %	4.1	4.9	11.8	4.2	28.8
2001-02	105	154349	282270	249	71244
Growth %	4.1	5.1	8.0	4.4	2.1
2002-03	110	162317	314850	260	86013
Growth %	4.1	5.2	11.5	4.4	20.7
2003-04	114	170219	364547	271	97644
Growth %	4.1	4.9	15.8	4.3	13.5
2004-05	119	178699	429796	283	124417
Growth %	4.0	5.0	17.9	4.1	27.4
2005-06	123	188113	497842	295	150242
Growth %	4.0	5.3	15.8	4.4	20.8
2006-07	261	500758	709398	595	182538
Growth %	111.5	166.2	42.5	101.6	21.5
2007-08	273	558190	790759	626	202017
Growth %	4.5	11.5	11.5	5.3	10.7
2008-09	285	621753	880805	659	na
Growth %	4.5	11.4	11.4	5.4	
2009-10	298	693835	982919	695	na
Growth %	4.5	11.6	11.6	5.5	

Note : na : not available.
Data upto 2005-06 refer to only Small Scale Industries (SSI). Subsequent to 2005-06 data refers to micro, small and medium industries.

Source : Ministry of Micro, Small and Medium Enterprises.

38 : Trends in Money Supply

(Rs. crore)

Year (as at end-March)	Money Supply (M3)		Currency with the Public		Deposit Money		As Per cent of GDP		
	Rs. crore	Growth (%)	Rs. crore	Growth (%)	Rs. crore	Growth (%)	Money Supply	Currency	Deposit Money
1950-51*	2352		1405		946		23.3	13.9	9.4
1960-61*	3964	5.4	2098	4.1	1865	7.0	22.8	12.1	10.7
1970-71*	11020	10.8	4371	7.6	6649	13.6	23.8	9.5	14.4
1980-81*	55774	17.6	13426	11.9	42348	20.3	38.4	9.2	29.1
1990-91*	265828	16.9	53048	14.7	212780	17.5	46.7	9.3	37.4
2000-01*	1313220	17.3	209550	14.7	1103671	17.9	62.5	10.0	52.5
2001-02	1498355	14.1	240794	14.9	1257561	13.9	65.7	10.6	55.2
2002-03	1717960	14.7	271581	12.8	1446378	15.0	70.0	11.1	58.9
2003-04	2005676	16.7	314971	16.0	1690705	16.9	72.8	11.4	61.4
2004-05	2245677	12.0	356314	13.1	1889363	11.8	69.3	11.0	58.3
2005-06	2719519	21.1	412124	15.7	2307395	22.1	73.7	11.2	62.5
2006-07	3310068	21.7	482854	17.2	2827213	22.5	77.1	11.2	65.8
2007-08	4017882	21.4	568410	17.7	3449472	22.0	80.6	11.4	69.2
2008-09	4794812	19.3	665450	17.1	4129363	19.7	85.9	11.9	74.0
2009-10	5602731	16.8	767492	15.3	4835239	17.0	85.5	11.7	73.8
2010-11	6499548	16.0	914197	19.1	5585351	17.0	82.5	11.6	70.9

Note: 1. * Growth between 1950-51 and 1960-01 and so on upto 2000-01 is CAGR (compounded annual growth rate). Thereafter the growth rates are annual. 2. Data for 2007-08 onwards are provisional. 3. Excluding the impact of merger on May 3, 2002, data on time deposits and broad money for the year 2002-03 works out to Rs. 12,14,708 crore and Rs. 16,88,289 crore, respectively. 4. Excluding the impact of conversion of a non-banking entity into a banking entity on October 11, 2004, data on time deposits and broad money for the year 2004-05 works out to Rs. 15,92,374 crore and Rs. 22,42,164 crore, respectively. 5. GDP upto 2004-05 is based on 1999-2000 series, thereafter it is based on the 2004-05 series. All at current prices.

Source: Reserve Bank of India.

39 : Sources of Changes in Money Supply

Year (as at end-March)	Net Bank Credit to Government		Bank Credit to Commercial Sector		Net Foreign Exchange Assets of the Banking Sector		Net Non-Monetary Liabilities of Banking Sector	
	Rs. crore	Share in M3 (%)	Rs. crore	Share in M3 (%)	Rs. crore	Share in M3 (%)	Rs. crore	Share in M3 (%)
1950-51*	808	34.4	588	25.0	860	36.6	145	6.2
1960-61*	2489	62.8	1503	37.9	178	4.5	413	10.4
1970-71*	5455	49.5	6522	59.2	551	5.0	1892	17.2
1980-81*	25718	46.1	36641	65.7	4730	8.5	11934	21.4
1990-91*	140193	52.7	171769	64.6	10581	4.0	58336	21.9
2000-01*	511955	39.0	679218	51.7	249820	19.0	133126	10.1
2001-02	589565	39.3	759647	50.7	311035	20.8	168258	11.2
2002-03	676523	39.4	898981	52.3	393715	22.9	258330	15.0
2003-04	742904	37.0	1016151	50.7	526586	26.3	287261	14.3
2004-05	752436	33.5	1275912	56.8	649255	28.9	439374	19.6
2005-06	759416	27.9	1688681	62.1	726194	26.7	462429	17.0
2006-07	827626	25.0	2128862	64.3	913179	27.6	567761	17.2
2007-08	899518	22.4	2578990	64.2	1295131	32.2	764980	19.0
2008-09	1277333	26.6	3014893	62.9	1352184	28.2	859652	17.9
2009-10	1669186	29.8	3491409	62.3	1281469	22.9	850602	15.2
2010-11	1982771	40.8	4235406	87.1	1393327	28.6	1124680	23.1

Note : * : Growth between 1950-51 and 1960-61 and so on upto 2000-01 is CAGR (compounded annual growth rate). Thereafter the growth rates are annual.

Source : Reserve Bank of India.

40 : Structural Changes in Reserve Bank of India's Balance Sheet

(Rs. crore)

End-March	Total Assets/Liabilities	*of which:* Notes in Circulation	Foreign Assets	GoI Securities	Loans & Advances
Outstandings					
1951	1612	1247	884	487	9
% to Total	100.0	77.3	54.8	30.2	0.6
1961	2257	1985	136	1632	171
% to Total	100.0	87.9	6.0	72.3	7.6
1971	5463	4212	350	3714	958
% to Total	100.0	77.1	6.4	68.0	17.5
1981	20275	13733	4320	11110	3504
% to Total	100.0	67.7	21.3	54.8	17.3
1991	120691	53784	4208	46924	18516
% to Total	100.0	44.6	3.5	38.9	15.3
2001	386541	212851	144013	110775	35442
% to Total	100.0	55.1	37.3	28.7	9.2
2007	980097	495938	836401	1046	6935
% to Total	100.0	50.6	85.3	0.1	0.7
2008	1364028	581577	1195828	1046	5250
% to Total	100.0	42.6	87.7	0.1	0.4
2009	1479515	681099	1231114	1046	23521
% to Total	100.0	46.0	83.2	0.1	1.6
2010	1472583	788279	1150574	1046	1620
% to Total	100.0	53.5	78.1	0.1	0.1
2011	1738785	936935	1225788	1046	7465
% to Total	100.0	53.9	70.5	0.1	0.4

Source : Reserve Bank of India, *Handbook of Statistics on the Indian Economy.*

41 : Monetary Policy Measures at Some Selected Dates

Effective Date	Bank Rate (%)	CRR	SLR (%)	Repo Rate	Reserve Repo Rate
31-03-1951	3.5	5% of DL & 2% of TL	20		
31-03-1961	4.0	do	20		
31-03-1971	6.0	3.00	28		
31-03-1981	9.0	6.00	34		
31-03-1991	10.0	15.00	38.5		
02-03-2001	7.0	8.25	24		
31-03-2002	6.5	7.50	24	8.50	6.50
30-04-2003	6.0	4.50	24	7.00	5.00
02-10-2004	6.0	5.00	24	6.00	4.50
23-12-2006	6.0	5.25	24	7.25	6.00
03-03-2007	6.0	6.00	24	7.50	6.00
26-04-2008	6.0	7.75	24	7.75	6.00
31-03-2009	6.0	5.00	24	5.50	4.00
31-03-2010	6.0	5.75	24	5.00	3.50
31-03-2011	6.0	6.00	24	6.75	5.75

Note : CRR: Cash Reserve Ratio, SLR: Statutory Liquidity Ratio, DL: Demand Liabilities and TL: Time Liabilities.

Source : Reserve Bank of India.

42 : Progress of Scheduled Commercial Banks at a Glance

	June/1969	June/1971	June/1981	March/1991	March/2001	March/2010
No. of Commercial Banks	89	85	187	276	300	169
1. Scheduled Commercial Banks	73	74	183	272	296	165
of which: Regional Rural Banks			102	196	196	82
2. Non-Scheduled Commercial Banks	16	11	4	4	5	4
Number of Offices in India	8262	12013	35707	60220	67937	85693
1. Rural	1833	4280	17656	35206	32585	32624
% Share	22.2	35.6	49.4	58.5	48.0	38.1
2. Semi-Urban	3342	4040	8474	11344	14843	20740
3. Urban	1584	1949	5454	8046	11193	17003
4. Metropolitan	1503	1744	4126	5624	9316	15026
Population per Office ('000)	64	46	19	14	15	14
No. of ATMs						60153
Off-Site						27474
On-Site						32679
Per Capita Deposit	88	113	587	2368	9770	38062
Per Capita Credit	68	86	385	1434	5228	27489
Share of Priority Sector Advances to Non-Food SC Bank Credit (%)	15.0	22.3	38.8	37.7	31.0	35.6
Credit-Deposit Ratio (%)	77.5	76.6	65.5	60.6	53.5	72.2
Investment Deposit Ratio (%)	29.3	29.1	35.1	37.7	37.1	36.2
Cash Deposit Ratio (%)	8.2	6.5	13.6	17.6	8.4	7.7

Source : Reserve Bank of India.

43 : Aggregate Deposits of Scheduled Commercial Banks

(Rs. crore)

Last Reporting Friday of March	Demand Deposits		Time Deposits		Aggregate Deposits		% of GDP
	Rs. crore	Growth (%)	Rs. crore	Growth (%)	Rs. crore	Growth (%)	
1950-51	593		290		882		8.7
1960-61	710	1.8	1026	13.5	1736	7.0	10.0
1970-71	2626	14.0	3280	12.3	5906	13.0	12.8
1980-81	7798	11.5	30190	24.9	37988	20.5	26.1
1990-91	33192	15.6	159349	18.1	192541	17.6	33.8
2000-01	142552	15.7	820066	17.8	962618	17.5	45.8
2001-02	153048	7.4	950312	15.9	1103360	14.6	48.4
2002-03	170289	11.3	1110564	16.9	1280853	16.1	52.2
2003-04	225022	32.1	1279394	15.2	1504416	17.5	54.6
2004-05	248028	10.2	1452171	13.5	1700198	13.0	52.4
2005-06	364640	47.0	1744409	20.1	2109049	24.0	57.1
2006-07	429731	17.9	2182203	25.1	2611933	23.8	60.8
2007-08	524310	22.0	2672630	22.5	3196939	22.4	64.1
2008-09	523085	(0.2)	3311025	23.9	3834110	19.9	68.7
2009-10	645610	23.4	3847216	16.2	4492826	17.2	68.6
2010-11	641705	(0.6)	4566264	18.7	5207969	15.9	66.1

Note: Growth for decades from 1950-51 to 2000-01 is based on CAGR, thereafter on annual growth.
Negative value in brackets.

Source: Reserve Bank of India.

44 : Investments by Scheduled Commercial Banks in SLR and Non-SLR Securities

(Rs. crore)

	SLR Securities			Non-SLR Securities						Total (SLR + Non-SLR Investment)	
	Investments in Government Securities	Investments in Other Approved Securities	Investment in SLR Securities	Commercial Paper	Shares of PSUs & Pvt. Corporate Sector	Bonds & Debentures	Mutual Funds	Financial Institutions	Investment in Non-SLR Securities	Total Investment	Investment Deposit Ratio (%)
1951-52	296		296							296	33.6
1960-61	559		559							559	32.2
1970-71	1362	410	1772							1772	30.0
1980-81	9219	3967	13186							13186	34.7
1990-91	49998	25067	75065							75065	39.0
2000-01	340035	30125	370160	8049	5690	62105			75844	446004	46.3
2001-02	411176	27093	438269	8497	5914	66589			81000	519269	47.1
2002-03	523417	24129	547546	4041	9230	81284	6455	31066	132076	679622	53.1
2003-04	654758	22830	677588	3835	9006	82918	11930	32988	140677	818265	54.4
2004-05	718982	20172	739154	3944	12219	85913	12744	31557	146377	885531	52.1
2005-06	700742	16712	717454	4837	13170	77721	10410	29203	135341	852795	40.4
2006-07	776058	15458	791516	9038	18428	74660	11761	26568	140455	931971	35.7
2007-08	958661	13053	971715	13270	26708	85865	18824	25942	170609	1142324	35.7
2008-09	1155786	10624	1166410	20001	28236	89660	37035	32585	207517	1373927	35.8
2009-10	1378395	6358	1384752	25188	30192	93679	52887	32597	234543	1619295	36.0
2010-11	1497148	4471	1501619	12309	41767	139590	47603	31296	272565	1774184	34.1

Source : Reserve Bank of India.

45 : Credit by Scheduled Commercial Banks

Last Reporting Friday of March	Food Credit	Non-Food Credit		Total Scheduled Commercial Bank Credit			
	Rs. crore	Rs. crore	Growth (%)	Rs. crore	Growth (%)	% to GDP*	Credit-Deposit Ratio (%)
1950-51				547		5.4	62
1960-61	.	.		1336	9.3	7.7	77
1970-71	214	4469		4684	13.4	10.1	79
1980-81	1759	23612	18.1	25371	18.4	17.5	67
1990-91	4506	111795	16.8	116301	16.4	20.4	60
2000-01	39991	471443	15.5	511434	16.0	24.3	53
2001-02	53978	535745	13.6	589723	15.3	25.9	53
2002-03	49479	679736	26.9	729215	23.7	29.7	57
2003-04	35961	804824	18.4	840785	15.3	30.5	56
2004-05	41121	1059308	31.6	1100428	30.9	33.9	65
2005-06	40691	1466386	38.4	1507077	37.0	40.8	71
2006-07	46521	1884669	28.5	1931189	28.1	45.0	74
2007-08	44399	2317515	23.0	2361914	22.3	47.4	74
2008-09	46211	2729338	17.8	2775549	17.5	49.7	72
2009-10	48489	3196299	17.1	3244788	16.9	49.5	72
2010-11	64283	3877800	21.3	3942083	21.5	50.1	76

Note: Growth for decades from 1950-51 upto 2000-01 based on CAGR, thereafter on annual growth.

* : GDP at current market prices.

Source: Reserve Bank of India.

46 : Sectoral Deployment of Non-Food Credit

Year	Non-Food Gross Bank Credit (Rs. crore)	Share of Priority Sector in Non-Food Bank Credit of which:							
		Total		Agriculture		Small Scale Industries		Medium & Large Industry	
		Rs. crore	% Share	Rs. crore	% Share	Rs. crore	% Share	Rs. crore	% Share
1979-80	19135	6730	35.2	2767	14.5	2635	13.8	8269	43.2
1980-81	23045	8504	36.9	3584	15.6	3229	14.0	9960	43.2
1990-91	113513	42915	37.8	16750	14.8	17181	15.1	44508	39.2
2000-01	429162	154414	36.0	51922	12.1	56002	13.0	162837	37.9
2001-02	482749	175259	36.3	60761	12.6	57199	11.8	172324	35.7
2002-03	620055	211609	34.1	73518	11.9	60394	9.7	235168	37.9
2003-04	728422	263834	36.2	90541	12.4	65855	9.0	247210	33.9
2004-05	999788	381476	38.2	125250	12.5	74588	7.5	352304	35.2
2005-06	1404840	510738	36.4	173972	12.4	91212	6.5	459232	32.7
2006-07	1801240	635966	35.3	230377	12.8	117910	6.5	579429	32.2
2007-08	2204801	748073	33.9	275342	12.5	132698	8.8	725646	32.9
2008-09	2601825	932459	35.8	338656	13.0	168997	9.9	885393	34.0
2009-10	3040007	1092179	35.9	416133	13.7	206401	6.8	1105051	36.4
2010-11	3667354	1258386	34.3	460333	12.6	229101	6.2	1391747	37.9

Source : Reserve Bank of India.

47 : Scheduled Commercial Banks' Direct Finance to Farmers (Short and Long Term)

End-June	Upto 2.5 Acres		2.5 Acres to 5 Acres		Above 5 Acres		Total	
	No. of ACs (in '000s)	Amount (Rs. crore)	No. of ACs (in '000s)	Amount (Rs. crore)	No. of ACs (in '000s)	Amount (Rs. crore)	No. of ACs (in '000s)	Amount (Rs. crore)
Disbursements								
1990-91	1960	1181	1219	952	899	1782	4078	3915
% to Total	48.1	30.2	29.9	24.3	22.0	45.5	100.0	100.0
2000-01	2382	3740	1860	3642	1599	7135	5841	14516
% to Total	40.8	25.8	31.8	25.1	27.4	49.2	100.0	100.0
2001-02	2679	4352	1933	4371	2359	7578	6970	16300
% to Total	38.4	26.7	27.7	26.8	33.8	46.5	100.0	100.0
2002-03	2494	4834	1934	5578	1983	11445	6411	21857
% to Total	38.9	22.1	30.2	25.5	30.9	52.4	100.0	100.0
2003-04	3711	7953	2695	7340	2259	16592	8665	31885
% to Total	42.8	24.9	31.1	23.0	26.1	52.0	100.0	100.0
2004-05	4478	10833	3172	10550	2535	19735	10185	41119
% to Total	44.0	26.3	31.1	25.7	24.9	48.0	100.0	100.0
2005-06	5004	16823	3670	17619	3670	32682	12344	67124
% to Total	40.5	25.1	29.7	26.2	29.7	48.7	100.0	100.0
2006-07	5963	23246	4008	21588	4379	49335	14350	94169
% to Total	41.6	24.7	27.9	22.9	30.5	52.4	100.0	100.0
2007-08	6605	25352	4463	23215	4932	48140	16000	96707
% to Total	41.3	26.2	27.9	24.0	30.8	49.8	100.0	100.0
2008-09	8544	34267	6641	33280	6811	72753	21996	140300
% to Total	38.8	24.4	30.2	23.7	31.0	51.9	100.0	100.0

contd...

...contd...

As of End-June	Upto 2.5 Acres		2.5 Acres to 5 Acres		Above 5 Acres		Total	
	No. of ACs (in '000s)	Amount (Rs. crore)	No. of ACs (in '000s)	Amount (Rs. crore)	No. of ACs (in '000s)	Amount (Rs. crore)	No. of ACs (in '000s)	Amount (Rs. crore)
Outstandings								
1990-91	6137	2895	4346	2870	3563	6624	14045	12389
% to Total	43.7	23.4	30.9	23.2	25.4	53.5	100.0	100.0
2000-01	4600	7215	3689	7308	3555	16963	11844	31486
% to Total	38.8	22.9	31.1	23.2	30.0	53.9	100.0	100.0
2001-02	4902	8759	3961	9686	3394	19083	12257	37529
% to Total	40.0	23.3	32.3	25.8	27.7	50.8	100.0	100.0
2002-03	4749	9813	4092	11316	3835	23831	12676	44961
% to Total	37.5	21.8	32.3	25.2	30.3	53.0	100.0	100.0
2003-04	6086	14805	4806	13974	4377	28786	15268	57565
% to Total	39.9	25.7	31.5	24.3	28.7	50.0	100.0	100.0
2004-05	7299	20499	5874	20759	5274	37218	18447	78476
% to Total	39.6	26.1	31.8	26.5	28.6	47.4	100.0	100.0
2005-06	8239	29719	6677	29255	6321	52769	21237	111743
% to Total	38.8	26.6	31.4	26.2	29.8	47.2	100.0	100.0
2006-07	9954	37336	7548	37815	6985	64810	24487	139961
% to Total	40.7	26.7	30.8	27.0	28.5	46.3	100.0	100.0
2007-08	11345	46457	9512	46631	8739	80956	29596	174044
% to Total	38.3	26.7	32.1	26.8	29.5	46.5	100.0	100.0
2008-09	11708	60199	9570	59792	10884	99349	32162	219340
% to Total	36.4	27.4	29.8	27.3	33.8	45.3	100.0	100.0

Source: Reserve Bank of India.

48 : Deposits of Scheduled Commercial Banks: According to Population Group

Year	Rural		Semi-Urban		Urban		Metropolitan	
	No. of Accounts (in '000s)	Amount Outstanding (Rs. crore)	No. of Accounts (in '000s)	Amount Outstanding (Rs. crore)	No. of Accounts (in '000s)	Amount Outstanding (Rs. crore)	No. of Accounts (in '000s)	Amount Outstanding (Rs. crore)
1991	108876	31010	98084	41439	80889	49140	67342	78979
2001	131723	139431	116400	186188	92769	217833	87137	405981
2002	133000	159423	117394	214990	94622	255478	94975	493501
2003	136733	176502	117537	241757	96099	290503	95711	567433
2004	138760	195082	120651	268217	99571	330296	98176	717679
2005	141908	213104	125198	295685	101376	374891	98310	863134
2006	139570	226061	121664	302213	106172	430813	117692	1132087
2007	149663	253014	132808	357395	113422	532592	123306	1454043
2008	168034	303423	148361	430280	128021	657699	137241	1858544
2009	199695	363910	169725	529758	142272	822914	150611	2205399
2010	224155	420338	189457	614047	152323	944992	168934	2581652

Source : Reserve Bank of India.

49 : Population Group-wise Number of Branches of Scheduled Commercial Banks

(number)

End-June	Rural	Share in Total (%)	Semi-Urban	Urban	Metropolitan	Total
1969	1833	22.2	3342	1584	1503	8262
1971	4280	35.6	4040	1949	1744	12013
1981	17656	49.4	8471	5454	4126	35707
1991	35206	58.5	11344	8046	5624	60220
2001	32562	49.4	14597	10293	8467	65919
2002	32380	48.9	14747	10477	8586	66190
2003	32303	48.6	14859	10693	8680	66535
2004	32121	47.8	15091	11000	8976	67188
2005	32082	46.9	15403	11500	9370	68355
2006	30579	44.0	15556	12032	11304	69471
2007	30551	42.5	16361	12970	11957	71839
2008	30914	40.7	17791	14416	13038	76159
2009	31576	39.6	19075	15479	13921	80051
2010	32497	38.4	20707	16884	14935	85023
2011	33495	37.4	22631	17712	15784	89622

Source : Reserve Bank of India.

50 : Statistics on Cheque Clearances

Year	All-India		All RBI Centres*		Mumbai		Kolkata		New Delhi		Chennai	
	Number (in million)	Amount (Rs. crore)	Number (in million)	Amount (Rs. crore)	Number (in million)	Amount (Rs. crore)	Number (in million)	Amount (Rs. crore)	Number (in million)	Amount (Rs. crore)	Number (in million)	Amount (Rs. crore)
1970-71	151	46332	112	36960	37	13344	13	6924	7	2628	8	2136
1980-81	315	243516	224	186252	66	56379	19	21324	16	16644	9	9133
1990-91	764	2287353	352	1839460	125	1182587	33	104051	55	239979	36	176123
2000-01	941	10747119	527	9189683	174	6667989	52	365280	101	818999	52	509292
2001-02	902	12575254	538	10947391	168	8217816	52	373131	108	990315	52	500872
2002-03	1014	13424313	598	10978762	202	7694748	53	419164	116	1319625	56	552913
2003-04	1023	11595960	624	9178751	216	5511293	47	465308	111	1354677	60	612158
2004-05	1167	10458895	739	8493321	230	3753670	60	560660	148	1773611	74	759883
2005-06	1287	11329134	794	8194977	239	3342829	64	658640	160	1697583	81	655278
2006-07	1367	12042426	831	8599494	252	3319090	68	682358	169	1773548	80	692201
2007-08	1461	13396066	878	9451748	265	3685407	73	778304	178	1800975	85	778854
2008-09	1397	12469135	835	8297385	251	2799765	69	753068	173	1664709	83	801964
2009-10	1380	10409942	813	6522135	248	1939327	68	658229	162	1299000	79	631101
2010-11P	1387	10134128	814	6195775	247	1706912	67	539311	160	1439116	79	549887

Note: * : RBI centres referes to all centres where RBI is the manager of clearing houses.
P: Provisional.

Source : Reserve Bank of India.

51 : Number of Kisan Credit Cards Issued

(million)

As of End-March	Cooperative Banks	Regional Rural Banks	Commercial Banks	Total
1998-99	0.16	0.01	0.62	0.78
1999-00	3.59	0.17	1.37	5.13
2000-01	5.61	0.65	2.39	8.65
2001-02	5.44	0.83	3.07	9.34
2002-03	4.58	0.96	2.70	8.24
2003-04	4.88	1.27	3.09	9.25
2004-05	3.56	1.73	4.40	9.68
2005-06	2.60	1.25	4.16	8.01
2006-07	2.30	1.41	4.81	8.51
2007-08	2.09	1.77	4.61	8.47
2008-09	1.34	1.41	5.83	8.59
2009-10	1.74	1.95	5.31	9.01
2010-11	2.81	1.78	2.67*	7.26
Cumulative Total#	40.70	15.20	45.03	100.93
% Share	40.32	15.06	44.62	100.00

Note : * : Data for commercial banks available upto 30th June 2010.

: Since inception of the scheme, i.e., August 1998.

Source : NABARD Annual Report.

52 : Retail Portfolio of Scheduled Commercial Banks

(Rs. crore)

End-March	Retail Loans	% to Total Loans & Advances	*of which:* Housing Loan	Consumer Durables	Credit Card	Auto Loans
2004	189041	22	89449	6256	6167	87170
2005	266610	24	134276	3810	8405	35043
2006	375683	26	179060	4469	12434	61369
2007	487860	26	224481	7296	18317	82562
2008	570776	25	252932	4802	27437	87998
2009	593815	21	263235	5431	29941	83915
2010	622752	19	315862	3032	21565	78346

Source : Reserve Bank of India.

53 : Non-Performing Assets of Scheduled Commercial Banks

(Rs. crore)

End-March	Non-Performing Assets					
	Gross Amount	As % of Gross Advances	As % of Total Assets	Net Amount	As % of Net Advances	As % of Total Assets
1996-97	47300	15.7	7.0	22340	8.1	3.3
1997-98	50815	14.4	6.4	23761	7.3	3.0
1998-99	58722	14.7	6.2	28020	7.6	2.9
1999-00	60408	12.7	5.5	30073	6.8	2.7
2000-01	63741	11.4	4.9	32461	6.2	2.5
2001-02	70861	10.4	4.6	35554	5.5	2.3
2002-03	68717	8.8	4.1	29692	4.0	1.8
2003-04	64812	7.2	3.3	24396	2.8	1.2
2004-05	59373	5.2	2.5	21754	2.0	0.9
2005-06	51097	3.3	1.8	18543	1.2	0.7
2006-07	50486	2.5	1.5	20101	1.0	0.6
2007-08	56309	2.3	1.3	24730	1.0	0.6
2008-09	68328	2.3	1.3	31564	1.1	0.6
2009-10	84747	2.4	1.4	39126	1.1	0.7

Source : Reserve Bank of India.

54 : Value of Coins and Notes Issued: Denomination-wise

(Rs. crore)

End-March	1950-51	1960-61	1970-71	1980-81	1990-91	2000-01	2009-10
Small Coins	76	71	137	243	685	1300	1458
Re. 1 Notes	1204	1942	219	207	335	307	299
Re. 1 Coins	130	142	43	141	616	1393	2968
Rs. 2 Coins	-	-	-	-	23	814	3068
Rs. 5 Coins	-	-	-	-	-	1544	4535
Rs. 10 Coins	-	-	-	-	-	-	300
Rs. 2 Notes	na	38	69	299	883	471	851
Rs. 5 Notes	na	203	310	634	1810	1016	3430
Rs. 10 Notes	na	814	1563	2097	3785	12336	21288
Rs. 20 Notes	na	-	-	1090	2952	1012	6040
Rs. 50 Notes	na	-	-	2206	14812	32818	15980
Rs. 100 Notes	na	865	2210	7406	24570	108141	140243
Rs. 500 Notes	na	-	-	-	2177	52947	445311
Rs. 1000 Notes	na	54	45	-	-	3719	302713

Note: - : not relevant.
Source : Reserve Bank of India.

55 : Retail Electronic Payments

	ECS Credit	ECS Debit	EFT/NEFT	Credit Cards	Debit Cards	Total
Volume of Transactions ('000)						
2003-04	20300	7900	819	100179	37757	166955
2004-05	40051	15300	2549	129472	41532	288904
2005-06	44216	35958	3067	156086	45686	285013
2006-07	69019	75202	4776	169536	60177	378710
2007-08	78365	127120	13315	228203	88306	535309
2008-09	88394	160055	32161	259561	127654	667825
2009-10	98133	149281	66338	234242	170168	718162
2010-11	117300	156739	132344	265145	237063	908591
Value of Transactions (Rs. crore)						
2003-04	10228	2254	17125	17663	4874	52143
2004-05	20180	2921	54601	25686	5361	108749
2005-06	32324	12986	61288	33886	5897	146381
2006-07	83273	25441	77446	41361	8172	235693
2007-08	782222	48937	140326	57984	12521	1041990
2008-09	97487	66976	251956	65356	18547	500322
2009-10	117613	69524	409507	61824	26418	684886
2010-11	181686	73646	939149	75516	38691	1308687

Note : The substantial increase in ECS credit in 2007-08 is due to refund of the oversubscription amount of IPOs floated by companies using electronic mode as mandated by stock exchange.

Source : Reserve Bank of India.

56 : Regional Rural Banks: Selected Indicators—Outstandings

(Rs. crore)

Year	Aggregate Deposits		Bank Credit		Investment		Credit-Deposit Ratio (%)	Investment-Deposit Ratio (%)
	Rs. crore	Growth (%)	Rs. crore	Growth (%)	Rs. crore	Growth (%)		
1980-81	232		285		0		122.8	0.0
1990-91	4560	(34.7)	3497	(28.5)	16		76.7	0.4
2000-01	35995	(22.9)	15211	(15.8)	7489	(84.9)	42.3	20.8
2001-02	42494	18.1	18033	18.6	6871	(8.3)	42.4	16.2
2002-03	47644	12.1	21359	18.4	12008	74.8	44.8	25.2
2003-04	53390	12.1	25057	17.3	17532	46.0	46.9	32.8
2004-05	58286	9.2	31651	26.3	20213	15.3	54.3	34.7
2005-06	64195	10.1	36050	13.9	19050	(5.8)	56.2	29.7
2006-07	81620	27.1	48420	34.3	22424	17.7	58.3	27.5
2007-08	94412	15.7	57417	18.6	25387	13.2	60.8	26.9
2008-09	113828	20.6	64011	11.5	29414	15.9	56.2	25.8
2009-10	135814	19.3	79086	23.6	39229	33.4	58.2	28.9
2010-11	156702	15.4	94626	19.6	45493	16.0	60.4	29.0

Note : Data as on last Friday of March upto 1984-85 and last reporting Friday of March thereafter.
Figures in brackets are CAGR.
P: Provisional.

Source : National Bank for Agriculture and Rural Development.

57 : Regional Rural Banks: Purpose-wise Outstanding Advances

(Rs. crore)

End-March	Total	Agriculture	Short Term	Long Term	Non-Agriculture	Rural Artisans	Other Industries	Retail Trade etc.	Others
1991	3804	1850	645	671	1954	321*		1143	490
2001	8823	3966	3095	871	4857	181	70	1123	3483
2002	18629	8405	4883	3522	10224	671	226	2984	6343
2003	22158	10261	6495	3766	11897	695	330	3264	7608
2004	26114	11722	7664	4058	14393	715	433	3607	9638
2005	32871	16710	10980	5730	16161	713	580	4364	10504
2006	39712	21509	13877	7632	18204	748	757	3452	13246
2007	48493	27452	18707	3745	21041	736	880	3677	15748
2008	58984	33216	22748	10468	25768	671	1227	4531	19339
2009	67802	37367	26652	10715	30435	772	1656	4690	23317
2010P	83562	45829	33208	12621	37733	857	1694	5285	29897

Note: * : Separate data not available. P: Provisional.
Source: National Bank for Agriculture and Rural Development.

58 : Regional Rural Banks: Financial Ratios (% to Assets)

(%)

Year	Income	of which:		of which:		of which:		Net Profit	Gross NPA
		Interest	Expenditure	Interest Expended	Operating Expenses	Wage Bill	Operating Profit		
1995-96	7.9	7.4	10.1	5.6	3.8	3.2	-1.5	-2.2	
2000-01	9.8	9.3	8.6	6.0	2.3	2.0	1.5	1.2	
2001-02	9.8	9.1	8.7	5.9	2.6	2.2	1.4	1.1	
2002-03	9.3	8.6	8.5	5.5	2.7	2.3	1.1	0.8	
2003-04	8.9	7.9	7.8	4.8	2.6	2.1	1.5	1.1	
2004-05	7.9	7.3	6.9	4.1	2.5	2.0	1.3	1.0	8.5
2005-06	7.3	6.8	6.6	3.6	2.6	2.1	1.0	0.7	7.3
2006-07	7.2	6.7	6.7	3.5	2.6	1.9	1.2	0.6	3.5
2007-08	7.5	7.0	6.7	3.8	2.2	1.6	1.5	0.8	6.1
2008-09	8.3	7.7	7.3	4.4	2.3	1.7	1.4	0.9	4.2
2009-10P	8.3	7.7	7.1	4.4	2.1	1.6	1.6	1.0	na

Note : na: not available. P: Provisional.
Source : National Bank for Agriculture and Rural Development.

59 : Capital Market Snapshot

As of End-March	Stock Exchanges (number)	Companies Listed		Brokers Cash Segment (number)	Registered FIIs (number)	Mutual Funds (number)	Market Capitalisation (% of GDP)	
		BSE (number)	NSE (number)				BSE	NSE
1993	21	2861		5200	18		21.7	
1994	22	3585		6413	158	12	36.2	
1995	22	4702	135	6711	308	22	36.5	
1996	22	5603	422	8476	367	27	38.2	
1997	22	5832	550	8867	439	37	36.6	30.4
1998	22	5853	612	9005	496	38	41.3	31.5
1999	23	5849	648	9069	450	41	35.4	28.0
2000	23	5815	720	9192	506	38	46.8	52.3
2001	23	5869	785	9782	527	39	29.3	33.7
2002	23	5782	793	9687	490	38	26.9	27.9
2003	23	5650	818	9519	502	38	23.3	21.9
2004	23	5528	909	9368	540	37	43.6	40.7
2005	22	4731	970	9128	685	39	52.4	48.9
2006	22	4781	1069	9335	882	38	81.8	76.2
2007	21	4821	1228	9443	1020	40	82.6	78.4
2008	19	4887	1381	9487	1319	40	103.0	97.4
2009	19	4929	1432	9628	1635	44	55.3	51.9
2010	19	4975	1470	9772	1713	47	94.1	91.7
2011	19	5067	1574	10203	1722	51	86.8	85.1

Note : BSE: Bombay Stock Exchange, NSF: National Stock Exchange.
Source : Securities and Exchange Board of India.

60 : New Capital Issues by Indian Private Sector

Type of Issues	Total		Equity Shares		Preference Shares		Debentures	
	No.	Rs. crore	No.	Rs. crore	No.	Rs. crore	No.	Rs. crore
1981-82	438	598	357	305	5	3	73	290
1991-92	514	61931	366	1916	3	2	145	4275
2001-02	19	5692	6	860	0	0	13	4832
2002-03	9	1878	5	460	0	0	4	1418
2003-04	38	3722	35	2471	0	0	3	1261
2004-05	54	13079	51	11452	0	0	3	1627
2005-06	131	21154	128	20899	1	10	2	245
2006-07	117	30606	114	29753	0	0	3	847
2007-08	115	63638	111	56848	1	5481	3	1309
2008-09	45	14671	45	14671	0	0	0	0
2009-10	67	25299	68	25479	0	0	1	180
2010-11	70	24830	70	24830	0	0	0	0

Source : Reserve Bank of India.

61 : Resources Raised by Corporate Sector

(Rs. crore)

	Equity Issues	Debt Issues			Total Resources Mobilised	Share of Private Placements (%)		Share of Debt to Total Resources (%)
		Public & Right Issues	Private Placements	Total		Debt	Total Resource Mobilised	
1995-96	14830	5974	13361	19335	34165	69.1	39.1	56.6
1996-97	7853	6286	15066	21352	29205	70.6	51.6	73.1
1997-98	1892	2678	30099	32777	34669	91.8	86.8	94.5
1998-99	935	4652	49679	54331	55266	91.4	89.9	98.3
1999-00	4566	3251	61259	64510	69076	95.0	88.7	93.4
2000-01	3368	2740	67836	70576	73944	96.1	91.7	95.4
2001-02	1272	6271	64876	71147	72419	91.2	89.6	98.2
2002-03	1457	2613	66948	69561	71018	96.2	94.3	97.9
2003-04	18948	4324	63901	68225	87173	93.7	73.3	78.3
2004-05	24388	3867	83405	87272	111660	95.6	74.7	78.2
2005-06	27372	10	96473	96483	123855	100.0	77.9	77.9
2006-07	32901	605	145865	146470	179371	99.6	81.3	81.7
2007-08	85427	1603	212726	214329	299756	99.3	71.0	71.5
2008-09	14721	1500	208557	210057	224778	99.3	92.8	93.5
2009-10	55046	2500	342445	344945	399991	99.3	85.6	86.2

Source : Securities and Exchange Board of India.

62 : Resource Mobilisation by Private Placements (Debt): By Borrower Categories

(Rs. crore)

	Private Sector		Public Sector		Total		Grand Total
	Financial Institution	Non-Financial Institution	Financial Institution	Non-Financial Institution	Financial Institution	Non-Financial Institution	
1995-96	2136	1934	4552	4739	6688	6673	13361
1996-97	1847	646	6541	6032	8388	6678	15066
1997-98	4324	4879	9660	11237	13984	16116	30100
1998-99	12174	4824	20382	12299	32556	17123	49679
1999-00	10875	8528	17981	23874	28856	32402	61258
2000-01	13263	9843	26201	18530	39464	28373	67837
2001-02	16019	12601	17358	18898	33377	31499	64876
2002-03	9454	15623	20407	21464	29861	37087	66948
2003-04	12551	6209	26461	18679	39012	24888	63900
2004-05	20974	14820	25531	22080	46505	36900	83405
2005-06	26463	14727	39165	16119	65628	30846	96474
2006-07	48414	33426	52117	11908	100531	45334	145865
2007-08	88291	41386	56186	26863	144477	68249	212726
2008-09	60586	35103	65615	47253	126201	82356	208557
2009-10	142441	90853	74290	35696	216731	126549	343280
2010-11	71975	49476	98983	17960	170958	67436	238394

Source : Reserve Bank of India.

63 : Resources Mobilised from the Primary Market (Equities)

	Total		Category-wise		Issuer Type		Pricing-Based		Sector-wise	
	Number	Amount (Rs. crore)	Public (Rs. crore)	Rights (Rs. crore)	Listed (Rs. crore)	IPOs (Rs. crore)	At Par	At Premium	Private*	Public
1993-94	1143	24372	15449	8923	16508	7864	3808	9220	..	..
1994-95	1692	27633	21045	6588	11061	16572	5529	12441	26270	1362
1995-96	1725	20804	14240	6564	9880	10924	4958	9727	16639	4165
1996-97	884	14285	11565	2719	8326	5959	3441	4412	10249	4035
1997-98	111	4570	2862	1708	3522	1048	271	1610	3852	718
1998-99	58	5586	5019	568	5182	404	197	660	5516	70
1999-00	93	7817	6257	1560	5098	2719	786	3780	7617	200
2000-01	151	6107	5378	729	3385	2722	818	2408	5893	215
2001-02	35	7543	6502	1041	6341	1202	151	1121	6601	942
2002-03	26	4071	3639	431	3032	1039	143	1314	1897	2173
2003-04	57	23272	22265	1007	19838	3434	360	18589	4612	18660
2004-05	60	28256	24640	3616	14507	13749	420	23968	17162	11094
2005-06	139	27382	23294	4088	16446	10936	372	27000	20199	7183
2006-07	124	33508	2997	3711	5004	28504	12	32889	31728	1779
2007-08	124	87029	54511	32518	44434	42595	387	79352	67311	19718
2008-09	47	16220	3582	12637	12637	2082	96	14176	16220	0
2009-10	76	57555	49236	8319	30359	24696	9	54866	26438	31117
2010-11	91	67609	58105	9503	22599	33559	50	57617	29385	38223

Note : * : Joint sector issues, if any, are clubbed with private sector issues. IPO : Initial Public Offers.

Source : Securities and Exchange Board of India.

64 : Resources Mobilised by Corporate through ADRs/GDRs and ECBs

(US $ mn)

	ADRs/GDRs	ECBs (net)
1992-93	240	(358)
1993-94	1597	607
1994-95	2080	1030
1995-96	683	1275
1996-97	1366	2848
1997-98	645	3999
1998-99	270	4362
1999-00	768	313
2000-01	831	3732
2001-02	477	1579
2002-03	600	(2353)
2003-04	459	(1856)
2004-05	613	5194
2005-06	2552	2508
2006-07	3776	16103
2007-08	6645	22609
2008-09	1162	7862
2009-10	3328	2808
2010-11	2049	11927

Note : Negative numbers in brackets. ADR: American Depository Receipt; GDR: Global Depository Receipt; ECB: External Commercial Borrowing.

Source : Reserve Bank of India.

65 : Net Resources Mobilised by Mutual Funds

(Rs. crore)

Year	Unit Trust of India	Bank-sponsored Mutual Funds	Financial Institution-sponsored Mutual Funds	Private Sector Mutual Funds	Total
1970-71	18	-	-	-	18
1980-81	52	-	-	-	52
1990-91	4553	2352	604	-	7509
2000-01	322	249	1273	9292	11136
2001-02	(7284)	863	406	16134	10119
2002-03	(9434)	1033	861	12122	4582
2003-04	1050	4526	787	41510	47873
2004-05	(2467)	706	(3384)	7933	2788
2005-06	3424	5365	2112	41581	52482
2006-07	7326	3033	4226	79477	94063
2007-08	10678	7597	2178	128032	148485
2008-09	(3659)	4489	5954	(31425)	(24641)
2009-10	15653	9855	4871	48166	78545
2010-11	(16636)	1304	(16988)	(15594)	(47914)

Note : Negative numbers in brackets.

Source : Securities and Exchange Board of India.

66 : Working of Clearing Corporation of India Limited

	Outright		Repo		Forex		CBLO	
	Number of Trades	Volume (Rs. crore)	Number of Trades	Volume (Rs. crore)	Number of Trades	Volume (Rs. crore)	Number of Trades	Volume (Rs. crore)
2002-03*	191843	1076147	11672	468229	100232	136102	159	852
2003-04	243585	1575133	20927	943189	330517	501342	3060	76851
2004-05	160682	1134222	24364	1557907	466327	899782	29351	976790
2005-06	125509	864751	25673	1694509	489649	1179688	67463	2953134
2006-07	137100	1021536	29008	2556501	606808	1776981	85881	4732271
2007-08	188843	1653851	26612	3948751	757074	3133665	113277	8110828
2008-09	245964	2160233	24280	4094286	837520	2758904	118941	8824784
2009-10	316956	2913890	28651	6072829	883949	2988971	142052	15541378
2010-11	332540	2870952	27409	4099284	1150037	4191037	145383	12259745

Note: * : February 2002 to March 2003.
CCIL commenced operations from February 2002.
Forex transactions commenced from November 8, 2002. Under it cash and tom settlement commenced from February 5, 2004. CBLO: Collateralised borrowing and lending obligation, commenced from January 20, 2003.

Source: Clearing Corporation of India.

67 : Trends in FII Investment in the Capital Market

Year	Gross Purchases (Rs. crore)	Gross Sales (Rs. crore)	Net Investment		Cumulative Net Investment ($ mn)
			Rs. crore	US $ mn.	
1992-93	17	4	13	4	4
1993-94	5593	466	5126	1634	1638
1994-95	7631	2835	4796	1528	3167
1995-96	9694	2752	6942	2036	5202
1996-97	15554	6979	8574	2432	7634
1997-98	18695	12737	5957	1650	9284
1998-99	16115	17699	-1584	-386	8898
1999-00	56856	46734	10122	2339	11237
2000-01	74051	64116	9935	2159	13396
2001-02	49920	41165	8755	1846	15242
2002-03	47061	44373	2688	562	15804
2003-04	144858	99094	45764	9950	25754
2004-05	216951	171071	45880	10352	36293
2005-06	346976	305509	41467	9363	45656
2006-07	520506	489665	30841	6821	52477
2007-08	948018	881839	66179	16442	69179
2008-09	614576	660386	-45811	-9837	59081
2009-10	846437	703779	142658	30252	89333
2010-11	992598	846161	146438	32226	121559

Note : FII : Foreign Institutional Investor.
Source : Securities and Exchange Board of India.

68 : Progress of Cash Segment in Bombay Stock Exchange

Year	No. of Companies Listed	No. of Trades (lakh)	Traded Quantity (lakh)	Turnover (Rs. crore)	Avg. Daily Turnover (Rs. crore)	Avg. Trade Size (Rs. crore)	Market Capitalisation (Rs. crore)
1992-93	2861	126	35031	45696	238	3632	188146
2000-01	5869	1428	258511	1000032	3984	7002	571553
2001-02	5782	1277	182196	307292	1244	24060	612224
2002-03	5650	1413	221401	314073	1251	22226	572197
2003-04	5528	2028	390441	503053	1981	24806	1201206
2004-05	4731	2374	477171	518715	2050	21849	1698428
2005-06	4781	2640	664455	816074	3251	30911	3022190
2006-07	4821	3462	560777	956185	3840	27618	3545041
2007-08	4887	5303	986010	1578857	6290	29771	5138014
2008-09	4929	5408	739600	1100074	4527	20342	3086075
2009-10	4975	6056	1136513	1378809	5651	22768	6165619
2010-11	5067	5285	990777	1105027	4333	20910	6839084

Source : Bombay Stock Exchange.

69 : Progress of Cash Segment in National Stock Exchange

Year	No. of Companies Listed	No of Trades (lakh)	Traded Quantity (lakh)	Turnover (Rs. crore)	Avg. Daily Turnover (Rs. crore)	Avg. Trade Size (Rs. crore)	Market Capitalisation (Rs. crore)
1995-96	422	66	39912	67287	276	101950	401459
2000-01	785	1676	329536	1339510	5337	86980	657847
2001-02	793	1753	278408	513167	2078	29270	636861
2002-03	818	2398	364065	617989	2462	25776	537133
2003-04	909	3780	713301	1099534	4329	29090	1120976
2004-05	970	4508	797685	1140072	4471	25283	1585585
2005-06	1069	6089	844486	1569558	6253	25044	2813201
2006-07	1228	7847	855456	1945287	7812	24790	3367350
2007-08	1381	11727	1498469	3551038	14148	30280	4858122
2008-09	1432	13650	1426355	2752023	11325	20161	2896194
2009-10	1470	16816	2215530	4138023	16959	24608	6009173
2010-11	1574	15507	1824515	3577410	14029	23070	6702616

Source : National Stock Exchange.

70 : Aggregate Deposits of NBFC Sector

(Rs. crore)

Year (end-March)	NBFC		RNBC		Total Public Deposits
	No. of Reporting Companies	Public Deposits	No. of Reporting Companies	Public Deposits	
1998	1420	13572	9	10249	23820
1999	1536	9785	11	10644	20429
2000	996	8338	9	11004	19342
2001	974	6459	7	11625	18085
2002	905	5933	5	12889	18822
2003	870	5035	5	15065	20100
2004	774	4317	3	15327	19644
2005	700	3926	3	16600	20526
2006	432	2447	3	20175	22622
2007	371	2075	3	22622	24697
2008	350	2042	2	22358	24400
2009	288	1941	2	19596	21567
2010	228	2727	2	14520	17247

Note : NBFC : Non-Banking Financial Company.
RNBC : Residuary Non-Banking Company.

Source : Reserve Bank of India.

71 : Derivative Segments at BSE and NSE (Equity)

	Bombay Stock Exchange				National Stock Exchange			
			Open Interest at the End of Fiscal				Open Interest at the End of Fiscal	
	No. of Contracts	Turnover (Rs. crore)	No. of Contracts	Turnover (Rs. crore)	No. of Contracts	Turnover (Rs. crore)	No. of Contracts	Turnover (Rs. crore)
2001-02	105527	1922			4196873	101925	93917	2150
2002-03	138037	2478	375	7	16768909	439865	97025	2194
2003-04	382258	12452	35	1	56886776	2130649	235792	7188
2004-05	531719	16112	0	0	77017185	2547053	592646	21052
2005-06	203	9	408	13	157619271	4824250	1028003	38469
2006-07	1545169	59006	408	13	216883573	7356271	1791549	38670
2007-08	7453371	242309	3175	74	425013200	13090478	2282671	48900
2008-09	496502	11775	22	0	657390497	11010482	3227759	57705
2009-10	9026	234	0	0	679293922	17663665	3489790	97978
2010-11	5623	154	4	0	1034212062	29248221	3690373	101816

Source : Securities and Exchange Board of India.

72 : Number of Joint Stock Companies and Paid-up Capital

31st March	Companies in Operation		Companies that Ceased Operation	
	Number	Paid-up Capital (Rs. crore)	Number	% to Operating Cos.
1951	28532	775	830	2.9
1961	26149	1819	2449	9.4
1971	30461	4423	472	1.5
1981	62714	15555	391	0.6
1991	224452	68111	173	0.1
2001	569100	341229	495	0.1
2002	589246	405753	760	0.1
2003	612155	457059	953	0.2
2004	641512	498791	498	0.1
2005	679649	654022	1777	0.3
2006	732169	619152	1380	0.2
2007	743678	649490	17818	2.4
2008	na	na	na	
2009	786774	na	32705	4.2
2010	872740	na	10185	1.2

Note : na : not available.
Data for 2010 pertains to end-December.

Source : Annual Report of Ministry of Company Affairs.

73 : Financial Assistance by All-India Finanical Institutions

(Rs. crore)

	Sanctions (Rs. crore)	Disbursements (Rs. crore)	Disbursement/ Sanctions (%)
1966-67	152	141	92.8
1970-71	254	160	62.9
1980-81	2927	1848	63.1
1990-91	19202	12810	66.7
2000-01	120548	75364	62.5
2001-02*	75089	58735	78.2
2002-03*	28311	26705	94.3
2003-04*	40759	30173	74.0
2004-05*	30404	21506	70.7
2005-06*	27665	21146	76.4
2006-07*	31259	38653	123.7
2007-08*	58733	46028	78.4
2008-09*	105228	94270	89.6
2009-10*	106760	92067	86.2
2010-11*	101448	87964	86.7

Note : * : The adoption of the system of universal banking and the merger of institutions have produced kinks in the data series.

Source : Reserve Bank of India.

74 : Selected Performance Indicators of Corporate Sector (RBI Sample)

	Public Limited Companies		
	1990-91	2000-01	2009-10
Number of Companies	1802	2031	3352
Capital Structure Ratios (%)			
1. Net Fixed Assets to Total Net Assets	41.7	47.3	37.7
2. Net Worth to Total Net Assets	29.6	37.6	44.8
3. Debt to Equity	98.1	68.3	43.6
4. Debt to Equity (Adjusted)	116.6	72.4	44.8
5. Short-Term Bank Borrowings to Inventory	51.2	70.1	82.7
Liquidity Ratios (%)			
1. Current Ratio (Current assets to current liabilities)	1.3	1.2	1.2
2. Quick Ratio % (Quick assets to current liabilities)	48.8	48.4	55.4
3. Current Assets to Total Net Assets	53.9	43.5	44.1
4. Sundry Creditors to Current Assets	27.1	28.5	26.4
5. Sundry Creditors to Net Working Capital	115.3	178.4	132.0
Asset Utilisation Ratios (%)			
1. Sales to Total Net Assets	93.6	78.0	69.0
2. Sales to Gross Fixed Assets	139.3	110.8	127.9
3. Exports to Sales	6.2	13.6	16.4
4. Gross Value Added to Gross Fixed Assets	35.0	23.5	31.6

contd...

...contd...

	Public Limited Companies		
	1990-91	2000-01	2009-10
Number of Companies	1802	2031	3352
Turnover Ratios (%)			
1. Inventory to Sales	25.6	19.1	17.0
2. Sundry Debtors to Sales	16.4	16.1	15.8
3. Raw Material Consumed to Value of Production	49.8	53.7	53.0
4. Remuneration to Employees to Sales	9.9	7.3	7.1
Profitability Ratios (%)			
1. Gross Profit to Total Net Assets	10.8	7.4	9.3
2. Gross Profit to Sales	11.6	9.8	13.5
3. Profit after Tax to Net Worth	13.9	6.3	12.2
Profit Allocation Ratios (%)			
1. Tax Provision to Gross Profit	16.7	13.9	22.2
2. Tax Provision to Profit After Tax	30.6	30.4	37.6
3. Profit Retained to Profit after Tax	64.6	49.4	75.5
4. Dividend to Net Worth	4.9	3.2	3.0
5. Ordinary Dividend to Ordinary Paid-up Capital	18.4	13.4	30.3
6. Interest to Gross Profit	50.8	63.2	23.3
7. Profit Retained to Gross Profit	24.5	15.7	44.6

Note : na : not available.
The number of companies indicates the number whose balance sheet have been included in this data and not the actual number of companies in existence.

Source : Reserve Bank of India.

75 : Financial Performance of Indian Corporate Sector

(Rs. crore)

	Public Limited Companies		
	(1990-91)	(2000-01)	(2009-10)
Number of Companies	1802	2031	3352
Sales	89912	326464	2262456
Operating Profits	5124	11738	233507
Depreciation	3792	15923	95688
Gross Profits	10407	31919	304536
Interest	5283	20181	71029
Profit Before Tax	5697	14605	247385
Profit After Tax	3955	10159	179825
Profit Retained	2554	5021	135773
Profitability Ratios			
Operating Margin (%)	5.7	3.6	10.3
Gross Margin (%)	11.6	9.8	13.5
Net Margin (%)	4.4	3.1	7.9
Interest Cover (times)	2.0	1.6	4.3
Cost Structure of Companies			
Manufacturing Expenses	59855	219421	1549977
of which: Fuel & Power	6775	22869	97485
Remuneration to Employees	8897	23819	160771
Other Operating Expenses	26709	97979	272505
of which: Advertisement	589	3932	22709
Depreciation	3792	15923	95688
Cost as % to Sales			
Manufacturing Expenses	66.6	67.2	68.5
of which: Fuel & Power	7.5	7.0	4.3
Remuneration to Employees	9.9	7.3	7.1
Other Operating Expenses	29.7	30.0	12.0
of which: Advertisement	0.7	1.2	1.0
Depreciation	4.2	4.9	4.2

Note: The data given here are indicative only and not exhaustive as the number of companies included in the study are limited.
Operating Margin is the per cent of operating profit to sales.
Gross margin is the per cent of gross profit to sales.
Net margin is the per cent of profit after tax to sales.
Interst cover measures the number of times gross profit can cover interest.

Source: Relevant Issues of Reserve Bank of India Bulletins.

76 : Trend in Forex Transaction of Indian Corporate Sector

(Rs. crore)

Public Limited Companies	1982-83	1990-91	2000-01	2009-10
Number of Companies	1838	1802	2031	3352
Expenditure in Foreign Currencies	2382	8068	69025	663746
% to Total Expenditure	*6.9*	*8.4*	*20.2*	*27.7*
Imports	1980	7077	57469	544396
Imports/Sales Ratio %	*6.0*	*8.0*	*17.6*	*24.1*
Raw Materials	1409	5587	47776	426705
% to Total Raw Materials	*8.1*	*12.2*	*27.1*	*35.1*
Earnings in Foreign Currencies	1904	6434	57369	526440
% to Total Income	*5.5*	*6.7*	*16.8*	*22.0*
Exports	1601	5569	44281	371064
Exports/Sales%	*4.8*	*6.3*	*13.6*	*16.4*
Net Inflow(+)/Net Outflow(-)	-478	-1634	-11656	-137306

Note : The data given here are indicative only and not exhaustive as the number of companies included in the study are limited.
Source : Reserve Bank of India.

77 : Decadal Inflationary Trends

	1. Wholesale Price Index				2. Consumer Price Index: Industrial Workers			
	March over March Basis		On an Average Basis		March over March Basis		On an Average Basis	
	Index	Growth	Index	Growth	Index	Growth	Index	Growth
Decadal Growth (Average Annual Increases)								
1951-60		1.7		1.7		5.0		2.3
1961-70		6.5		6.4		5.9		4.1
1971-80		9.7		9.0		8.0		7.2
1981-90		7.3		8.0		9.0		10.2
1991-00		8.6		8.1		9.4		9.5
2001-10		5.9		5.3		6.2		5.9

Source : Office of the Economic Adviser and Labour Bureau.

78 : Annual Inflationary Trends

	1. Wholesale Price Index (New series with Base 2004-05=100)				2. Consumer Price Index: Industrial Workers			
	March over March Basis		On an Average Basis		March over March Basis		On an Average Basis	
	Index	Growth	Index	Growth	Index	Growth	Index	Growth
2004-05	101.4		100.0		113	3.7	520	3.9
2005-06	105.7	4.2	104.5	4.5	119	5.3	542	4.3
2006-07	112.8	6.7	111.4	6.6	127	6.7	579	6.8
2007-08	121.5	7.7	116.6	4.7	137	7.9	133	6.4
2008-09	123.5	1.6	126.0	8.1	148	8.0	145	9.0
2009-10	136.3	10.4	130.8	3.8	170	14.9	163	12.4
2010-11	149.5	9.7	143.3	9.6	185	8.8	180	10.4

Note: With effect from October 17, 2009 Office of the Economic Adviser discontinued to issue price index on all commodities on a weekly basis instead monthly price index were dessiminated. Hence in this table and the subsequent tables point-to-point basis is worked out by using March data and not end-March data.

The base of WPI is changed from 1993-94 to 2004-05 with effect from 14 September 2010.

Source : Office of the Economic Adviser and Labour Bureau.

79 : Changing Weights of Selected Primary Commodities Over the Years in Different Wholesale Price Indices

	1952-53=100	1961-62=100	1970-71=100	1981-82=100	1993-94=100	2004-05=100
All Commodities	100.00	100.00	100.00	100.00	100.00	100.00
Primary Articles	54.04	38.78	41.67	32.30	22.03	20.12
Fuel, Power, Light & Lubricants	2.84	6.04	8.46	10.66	14.23	14.91
Manufacturing Products	39.03	55.18	49.87	57.04	63.75	64.97
Food Grains	23.48	14.78	12.92	7.92	5.01	4.09
Cereals	19.25	12.10	10.74	6.82	4.41	3.37
Rice	11.30	6.69	5.13	3.69	2.45	1.79
Wheat	5.34	3.22	3.42	2.25	1.38	1.12
Pulses	4.23	2.68	2.18	1.09	0.60	0.72
Gram	1.51	1.07	1.04	0.41	0.22	0.33
Arhar	na	0.66	0.52	0.27	0.13	0.14
Moong	na	0.21	0.26	0.20	0.11	0.08
Fruits & Vegetables	2.27	2.36	6.13	4.09	2.92	3.84
Potato	0.46	0.62	1.01	0.47	0.26	0.20
Onions	0.15	0.08	0.19	0.16	0.09	0.18
Banana	1.21	0.99	0.65	0.47	0.28	0.34
Milk	4.69	2.97	4.52	1.78	2.21	3.24
Condiments & Spices	2.17	1.20	1.09	0.95	0.66	0.57
Chillies	na	na	0.50	0.32	0.19	0.16
Tea	1.92	1.94	1.15	0.56	0.16	0.11
Sugar Group	4.79	6.49	7.24	4.06	3.93	2.09
Sugar	1.76	3.68	2.19	2.01	3.62	1.74
Gur	3.03	2.44	4.56	1.75	0.06	0.08
Edible Oils	4.69	5.37	3.72	2.45	2.76	3.04
Groundnut Oil	1.92	2.48	1.42	0.53	0.17	0.30
Rapeseed & Mustard Oil	1.31	1.03	0.67	0.28	0.49	0.45
Fibres	6.09	4.11	3.17	1.79	1.52	0.88
Raw Cotton	3.16	2.24	2.25	1.34	1.36	0.70
Oilseeds	6.01	5.26	4.20	3.86	2.67	1.78
Groundnut	2.74	2.52	1.82	1.82	1.03	0.40
Rapeseed & Mustard	1.04	0.90	0.82	1.75	0.58	0.34
Mineral Oils	1.44	3.02	4.91	6.67	6.99	9.36

Note : Weight of primary articles, fuel, power, light & lubricants and manufactured products for the base year=1952-53 and 1961-62 are worked out by Economic and Political Weekly Research Foundation.

Source : Office of the Economic Adviser, (GoI).

80 : Average Price of Gold and Silver: India and International

Year	Gold				Silver			
		London				New York		
	Mumbai Rs. per 10 gms	$ per Troy oz.	In Re. Terms/10 gms	Difference in Prices (Rs.)	Mumbai Rs. per kg	Cents per Troy oz.	In Re. Terms/kg	Difference in Prices (Rs.)
1950-51	97	..	..	..	159	..	..	..
1960-61	115	..	..	..	194	..	..	..
1970-71	185	37	89	96	536	171	415	121
1980-81	1522	585	1485	38	2618	1585	4020	(1403)
1990-91	3452	375	2164	1287	6761	450	2579	4182
2000-01	4474	272	4008	466	7868	484	7110	758
2001-02	4579	278	4260	319	7447	437	6709	738
2002-03	5332	325	5062	270	7991	467	7268	722
2003-04	5719	378	5574	145	8722	542	7982	739
2004-05	6145	414	5976	169	10681	676	9767	914
2005-06	6901	477	6790	110	11829	801	11417	411
2006-07	9240	628	9138	103	19057	1248	18134	923
2007-08	9996	766	9897	99	19427	1449	18738	689
2008-09	12890	867	12817	73	21248	1375	20059	1188
2009-10	15756	1023	15570	186	25321	1576	23980	1341
2010-11	19227	1294	18937	290	37290	2391	35051	2239

Source : Reserve Bank of India.

81 : Receipt Budget of Centre

(Rs. crore)

Year	Revenue Receipts	Capital Receipts	Total Receipts	Growth (%)			Total Receipts as % of GDP
				Revenue	Capital	Total	
1950-51	406	106	512				5.1
1960-61	877	1156	2033	8.0	27.0	14.8	11.7
1970-71	3293	2046	5339	14.1	5.9	10.1	11.5
1980-81	12373	7918	20291	14.2	14.5	14.3	14.0
1990-91	54954	38997	93951	16.1	17.3	16.6	16.5
2000-01	192605	134184	326789	13.4	13.2	13.3	15.5
2001-02	201306	162500	363806	4.5	21.1	11.3	16.0
2002-03	230834	180531	411365	14.7	11.1	13.1	16.8
2003-04	263813	211333	475146	14.3	17.1	15.5	17.2
2004-05	305991	200391	506382	16.0	-5.2	6.6	15.6
2005-06	347077	179549	526626	13.4	-10.4	4.0	14.3
2006-07	434387	144482	578869	25.2	-19.5	9.9	13.5
2007-08	541864	197978	739842	24.7	37.0	27.8	14.8
2008-09	540259	299863	839935	-0.3	51.5	13.5	15.0
2009-10	572811	453063	1025883	6.0	51.1	22.1	15.7
2010-11RE	783833	563685	1231576	36.8	24.4	20.1	15.6
2011-12BE	789892	664457	1237728	0.8	17.9	0.5	

Note : 1. RE: Revised Estimates, BE: Budget Estimates.
2. Tax Revenue, Direct Tax and Indirect Tax are the Net of State Governments' share and amount assigned to National Calamity Contingency Fund (NCCF).
3. Capital Receipts and Total Receipts of 2007 includes an amount of Rs. 34,309 crore which represents the Reserve Bank's surplus transferred to the Central Government on account of transfer of its stake in SBI to the Central Government.
4. The taxes and duties referred to in the Union list are now distributed in the same manner as laid down by the Constitution (Eighteenth Amendment) Act, 2000 read along with the recommendations of the Twelfth Finance Commission.
5. GDP data upto 2004-05 pertains to 1993-94 series thereafter it is 2004-05 series.

Source : RBI (2009). *Handbook of Statistics on the Indian Economy, Report on Currency and Finance 1970-71* and Budget Document (2011-12).

82 : Trends in Tax Revenue of Centre

(Rs. crore)

Year	Gross Tax Revenue	% to GDP	States Share	NCCF Expenditure	Net Tax Revenues	Non-Tax Revenues	Revenue Receipts
1950-51	405	4.02	48		357	49	406
1960-61	895	5.14	179		730	147	877
1970-71	3206	6.93	755		2451	891	3293
1980-81	13179	9.07	3791		9388	3442	12373
1990-91	57577	10.11	14598		43042	11976	54954
2000-01	188605	8.97	51688		136658	55947	192605
2001-02	187060	8.21	52842	686	133532	67774	201306
2002-03	216266	8.81	56122	1600	158544	72290	230834
2003-04	254348	9.23	65766	1600	186982	76831	263813
2004-05	304958	9.41	78595	1565	224798	81193	305991
2005-06	366151	9.92	94385	2825	268941	76813	347077
2006-07	473512	11.03	120330	2000	351182	83205	434387
2007-08	593147	11.90	151800	1800	439547	102317	541864
2008-09	605299	10.84	160179	1800	443320	96940	540260
2009-10	624528	9.53	164832	3160	456536	116275	572811
2010-11RE	786888	9.99	219303	3900	563685	220149	783834
2011-12BE	932440		263458	4525	664457	125435	789892

Note : RE: Revised Estimates, BE: Budget Estimates.
GDP data upto 2004-05 pertains to 1993-94 series thereafter it is 2004-05 series.

Source : RBI (2009). *Handbook of Statistics on the Indian Economy*, *Report on Currency and Finance 1970-71* and Budget Document (2010-11).

83 : Trends in Gross Tax Revenue of Centre

(Rs. crore)

Year	Gross Tax Revenue	*of which:* Corporate Tax	Taxes on Income other than Corporation Tax	Customs Duty	Union Excise Duties	Service Tax
1950-51	405	41	133	157	68	0
	(100.0)	(10.1)	(32.8)	(38.8)	(16.8)	(0.0)
1960-61	895	111	167	170	416	0
	(100.0)	(12.4)	(18.7)	(19.0)	(46.5)	(0.0)
1970-71	3206	371	473	524	1759	0
	(100.0)	(11.6)	(14.8)	(16.3)	(54.9)	(0.0)
1980-81	13179	1311	1506	3410	6500	0
	(100.0)	(9.9)	(11.4)	(25.9)	(49.3)	(0.0)
1990-91	57577	5335	5371	20644	24514	0
	(100.0)	(9.3)	(9.3)	(35.9)	(42.6)	(0.0)
2000-01	188605	35696	31764	47542	68526	2613
	(100.0)	(18.9)	(16.8)	(25.2)	(36.3)	(1.4)
2001-02	187060	36609	32004	40268	72555	3302
	(100.0)	(19.6)	(17.1)	(21.5)	(38.8)	(1.8)
2002-03	216266	46172	36866	44852	82310	4122
	(100.0)	(21.3)	(17.0)	(20.7)	(38.1)	(1.9)
2003-04	254348	63562	41387	48629	90774	7891
	(100.0)	(25.0)	(16.3)	(19.1)	(35.7)	(3.1)

contd...

...contd...

Year	Gross Tax Revenue	*of which:* Corporate Tax	Taxes on Income other than Corporation Tax	Customs Duty	Union Excise Duties	Service Tax
2004-05	304958	82680	49268	57611	99125	14200
	(100.0)	(27.1)	(16.2)	(18.9)	(32.5)	(4.7)
2005-06	366151	101277	55985	65067	111226	23055
	(100.0)	(27.7)	(15.3)	(17.8)	(30.4)	(6.3)
2006-07	473512	144318	75093	86327	117613	37598
	(100.0)	(30.5)	(15.9)	(18.2)	(24.8)	(7.9)
2007-08	593147	192911	102644	104119	123611	51301
	(100.0)	(32.5)	(17.3)	(17.6)	(20.8)	(8.6)
2008-09	605298	213395	106046	99879	108613	60941
	(100.0)	(35.3)	(17.5)	(16.5)	(17.9)	(10.1)
2009-10	633095	244725	122370	83324	102991	58422
	(100.0)	(38.7)	(19.3)	(13.2)	(16.3)	(9.2)
2010-11RE	746651	296377	141566	131800	137263	69400
	(100.0)	(39.7)	(19.0)	(17.7)	(18.4)	(9.3)
2011-12BE	932440	359990	164526	151700	163550	82000
	(100.0)	(38.6)	(17.6)	(16.3)	(17.5)	(8.8)

Note : Figures in brackets are percentages to Gross Tax Revenue. BE: Budget Estimates, RE: Revised Estimates.
Source : Budget Documents 2011-12.

84 : Trends in Non-Tax Revenue of Centre

(Rs. crore)

Year	Non-Tax Revenue	% to GTR	% to GDP	Interest Receipt	Profit & Dividend	Others
1950-51	49	12.1	0.49	0	23	26
1960-61	147	16.4	0.84	15	53	9
1970-71	891	27.8	1.93	575	121	195
1980-81	3442	26.1	2.37	1795	292	1355
1990-91	11976	20.8	2.10	8730	774	2472
2000-01	55947	29.7	2.66	33895	9553	9763
2001-02	67774	36.2	2.97	35538	17290	14946
2002-03	72290	33.4	2.95	37622	21230	13438
2003-04	76831	30.2	2.79	38538	21160	17133
2004-05	81193	26.6	2.50	32387	22939	25867
2005-06	76813	21.0	2.08	22032	25451	29330
2006-07	83205	17.6	1.94	22524	29309	31372
2007-08	102317	17.2	2.05	21060	34499	46758
2008-09	96940	16.0	1.74	20717	38607	37616
2009-10	116275	18.4	1.78	21756	50248	44271
2010-11RE	220149	29.5	2.80	19728	48727	151694
2011-12BE	125435	13.5		19578	42624	63233

Note : RE: Revised Estimates, BE: Budget Estimates, GTR: Gross Tax Revenue. GDP data upto 2004-05 pertains to 1993-94 series thereafter it is 2004-05 series.

Source : Budget Documents 2011-12.

85 : Capital Receipts of Centre

(Rs. crore)

Year	Market Borrowings (net)	Small Savings; PF, Special Deposit	Recovery of Loans	Disinvestment Receipts	External Loans (net)	Other Capital Receipts	Total Capital Receipts	% of GDP
1950-51	30	60	10	nr	8		106	1.05
1960-61	181	344	126	nr	505		1156	6.64
1970-71	238	275	923	nr	332	278	2046	4.42
1980-81	2679	1997	2096	nr	1281	-135	7918	5.45
1990-91	8001	18027	5712	nr	3181	4076	38997	6.85
2000-01	73431	21690	12046	2125	7505	17387	134184	6.38
2001-02	87724	20998	16403	3646	5601	28128	162500	7.13
2002-03	97588	13947	34191	3151	-11934	43588	180531	7.35
2003-04	88860	5002	67165	16953	-13488	46841	211333	7.67
2004-05	46031	-440	62043	4424	14753	73580	200391	6.18
2005-06	95374	6032	10645	1581	7472	58445	179549	4.86
2006-07	110446	5178	5893	534	8472	13959	144482	3.36
2007-08	131768	-7405	5100	38795	9315	20405	197978	3.97
2008-09	233630	6739	6139	566	11015	41774	299863	5.37
2009-10	398424	29312	8613	24581	11038	-18905	453063	6.92
2010-11RE	355414	27781	9001	22744	22264	10539	447743	5.69
2011-12BE	343000	34182	15020	40000	14500	1134	447836	

Note : RE: Revised Estimates, BE: Budget Estimates, nr: not relevant.
GDP data upto 2004-05 pertains to 1993-94 series thereafter it is 2004-05 series.

Source : Budget Documents 2011-12.

86 : Central Government Total Expenditure

(Rs. crore)

Year	Revenue Expenditure		Capital Expenditure		Total Expenditure		
	Rs. crore	% to GDP	Rs. crore	% to GDP	Rs. crore	Growth (%)	% to GDP
1950-51	346	3.4	184	1.8	530		5.3
1960-61	826	4.7	1029	5.9	1855	13.3	10.7
1970-71	3130	6.8	2494	5.4	5624	11.7	12.2
1980-81	14410	9.9	8358	5.7	22768	15.0	15.7
1990-91	73516	12.9	31782	5.6	105298	16.5	18.5
2000-01	277839	13.2	47753	2.3	325592	12.0	15.5
2001-02	301468	13.2	60842	2.7	362310	11.3	15.9
2002-03	338713	13.8	74535	3.0	413248	14.1	16.8
2003-04	362074	13.1	109129	4.0	471203	14.0	17.1
2004-05	384329	11.9	113923	3.5	498252	5.7	15.4
2005-06	439376	11.9	66362	1.8	505738	1.5	13.7
2006-07	514609	12.0	68778	1.6	583387	15.4	13.6
2007-08	594433	11.9	118238	2.4	712671	22.2	14.3
2008-09	793798	14.2	90158	1.6	883956	24.0	15.8
2009-10	911809	13.9	112678	1.7	1024487	15.9	15.6
2010-11RE	1053678	13.4	162898	2.1	1216576	18.7	15.4
2011-12BE	1097162		160567		1257729	3.4	

Note : RE: Revised Estimates, BE: Budget Estimates.
GDP data upto 2004-05 pertains to 1993-94 series thereafter it is 2004-05 series.

Source : Budget Documents 2011-12.

87 : Selected Heads of Expenditure

Year	Centre's Expenditure (Rs. crore)	Defence		Interest Payments		Subsidies	
		Rs. crore	% to Total	Rs. crore	% to Total	Rs. crore	% to Total
1950-51	530	168	31.7	37	7.0		0.0
1960-61	1855	281	15.0	77	4.2		0.0
1970-71	5624	1206	21.4	606	10.8	94	1.7
1980-81	22768	3604	15.8	2604	11.4	2028	8.9
1990-91	105298	15426	14.6	21498	20.4	12158	11.5
2000-01	325592	49622	15.2	99314	30.5	26839	8.2
2001-02	362310	24266	6.7	107460	29.7	31210	8.6
2002-03	413248	55662	13.5	117804	28.5	43533	10.5
2003-04	471203	60066	12.7	124088	26.3	44323	9.4
2004-05	498252	75856	15.2	126934	25.5	45957	9.2
2005-06	505738	80549	15.9	132630	26.2	47522	9.4
2006-07	583387	85510	14.7	150272	25.8	57125	9.8
2007-08	712671	91681	12.9	171030	24.0	70926	10.0
2008-09	883956	114223	12.9	192204	21.7	129708	14.7
2009-10	1024487	141781	13.8	213093	20.8	143151	14.0
2010-11RE	1216576	151582	12.5	240757	19.8	164153	13.5
2011-12BE	1257729	164415	13.1	267986	21.3	143570	11.4

Note: RE: Revised Estimates, BE: Budget Estimates, % to Total = per cent to total expenditure.
Source: Budget Documents 2011-12.

88 : Major Deficit Indicators of Centre

(Rs. crore)

Year	Revenue Deficit		Fiscal Deficit		Primary Deficit		Net RBI Credit to Centre
		% to GDP		% to GDP		% to GDP	
1951-52	-126	-1.2		0.0		0.0	
1960-61	-50	-0.3		0.0		0.0	
1970-71	-163	-0.4	1408	3.0	803	1.7	376
1980-81	2037	1.4	8299	5.7	5695	3.9	3551
1990-91	18561	3.3	44632	7.8	23134	4.1	14746
2000-01	85234	4.1	118816	5.7	19502	0.9	6705
2001-02	100162	4.4	140955	6.2	33495	1.5	-5150
2002-03	107879	4.4	145072	5.9	27268	1.1	-28399
2003-04	98262	3.6	123273	4.5	-815	0.0	-76065
2004-05	78338	2.4	125794	3.9	-1140	0.0	-60177
2005-06	92300	2.5	146435	4.0	13805	0.4	28417
2006-07	80222	1.9	142573	3.3	-7699	-0.2	-3024
2007-08	52569	1.1	126912	2.5	-44118	-0.9	-116772
2008-09	253539	4.5	336992	6.0	144788	2.6	176397
2009-10	338998	5.2	418482	6.4	205389	3.1	149820
2010-11RE	269844	3.4	400998	5.1	160241	2.0	182454
2011-12BE	307270		412817		144831		149483*

Note: Negative sign indicates surplus in the deficit indicators. * : upto July 29, 2011, RE: Revised Estimates, BE : Budget Estimates.
GDP data upto 2004-05 pertains to 1993-94 series thereafter it is 2004-05 series.

Source: Budget Documents 2011-12.

89 : Financing Gross Fiscal Deficit (GFD)

(Rs. crore)

Year	Gross Fiscal Deficit	Financing of GFD				
		External Finance	Internal Finance			
			Market Borrowings	% to Gross Fiscal Deficit	Other Borrowings	Draw Down on Cash Balances
1980-81	8299	1281	2679	32.3	1862	2477
1990-91	44632	3181	8001	17.9	22103	11347
2000-01	118816	7505	73431	61.8	39077	-1197
2001-02	140955	5601	90812	64.4	46038	-1496
2002-03	145072	-11934	104126	71.8	50997	1883
2003-04	123273	-13488	88870	72.1	51833	-3942
2004-05	125794	14753	50940	40.5	68231	-1461
2005-06	146435	7472	106241	72.6	53610	-20888
2006-07	142573	8472	114801	80.5	14782	4517
2007-08	126912	9315	130600	102.9	-39597	-27171

contd...

(Rs. crore)

...contd...

Year	Gross Fiscal Deficit	Financing of GFD				
		External Finance	Internal Finance			
			Market Borrowings	% to Gross Fiscal Deficit	Other Borrowings	Draw Down on Cash Balances
2008-09	336992	11015	233630	69.3	39751	43834
2009-10	418482	11038	398424	95.2	10407	-1386
2010-11RE	400998	22464	335414	83.6	58320	-15000
2011-12BE	412817	14500	343000	83.1	35317	20000

Note : RE: Revised Estimates, BE: Budget Estimates.
1) Data for 2011-12 are budget estimates & 2010-11 are revised estimates.
2) Market Borrowing include dated securities and 364-day treasury bills.
3) Other borrowings comprise small savings, state provident fund, special deposits, reserve funds, treasury bills excluding 364-day.
4) Market Borrowing is exclusive of amount raised under Market Stabilisation Scheme.

Source : Budget Documents 2011-12.

90 : Total Liabilities of Centre

(Rs. crore)

Year	Internal Liabilities	% GDP	External Liabilities	% GDP	Total Liabilities	% GDP
1950-51	2833	28.1	32	0.3	2865	28.4
1960-61	5784	33.2	761	4.4	6244	35.9
1970-71	13379	28.9	6485	14.0	19864	43.0
1980-81	48451	33.3	11298	7.8	59749	41.1
1990-91	283033	49.7	31525	5.5	314558	55.2
2000-01	1102596	56.5	65945	3.4	1168541	59.9
2001-02	1294862	56.8	71546	3.1	1366408	60.0
2002-03	1499589	61.1	59612	2.4	1559201	63.5
2003-04	1690554	61.4	46124	1.7	1736678	63.0
2004-05	1933544	59.6	60877	1.9	1994421	61.5
2005-06	2165902	58.7	94243	2.6	2260145	61.2
2006-07	2435880	56.7	102716	2.4	2538596	59.1
2007-08	2725394	54.7	112031	2.2	2837426	56.9
2008-09	3036132	54.4	123046	2.2	3159178	56.6
2009-10	3383761	51.7	134083	2.0	3517844	53.7
2010-11RE	3774758	47.9	156347	2.0	3931105	49.9
2011-12BE	4181842		170847		4352689	

Note : RE: Revised Estimates, BE: Budget Estimates.
GDP data upto 2004-05 pertains to 1993-94 series thereafter to the 2004-2005 series.

Source : Reserve Bank of India and Budget Documents.

91 : Components of Centre's Internal Liabilities

(Rs. crore)

Year	Internal Debt	% to GDP	Small Savings & PF	% to GDP	Other Liabilities	% to GDP
1950-51	2022	20.0	337	3.3	474	4.7
1960-61	3975	22.8	973	5.6	835	4.8
1970-71	7663	16.6	3050	6.6	2666	5.8
1980-81	30864	21.2	10621	7.3	6966	4.8
1990-91	154004	27.0	61771	10.8	67258	11.8
2000-01	803698	41.2	96343	4.9	202555	10.4
2001-02	913061	40.1	144511	6.3	237290	10.4
2002-03	1020689	41.6	226400	9.2	252500	10.3
2003-04	1141706	41.4	288378	10.5	260470	9.5
2004-05	1275971	39.4	390477	12.0	267096	8.2
2005-06	1389758	37.6	479761	13.0	296383	8.0
2006-07	1544975	36.0	539450	12.6	351455	8.2
2007-08	1808359	36.3	553620	11.1	363416	7.3
2008-09	2028549	36.3	553518	9.9	454065.04	8.1
2009-10	2349147	35.9	581033	8.9	453581	6.9
2010-11RE	2703844	34.3	590809	7.5	480105	6.1
2011-12BE	3110618		600903		470321	

Note : RE: Revised Estimates, BE: Budget Estimates; PF: Provident Fund.
Other liabilities include others and reserve fund and deposits.
GDP data upto 2004-05 pertains to 1993-94 series thereafter it is 2004-05 series.

Source : Reserve Bank of India and Budget Documents.

92 : Receipts of State Governments

(Rs. crore)

Year	Total Revenue Receipts	Tax Receipts	Non-Tax Receipts	Total Capital Receipts	Total Receipts
1951-52	396	281	115	135	531
1960-61	1012	625	387	580	1592
1970-71	3371	2284	1087	1662	5033
1980-81	16294	10405	5888	5473	21767
1990-91	66467	44586	21881	24693	91160
2000-01	232509	164314	68195	109705	342214
2001-02	249422	175415	74007	115714	365136
2002-03	273674	193474	80200	140866	414539
2003-04	309187	221117	88074	205641	514828
2004-05	363512	260577	102935	200148	563660
2005-06	431021	306332	124690	164607	595628
2006-07	530556	372841	157714	143049	673605
2007-08	623748	437948	185799	141987	765735
2008-09	694657	482983	211675	196634	891292
2009-10RE	807388	531004	276384	237355	1044743
2010-11BE	913038	627147	285891	242860	1155898

Note : RE: Revised Estimates, BE: Budget Estimates.
Source : Reserve Bank of India study on State Finances.

93 : Components of State Tax Receipts

(Rs. crore)

Year	Total Tax Receipts of States		of which:					
		% to GDP	Sales Tax	% Share of Total Tax Receipts	State Excise Duties	% Share of Total Tax Receipts	Transfer of Resources from Central Taxes	% Share of Total Tax Receipts
1951-52	281	2.6	54	19.2	49	17.4	53	18.9
1960-61	625	3.6	142	22.7	53	8.5	165	26.4
1970-71	2284	4.9	755	33.1	194	8.5	756	33.1
1980-81	10405	7.2	3888	37.4	824	7.9	3789	36.4
1990-91	44586	7.8	17667	39.6	4795	10.8	14242	31.9
2000-01	164314	7.8	69976	42.6	15479	9.4	50734	30.9
2001-02	175415	7.7	73181	41.7	16504	9.4	52215	29.8
2002-03	193474	7.9	82155	42.5	18268	9.4	56655	29.3
2003-04	221117	8.0	93172	42.1	18928	8.6	67080	30.3
2004-05	260577	8.0	111554	42.8	21096	8.1	78550	30.1
2005-06	306332	8.3	128769	42.0	25036	8.2	94024	30.7
2006-07	372841	8.7	153573	41.2	29316	7.9	120293	32.3
2007-08	437948	8.8	173422	39.6	34127	7.8	151402	34.6
2008-09	482983	8.7	198327	41.1	40990	8.5	161052	33.3
2009-10RE	531004	8.1	225227	42.4	47729	9.0	166477	31.4
2010-11BE	627147	8.0	264848	42.2	55478	8.8	200466	32.0

Note : RE: Revised Estimates, BE: Budget Estimates.

Source : Reserve Bank of India study on State Finances.

94 : Details of Non-Tax Receipts of States

(Rs. crore)

Year	Non-Tax Receipts	% to Total Receipts	Interest Receipts	% Share to Non-Tax Receipts	Grants from the Centre	% Share to Non-Tax Receipts
1951-52	115	1.1	27	0.3	38	0.4
1960-61	387	2.2	78	0.5	140	0.8
1970-71	1087	2.4	183	0.4	566	1.2
1980-81	5888	4.1	824	0.6	2623	1.8
1990-91	21881	3.8	2403	0.4	12643	2.2
2000-01	68195	3.2	10961	0.5	37289	1.8
2001-02	74007	3.2	8415	0.4	42602	1.9
2002-03	80200	3.3	8761	0.4	45170	1.8
2003-04	88074	3.2	7748	0.3	50836	1.8
2004-05	102935	3.2	8648	0.3	56322	1.7
2005-06	124690	3.4	9380	0.3	76750	2.1
2006-07	157714	3.7	11825	0.3	94451	2.2
2007-08	185799	3.7	12637	0.3	108622	2.2
2008-09	211675	3.8	16356	0.3	129923	2.3
2009-10RE	276384	4.2	16812	0.3	179206	2.7
2010-11BE	285891	3.6	16356	0.2	183282	2.3

Note : RE: Revised Estimates, BE: Budget Estimates.
Source : Reserve Bank of India study on State Finances.

95 : States' Expenditure Pattern

(Rs. crore)

Year	Total Expenditure	% to GDP	of which: Interest	% to Total Expenditure	Pension etc.	% to Total Expenditure
1970-71	5174	11.2	398	7.7	165	3.2
1980-81	22664	15.6	1225	5.4	375	1.7
1990-91	91088	16.0	8655	9.5	3593	3.9
2000-01	339835	16.2	50985	15.0	28483	8.4
2001-02	368680	16.2	61596	16.7	32754	8.9
2002-03	410249	16.7	69027	16.8	36563	8.9
2003-04	514302	18.7	80396	15.6	39110	7.6
2004-05	553428	17.1	86421	15.6	44747	8.1
2005-06	561682	15.2	84024	15.0	48401	8.6
2006-07	657280	15.3	93164	14.2	52646	8.0
2007-08	752324	15.1	99831	13.3	56098	7.5
2008-09	882333	15.8	102955	11.7	65440	7.4
2009-10RE	1080632	16.5	115904	10.7	87271	8.1
2010-11BE	1174584	14.9	128656	11.0	95018	8.1

Note : RE: Revised Estimates, BE: Budget Estimates.
Source : Reserve Bank of India study on State Finances.

96 : Deficit Indicators of State Governments

(Rs. crore)

Year	Fiscal Deficit	% to GDP	Revenue Deficit	% to GDP	Primary Deficit	% to GDP	Net RBI Credit
1970-71	901	1.9	19	0.0	503	1.1	-
1980-81	3713	2.6	-1486	-1.0	2488	1.7	487
1990-91	18151	3.2	5309	0.9	10132	1.8	420
2000-01	82412	3.9	55316	2.6	36937	1.8	-1092
2001-02	89298	3.9	60398	2.7	32665	1.4	3451
2002-03	95255	3.9	57179	2.3	30399	1.2	-3100
2003-04	117494	4.3	63407	2.3	40235	1.5	293
2004-05	100743	3.1	39158	1.2	21353	0.7	-2705
2005-06	86054	2.3	7013	0.2	6060	0.2	2425
2006-07	78219	1.8	-24857	-0.6	-15672	-0.4	640
2007-08	75455	1.5	-42943	-0.9	-24376	-0.5	1140
2008-09	134589	2.4	-12672	-0.2	31634	0.6	602
2009-10RE	216101	3.3	46663	0.7	100197	1.5	
2010-11BE	198539	2.5	24370	0.3	69883	0.9	

Note : RE: Revised Estimates, BE: Budget Estimates.
Source : RBI study on State Finances.

97 : Liabilities of State Governments

(Rs. crore)

Year (end-March)	Total Internal Debt	% to GDP	of which: Market Loans	Loans & Advances: Centre	Provident Funds etc.	Reserve Funds	Deposits and Advances	Contingency Funds	Total Liabilities	% to GDP
1980-81	4443	3.1	2988	16980	2536	449	2338	37	26783	18.4
1990-91	19274	3.4	15652	73521	16861	4734	12769	995	128155	22.5
2000-01	181623	8.6	86767	238655	93629	22868	59328	714	594148	28.3
2001-02	249069	10.9	104027	249551	103815	27389	64325	1042	690747	30.3
2002-03	333753	13.6	133066	249179	113678	32188	65036	314	786427	32.0
2003-04	476772	17.3	208901	192981	121841	42217	69116	246	913376	33.2
2004-05	595064	18.4	243362	160045	130828	52311	75290	527	1029174	31.7
2005-06	698773	18.9	260506	157004	140806	63120	86691	1322	1167866	31.6
2006-07	763855	17.8	268828	146653	149920	78761	101068	1319	1250819	29.1
2007-08	824304	16.5	321651	145098	161972	78265	116591	2073	1328302	26.6
2008-09	933762	16.7	423615	143870	177434	83927	128350	2853	1470195	26.3
2009-10	1073163	16.4	534569	148729	201723	76719	134586	3554	1638474	25.0
2010-11	1217959	15.5	664303	155698	224149	80458	138152	3739	1820155	23.1

Note : Market loans data with effect from 2004 contains power bonds also in addition to market loans.
Data for 2009-10 is revised estimates and 2010-11 is budget estimates.

Source : RBI, *Handbook of Statistics on Indian Economy 2010-11.*

98 : Deficit Indicators of Centre and States

(Rs. crore)

Year	Revenue Deficit		Gross Fiscal Deficit		Primary Deficit	
		% to GDP		% to GDP		% to GDP
1990-91	23668	4.2	52913	9.3	27907	4.9
2000-01	135409	6.4	192429	9.2	69637	3.3
2001-02	157105	6.9	219727	9.6	78837	3.5
2002-03	162099	6.6	228631	9.3	74232	3.0
2003-04	157278	5.7	229956	8.4	53583	2.0
2004-05	112540	3.5	228664	7.1	36297	1.1
2005-06	93052	2.5	235634	6.4	29244	0.8
2006-07	50510	1.2	218857	5.1	(14163)	(0.3)
2007-08	4000	0.1	198137	4.0	(51058)	(1.0)
2008-09	237838	4.3	459831	8.2	182193	3.3
2009-10RE	365050	5.6	616317	9.4	297825	4.6
2010-11BE	288611	3.7	567287	7.2	207299	2.6

Note: Number in brackets represent negative values and indicates surplus.
RE: Revised Estimates, BE: Budget Estimates.

Source: Indian Public Finance Statistics, Ministry of Finance.

99 : Combined Receipts and Disbursements of Centre and States

Year	Aggregate Receipts		Aggregate Disbursements	
	Rs. crore	% to GDP	Rs. crore	% to GDP
1990-91	141666	24.9	153152	26.9
2000-01	547257	28.0	546348	28.0
2001-02	543732	23.9	606582	26.6
2002-03	655438	26.7	658481	26.8
2003-04	761052	27.6	748476	27.2
2004-05	902260	27.8	825687	25.5
2005-06	907894	24.6	935648	25.3
2006-07	1009226	23.5	1091734	25.4
2007-08	1257820	25.2	1245391	25.0
2008-09	1366015	24.5	1513363	27.1
2009-10RE	1809629	27.6	1839359	28.1
2010-11BE	1970036	25.0	1988371	25.2

Note: RE: Revised Estimates, BE: Budget Estimates.
1. Aggregate Receipts and Disbursement include discharge of internal debt.
2.Tax Revenue from Year 2000-01 to 2009-10 are excluding the amount transferred to National Calamity Contingency Fund.

Source: Indian Public Finance Statistics, Ministry of Finance.

100 : Trends in Revenue Receipts of Centre and States

(Rs. crore)

Year	Total Tax Revenue (All-India)		Central Taxes (Gross)		States' Own Taxes	
	Rs. crore	% to GDP	Rs. crore	% to GDP	Rs. crore	% to GDP
1990-91	87722	15.40	57577	10.11	30145	5.29
2000-01	305322	14.52	188605	8.97	116717	5.55
2001-02	314535	13.80	187060	8.21	127475	5.59
2002-03	356277	14.51	215905	8.80	140372	5.72
2003-04	414084	15.03	254348	9.23	159736	5.80
2004-05	494370	15.25	304957	9.41	189413	5.84
2005-06	587688	15.92	366151	9.92	221537	6.00
2006-07	736708	17.16	473513	11.03	263195	6.13
2007-08	870329	17.45	593147	11.90	277182	5.56
2008-09	915450	16.40	605298	10.84	310152	5.56
2009-10RE	987510	15.08	633095	9.67	354415	5.41
2010-11BE	1160267	14.73	746651	9.48	413616	5.25

Note : RE: Revised Estimates, BE: Budget Estimates.
1. The ratios to GDP at market prices are based on CSO's *National Accounts 2004-05* series and prior to 2004-05 are based on old (1999-2000) series.

Source : Indian Public Finance Statistics, Ministry of Finance.

101 : Combined Liabilities of Centre and States

(Rs. crore)

Year	Total Liabilities of the Centre	% to GDP	Total Liabilities of the States	% to GDP	Combined Total Liabilities of the Centre & States	% to GDP
1990-91	314558	55.2	128155	22.5	368824	64.7
2000-01	1168541	59.9	355492	18.2	1524033	78.1
2001-02	1366409	60.0	441196	19.4	1807605	79.3
2002-03	1559201	63.5	537248	21.9	2096449	85.4
2003-04	1736678	63.0	710192	25.8	2446870	88.8
2004-05	1994421	61.5	854021	26.3	2848442	87.9
2005-06	2260145	61.2	990712	26.8	3250857	88.0
2006-07	2538596	59.1	1094924	25.5	3633520	84.6
2007-08	2837425	56.9	1183204	23.7	4020629	80.6
2008-09	3159178	56.6	1326326	23.8	4485504	80.3
2009-10RE	3515906	53.7	1489746	22.7	5005652	76.4
2010-11BE	3944598	50.1	1664458	21.1	5609056	71.2

Note : RE: Revised Estimates, BE: Budget Estimates.
Inter-governmental transfers have been netted. Hence the sub-total do not add up to the combined total.

Source : Indian Public Finance Statistics, Ministry of Finance.

102 : Distribution of Total Expenditure

(Rs. crore)

Year	Total Expenditure*	of which:									
		Interest Payments		Defence		Pension		Education		Health	
			% to Total		% to Total		% to Total		% to Total		% to Total
1990-91	143196	25006	17.5	15426	10.8	5184	3.6	17378	12.1	7496	5.2
2000-01	534944	122792	23.0	49622	9.3	38819	7.3	63756	11.9	27187	5.1
2001-02	590451	140890	23.9	54266	9.2	40321	6.8	67881	11.5	28440	4.8
2002-03	640169	154399	24.1	55662	8.7	43038	6.7	71117	11.1	29420	4.6
2003-04	729843	176373	24.2	60066	8.2	45227	6.2	76160	10.4	32919	4.5
2004-05	799197	192367	24.1	75856	9.5	55437	6.9	85717	10.7	37702	4.7
2005-06	909474	206390	22.7	80549	8.9	60871	6.7	98184	10.8	45486	5.0
2006-07	1064457	233020	21.9	85510	8.0	69069	6.5	117312	11.0	53058	5.0
2007-08	1221437	249195	20.4	91681	7.5	77634	6.4	126532	10.4	60755	5.0
2008-09	1492017	277638	18.6	114223	7.7	94668	6.3	160275	10.7	72153	4.8
2009-10RE	1802652	318492	17.7	136264	7.6	124774	6.9	202869	11.3	88998	4.9
2010-11BE	1943008	359988	18.5	147344	7.6	132537	6.8	231158	11.9	96673	5.0

Note : RE: Revised Estimates, BE: Budget Estimates.
* Total expenditure exludes loans and balances, self-balancing items and transfer to funds.
Health includes medical & public health, water supply & sanitation and family welfare.

Source : Indian Public Finance Statistics 2010-11, Ministry of Finance.

103 : Small Savings

(Rs. crore)

Year	Outstandings	% to GDP	Net Receipts	% to GDP	Gross Receipts	% to GDP
1950-51	336	1.2	34	0.3	101	1.0
1960-61	982	4.5	105	0.6	239	1.4
1970-71	2222	4.8	192	0.4	783	1.7
1980-81	8244	5.7	1266	0.9	3119	2.1
1990-91	50279	8.8	5950	1.0	17700	3.1
2000-01	225087	10.7	37577	1.8	79311	3.8
2001-02	262856	11.5	37769	1.7	81753	3.6
2002-03	313793	12.8	50937	2.1	105601	4.3
2003-04	375737	13.6	61944	2.2	135970	4.9
2004-05	457732	14.1	81995	2.5	158519	4.9
2005-06	527611	14.2	69897	1.9	173283	4.7
2006-07	564372	13.2	36743	0.9	154836	3.6
2007-08	509411	10.3	-54961	-1.1	123652	2.5
2008-09	545873	9.8	34929	0.6	146801	2.6
2009-10	583789	9.2	24886	0.4	215562	3.3
2010-11*	616692	7.8	32903	0.4	218744	2.8

Note: * : data pertains to April-February 2011.
Source: Accountant General, Post & Telegraph.

104 : Foreign Trade

(US $ million)

Year	DGCI&S Data					RBI BoP Data		
	Exports	Growth (%)	Imports	Growth (%)	Trade Balance	Exports	Imports	Trade Balance
1950-51	1016		1292		(276)	1355	1366	(11)
1960-61*	1346	2.9	2353	6.1	(1007)	1326	2324	(998)
1970-71*	2031	4.2	2162	(0.1)	(131)	1876	2416	(540)
1980-81*	8485	15.4	15867	22.1	(7382)	8429	16284	(7855)
1990-91*	18145	7.9	24073	4.3	(5927)	18477	27915	(9438)
2000-01*	44560	9.4	50537	7.7	(5976)	45452	57912	(12460)
2010-11*	245868	18.6	350695	21.4	(104827)			
2000-01	44560	21.0	50537	1.7		45452	57912	(12460)
2001-02	43827	(1.6)	51413	1.7	(7587)	44703	56277	(11574)
2002-03	52719	20.3	61412	19.4	(8693)	53774	64464	(10690)
2003-04	63843	21.1	78149	27.3	(14307)	66285	80003	(13718)
2004-05	83536	30.8	111517	42.7	(27982)	85206	118908	(33702)
2005-06	103091	23.4	149166	33.8	(46075)	105152	157056	(51904)
2006-07	126414	22.6	185735	24.5	(59321)	128888	190670	(61782)
2007-08	162904	28.9	251439	35.4	(88535)	166162	257629	(91467)
2008-09	182800	12.2	298834	18.8	(116034)	189001	308521	(119520)
2009-10	178751	(3.5)	288373	(5.0)	(109622)	182235	300609	(118374)
2010-11	254402	42.3	352575	22.3	(98173)	250468	380935	(130467)

Note: * : Growth for decades from 1950-51 to 2010-11 is compounded annual growth rate, that from 2000-01 onwards is the annual growth rate.

Source: Directorate General of Commercial Intelligence and Statistics (DGCI&S), Calcutta, Reserve Bank of India for balance of payment data.

105 : Imports of Some Selected Commodities

($ million)

	1960-61	1970-71	1980-81	1990-91	2000-01	2010-11
Total Imports	2353	2162	15869	24075	50536	352575
Pulses			268	109	1532	
% of Total			1.1	0.2	0.4	
Edible Oils	8	31	857	182	1334	6462
% of Total	0.3	1.4	5.4	0.8	2.6	1.8
Raw Materials and Intermediates						
Petroleum Oil & Lubricants	145	180	6656	6028	15650	106068
% of Total	6.2	8.3	41.9	25.0	31.0	30.1
Fertilisers	27	113	1034	984	664	6983
% of Total	1.1	5.2	6.5	4.1	1.3	2.0
Medicinal &	21	32	107	261	377	2376
Pharmaceuticals	0.9	1.5	0.7	1.1	0.7	0.7
Iron & Steel	258	194	1078	1178	781	10279
% of Total	11.0	9.0	6.8	4.9	1.5	2.9
Pearl, Precious & Semi-Precious Stones	2	33	527	2083	4838	31262
% of Total	0.1	1.5	3.3	8.7	9.6	8.9
Gold & Silver				4638	35611	
% of Total				9.2	10.1	
Capital Goods*	747	534	2416	6495	8941	71627
% of Total	31.7	24.7	15.2	27.0	17.7	20.3

Note: * : Capital goods include manufacture of metals, machinery, electronic goods, computer goods.

Source: *Economic Survey, Handbook of Statistics on Indian Economy* and Department of Commerce.

106 : Exports of Some Selected Commodities

($ million)

	1960-61	1970-71	1980-81	1990-91	2000-01	2009-10
Total Exports	1346	2041	8486	18143	44560	254402
Tea and Mate	260	196	538	596	433	691
% of Total	11.0	9.1	3.4	2.5	0.9	0.2
Tobacco	34	43	178	147	191	835
% of Total	1.4	2.0	1.1	0.6	0.4	0.2
Sugar & Molasses	60	39	50	21	112	2488
% of Total	2.5	1.8	0.3	0.1	0.2	0.7
Iron Ore	36	155	384	585	358	4617
% of Total	1.5	7.2	2.4	2.4	0.7	1.3
Textile	153	192	1179	3807	11285	23312
% of Total	6.5	8.9	7.4	15.8	22.3	6.6
Gems & Jewellery	2	59	782	2924	7384	40791
% of Total	0.1	2.7	4.9	12.1	14.6	11.6
Chemicals & Products	15	39	284	1176	5002	28980
% of Total	0.6	1.8	1.8	4.9	9.9	8.2
Machinery **	46	261	1045	2158	6819	68784
% of Total	2.0	12.1	6.6	9.0	13.5	19.5
Mineral Fuel & Lubricants*	15	17	35	528	1870	41918
% of Total	0.6	0.8	0.2	2.2	3.7	11.3

Note: ** : Machinery includes machinery and electronic goods. * Data pertains to petroleum products mainly.

Source: *Economic Survey*, *Handbook of Statistics on Indian Economy* and Department of Commerce.

107 : Index Numbers and Terms of Foreign Trade

Year	Unit Value Index		Quantum Index		Terms of Trade		
	Exports	Imports	Exports	Imports	Gross	Net	Income
Base: 1999-2000 =100							
2000-01	102	109	125	99	79	94	118
2001-02	103	112	126	103	82	92	116
2002-03	106	128	150	109	73	83	125
2003-04	114	132	161	128	80	86	138
2004-05	131	157	179	150	84	83	149
2005-06	139	179	206	174	84	78	161
2006-07	158	206	227	191	84	77	175
2007-08	166	210	245	218	89	79	194
2008-09	194	239	267	262	98	81	216
2009-10	196	215	264	288	109	91	240

Note: Index number of foreign trade of a country is an instrument which indicate the temporal fluctuations in export/import in terms of volume and unit price. It may be defined as a measure of average change in a group of related variables over two different situations.

1. Gross Terms of Trade is the ratio of overall import quantum index to similar export index.
2. Net Terms of Trade is the ratio of overall export unit value index to similar import index.
3. Income Terms of Trade = (NTT X QIE)/100.

Source: *Economic Survey, Handbook of Statistics on Indian Economy.*

108 : India's Share in World Exports of Principal Commodities

	World Exports (US $ billion)			India's Share (% of World Exports)		
	1900	2000	2008	1900	2000	2008
Meat & Preparations	34	45	114	0.2	0.7	1.1
Fish etc. & Preparations	33	51	93	1.6	2.7	1.7
Rice	4	6	20	6.4	10.2	14.3
Vegetables & Fruits	50	68	172	0.8	1.3	1.2
Sugar, Honey, etc.	14	14	33	0.1	0.9	4.8
Coffee & Substitute	9	12	27	1.7	2.3	2.0
Tea & Mate	3	3	7	22.1	14.0	9.0
Spices	1	3	6	7.7	10.3	14.5
Animal Feed	16	20	55	2.2	2.3	5.1
Tobacco & Manufactures	18	22	34	0.8	0.7	1.6
Oilseeds & Oleaginous Fruit	11	14	53	0.8	1.7	1.5
Iron Ore & Concentrates	8	9	66	7.6	3.9	8.6
Organic Chemicals	71	134	334	0.3	1.1	2.1
Medicine & Pharmaceuticals	38	108	112	1.2	1.2	0.9

contd...

...contd...

	World Exports (US $ billion)			India's Share (% of World Exports)		
	1900	2000	2008	1900	2000	2008
Leather & Products	13	24	28	6.3	3.3	3.3
Textiles	105	168	257	2.1	3.6	4.0
Pearls, Precious Stones	28	54	117	9.9	12	13
Iron & Steel	106	146	579	0.3	1.0	1.9
Metal Manufacturers	66	125	346	0.5	0.9	1.4
Machinery	775	2462	3833	0.1	0.1	0.4
Road Vehicles	96	158	1214	2.3	3.5	0.5
Apparel	95	201	378	2.3	3.5	2.9
Total Exports	3304	6255	15926	0.5	0.7	1.1

Source : United Nations, *International Trade Statistics Year Book 2009.*

109 : Direction of Trade from India

(US $ million)

Year	2000-01				2010-11			
	Export		Import		Export		Import	
	US $ mn	Share in Total (%)	US $ mn	Share in Total (%)	US $ mn	Share in Total (%)	US $ mn	Share in Total (%)
Total	44560	100.0	50536	100.0	252354	100.0	352575	100.0
Australia	406		1063	2.1	1385	0.5	10233	2.9
Bangladesh	935	2.1	81	0.2	3571	1.4	413	0.1
Brazil	226	0.5	145	0.3	4443	1.8	3491	1.0
Canada	656	1.5	397	0.8	1365	0.5	1932	0.5
China	831	1.9	1502	3.0	19396	7.7	40225	11.4
Egypt	357	0.8	39	0.1	2260	0.9	1348	0.4
France	1020	2.3	641	1.3	5077	2.0	3534	1.0
Germany	1908	4.3	1760	3.5	6784	2.7	42446	12.0
Hongkong	2641	5.9	852	1.7	10359	4.1	8523	2.4
Indonesia	400	0.9	910	1.8	6426	2.5	9490	2.7
Italy	1309	2.9	724	1.4	4577	1.8	4076	1.2
Japan	1794	4.0	1842	3.6	5212	2.1	8151	2.3
Korea, Rep. of	451	1.0	894	1.8	4133	1.6	10059	2.9
Malaysia	608	1.4	1177	2.3	3996	1.6	6291	1.8
Mexico	209	0.5	54	0.1	914	0.4	1129	0.3

contd...

...contd...

(US $ million)

Year	2000-01				2010-11			
	Export		Import		Export		Import	
	US $ mn	Share in Total (%)	US $ mn	Share in Total (%)	US $ mn	Share in Total (%)	US $ mn	Share in Total (%)
Netherlands	880	2.0	438	0.9	7770	3.1	1787	0.5
Pakistan	187	0.4	64	0.1	2322	0.9	334	0.1
Phillipines	203	0.5	63	0.1	886	0.4	396	0.1
Russia	889	2.0	518	1.0	1597	0.6	3453	1.0
Saudi Arabia	823	1.8	621	1.2	5246	2.1	20114	5.7
Singapore	877	2.0	1464	2.9	10631	4.2	6690	1.9
South Africa	311	0.7	1022	2.0	4162	1.6	6482	1.8
Spain	666	1.5	142	0.3	2566	1.0	1446	0.4
Sri Lanka	640	1.4	45	0.1	4046	1.6	442	0.1
Thailand	530	1.2	338	0.7	2823	1.1	4168	1.2
Turkey	334	0.7	43	0.1	2753	1.1	795	0.2
UAE	2598	5.8	659	1.3	34105	13.5	28298	8.0
UK	2299	5.2	3168	6.3	7219	2.9	5116	1.5
USA	9305	20.9	3015	6.0	25673	10.2	18530	5.3

Source : Department of Commerce, Government of India.

110 : Foreign Exchange Rate (End-Year)

Year	(Rupees per Unit of Foreign Currency)					US $ (Average)
	SDR	US Dollar	Pound Sterling	Deutsche Mark/Euro	Japanese Yen	
1970-71	7.50	7.50	18.13	2.07	2.10	7.56
1980-81	10.06	8.19	18.38	3.90	3.90	7.91
1990-91	26.41	19.64	34.05	11.43	13.90	17.94
2000-01	58.80	46.64	66.58	41.01	37.43	45.68
2001-02	60.84	48.80	69.59	42.64	36.81	47.69
2002-03	65.26	47.51	74.92	51.49	39.89	48.40
2003-04	64.24	43.45	79.68	53.17	41.67	45.95
2004-05	66.10	43.76	82.11	56.59	40.81	44.93
2005-06	64.26	44.61	77.80	54.19	38.02	44.27
2006-07	65.83	43.60	85.59	58.15	37.03	45.28
2007-08	65.73	39.99	79.51	63.10	40.07	40.24
2008-09	76.17	50.95	72.86	67.47	51.89	45.92
2009-10	68.53	45.14	68.39	60.84	48.45	47.42
2010-11	70.79	44.65	71.92	63.24	54.02	45.58

Note : 1 . Exchange rate for Yen is in Rs. per 100.
2. Data from 1970-71 to 1991-92 are based on official exchange rate and for later years based on FEDAI Rate.
3. Euro replaced Deutsche Mark with effect from 1-1-1999.

Source : *Handbook of Statistics on Indian Economy.*

111: India's Share in World Merchandise Trade

	Imports		Exports	
	World (US $ billion)	India (%)	World (US $ billion)	India (%)
1948	62	2.2	59	2.2
1953	85	1.3	84	1.3
1963	164	1.0	157	1.0
1973	595	0.5	579	0.5
1983	1882	0.5	1838	0.5
1993	3787	0.6	3676	0.6
2003	7611	1.0	7452	0.8
2010	15021	2.2	14879	1.5

Source : International Merchandise Trade Statistics, UNO.

112 : Indices of Real Effective Exchange Rate (REER) and Nominal Effective Exchange Rate (NEER)

Year	36-Currency Export & Trade-Based Weights (Base: 1993-94=100)(Financial Year Average)							
	Trade-Based Weights				Export-Based Weights			
	REER	Change (+/-)*	NEER	Change (+/-)*	REER	Change (+/-)*	NEER	Change (+/-)*
2004-05	100.00		100.00		100.00		100.00	
2005-06	103.10	3.1	102.24	2.2	102.74	2.7	102.20	2.2
2006-07	101.29	(1.8)	97.63	(4.5)	101.05	(1.6)	98.00	(4.1)
2007-08	108.52	7.1	104.75	7.3	108.57	7.4	105.62	7.8
2008-09	97.80	(9.9)	93.34	(10.9)	97.77	(9.9)	94.00	(11.0)
2009-10	94.74	(3.1)	90.94	(2.6)	95.28	(2.5)	91.42	(2.7)
2010-11	102.04	7.7	93.56	2.9	103.27	8.4	94.75	3.6

Note: Change (+/-)* indicates appreciation (+)/depreciation of the rupee over the year.
1. Data in brackets indicates negative value i.e., depreciation of the rupee over the year.
2. Data for 2009-10 and 2010-11 are provisional.
3. The 36-country indices are revised as 36-currency indices.

Source: RBI Bulletin.

113 : Balance of Payments

(US $ million)

	1990-91	2000-01	2009-10	2010-11
Current Account	(9680)	(2666)	(38383)	(44281)
Export f.o.b	18477	45452	182235	250468
Import c.i.f	27915	57912	300609	380935
Trade Balance	(9438)	(12460)	(118374)	(130467)
Invisibles				
Receipt	7464	32267	163404	197583
Payment	7706	22473	83413	111397
Net	(242)	9794	79991	86186
Capital Account	7056	8840	53397	59747
Foreign Investment (net)	103	5862	51167	37434
In India (net)	103	5862	65500	54835
Direct (net)	97	3272	33124	23364
Portfolio (net)	6	2590	32396	31471
Abroad	0	(759)	(14333)	(17401)
Loans (net)	5533	5264	13259	27859
External Assistance (net)	2204	410	2893	4941
Commercial Borrowings (net)	2254	4303	2808	11927
Short Term to India (net)	1075	551	7558	10991
Banking Capital (net)	682	(1961)	2084	4963
Commercial Banks (net)	904	(1882)	1927	4434
of which: NRI Deposits (net)	1537	2316	2924	3239
Others (net)	(222)	(79)	157	529
Rupee Debt Service (net)	(1193)	(617)	(97)	-69
Other Capital (net)	1931	292	(13016)	(10440)
Errors & Omissions	132	(305)	(1573)	(2416)
Overall Balances	(2492)	5869	13441	13050
Monetary Movements	2492	(5869)	(13441)	(13050)
IMF	1214	(26)		
Foreign Exchange Reserves (Increase - /Decrease +)	1278	(5842)	(13441*)	(13050)

Note: Negative values in brackets.
*: Includes SDR allocation of US $ million 5160, f.o.b. : Free on Board, c.i.f. : Cost, Insurance & Freight.

Source: RBI Bulletins.

114 : Selected Balance of Payment Indicators

(%)

	Per cent to Gross Domestic Product at Current Market Prices					
	Net Current Account	Net Capital Account	Merchandise Trade			Invisibles
			Export	Import	Merchandise (Total)	Net
1950-51	0.39	-0.04	6.4	6.4	12.9	0.4
1960-61	(2.25)	2.01	3.6	6.4	10.0	0.5
1970-71	(0.96)	1.09	3.1	3.9	7.0	(0.1)
1980-81	(1.52)	0.99	4.6	8.9	13.4	2.7
1990-91	(3.05)	2.22	5.8	8.8	14.6	(0.1)
2000-01	(0.55)	1.93	9.8	12.9	22.6	2.3
2005-06	(1.18)	3.02	12.6	18.8	31.3	5.0
2006-07	(1.04)	4.75	13.6	20.1	33.7	5.5
2007-08	(1.39)	8.77	13.5	20.9	34.4	6.1
2008-09	(2.37)	0.58	14.3	24.1	38.4	7.4
2009-10	(2.80)	3.80	13.2	21.7	34.9	5.8
2010-11	(2.57)	3.47	14.5	22.0	36.5	5.0

Note : Negative value in brackets.
Source : *Economic Survey*.

115 : Foreign Exchange Reserves

(US $ million)

End-March	SDRs	Gold	Foreign Currency Assets*	Reserve Tranche Position	Total	Import Cover: No. of Months
1950-51	.	247	1914	.	2161	20
1960-61	.	247	390	.	637	3
1970-71	148	243	584	.	975	5
1980-81	603	370	5850	.	6823	5
1990-91	102	3496	2236	.	5834	3
2000-01	2	2725	39554	.	42281	10
2001-02	10	3047	51049	.	54106	13
2002-03	4	3534	71890	672	76100	15
2003-04	2	4198	107448	1311	112959	17
2004-05	5	4500	135571	1438	141514	15
2005-06	3	5755	145108	756	151622	12
2006-07	2	6784	191924	469	199179	13
2007-08	18	10039	299230	436	309723	14
2008-09	1	9577	241426	981	251985	10
2009-10	5006	17986	254685	1380	279057	11
2010-11	4569	22972	274330	2947	304818	10

Source : RBI Bulletin.

116 : Trend in Invisibles

(US $ million)

	Receipts	Growth	Payments	Growth	Net
1950-51	293		203		90
1960-61	548	(7.0)	375	(6.9)	173
1970-71	663	(3.1)	712	(6.8)	-49
1980-81	7183	(49.1)	2118	(11.9)	5065
1990-91	7464	(0.6)	7706	(14.3)	-242
2000-01	32267	(16.2)	22473	(12.0)	9794
2001-11	197583	(20.3)	111397	(18.3)	86186
2000-01	32267	6.4	22473	30.9	9794
2001-02	36737	13.9	21763	-3.2	14974
2002-03	41925	14.1	24890	14.4	17035
2003-04	53508	27.6	25707	3.3	27801
2004-05	69533	29.9	38301	49.0	31232
2005-06	89687	29.0	47685	24.5	42002
2006-07	114558	27.7	62341	30.7	52217
2007-08	148875	30.0	73144	17.3	75731
2008-09	167819	12.7	76214	4.2	91605
2009-10	163404	-2.6	83413	9.4	79991
2010-11	197583	20.9	111397	33.5	86186

Note : Growth in brackets represents annual average growth.
Source : RBI Bulletins.

117 : NRI Deposit Outstandings Under Various Schemes

(US $ million)

Year (End-March)	NR(E)RA	FCNR Accounts	Others	Total
1991	3618	10103	265	13986
2000	6758	8172	6754	21684
2001	7147	9076	6849	23072
2002	8449	9673	7052	25174
2003	14923	10199	3407	28529
2004	20559	10961	1746	33266
2005	21291	11452	232	32975
2006	22070	13064	1148	36282
2007	24495	15129	1616	41240
2008	26716	14168	2788	43672
2009	23570	13211	4773	41554
2010	26251	14258	7381	47890
2011	26378	15597	9707	51682

Note : NR(E)RA: Non-Resident (External) Rupee Accounts.
FCNR A/c includes both Foreign Currency Non-Resident Accounts and Banks.
Others include Foreign Currency Non-Resident (Banks), Foreign Currency (Bank & Other) Deposits, Foreign Currency (Ordinary) Non-Repartiable Deposits and Non-Resident Ordinary Rupee Accounts.
Source : *Handbook of Statistics on Indian Economy.*

118 : Invisibles by Categories of Transaction (Net)

(US $ million)

Year/Item	Non-Factor Services	Investment Income	Compensation to Employees	Private Transfers	Official Transfers	Invisibles
1950-51	59	-50	.	73	4	86
1960-61	120	-101	.	59	95	173
1970-71	11	-338	.	116	162	-49
1980-81	1297	325	.	2693	750	5065
1990-91	980	-3752	.	2069	461	-242
2000-01	1692	-4664	-340	12854	252	9794
2001-02	3324	-3844	-362	15398	458	14974
2002-03	3643	-3544	98	16387	451	17035
2003-04	10144	-3757	-748	21608	554	27801
2004-05	15426	-4095	-884	20525	260	31232
2005-06	23170	-5262	-593	24493	194	42002
2006-07	29469	-6762	-569	29825	254	52217
2007-08	38853	-4433	-635	41706	239	75731
2008-09	53916	-6626	-484	44567	232	91605
2009-10	35726	-7249	-791	52055	250	79991
2010-11	47664	-13900	-963	53368	17	86186

Note : G.n.i.e: Government not included elsewhere.
Source : RBI Bulletins.

119 : Non-Factor Services by Components (Net)

(US $ million)

Year/Item	Non-Factor Services	Travel	Transport	Insurance	Gnie	Misc.
1950-51	59	-25	44	11	6	23
1960-61	120	7	42	4	63	4
1970-71	11	25	40	0	9	-63
1980-81	1297	1107	7	21	51	111
1990-91	980	1064	-110	23	-158	161
2000-01	1692	693	-1512	47	332	2132
2001-02	3324	123	-1306	8	235	4264
2002-03	3643	-29	-736	19	65	4324
2003-04	10144	1435	879	56	28	7746
2004-05	15426	1417	144	148	-10	13727
2005-06	23170	1215	-2012	-54	-215	24236
2006-07	29469	2439	-94	553	-150	26721
2007-08	38853	2091	-1500	595	-45	37712
2008-09	53916	1469	-1509	292	-404	54070
2009-10	35726	2517	-757	317	-86	33735
2010-11	47664	4043	397	549	-286	42961

Note : Non-factor services include travel, transport, insurance, government not elsewhere classified and miscellaneous.
Source : RBI Bulletin.

120 : Foreign Investment Inflows (Incl: Advance)

	Foreign Direct Investments		Portfolio Investment	
	In Rs. crore	In US $ mn	In Rs. crore	In US $ mn
1990-91	174	97	11	6
2000-01	18406	4029	12609	2760
2001-02	29235	6130	9639	2021
2002-03	24367	5035	4738	979
2003-04	19860	4322	52279	11377
2004-05	27188	6051	41854	9315
2005-06	39674	8961	55307	12492
2006-07	103367	22826	31713	7003
2007-08	140180	34835	109741	27271
2008-09	161536	37838	-63618	-13855
2009-10	176304	37763	153511	32376
2010-11	135647	30380	140518	31471

Source : RBI Bulletin.

121 : Inflow (+) and Outflow (-) Under Various NRI Deposit Schemes

(US $ million)

Year (End-March)	NR(E)RA	FCNR Accounts	Others	Total
1991-92	324	-311	564	577
2000-01	860	904	553	2317
2001-02	1626	594	508	2728
2002-03	6195	526	-3745	2976
2003-04	4695	762	-1816	3641
2004-05	84	492	-1538	-962
2005-06	1177	1612	930	3719
2006-07	1830	2065	426	4321
2007-08	109	-960	1030	179
2008-09	2508	-957	2738	4289
2009-10	-71	1047	1946	2922
2010-11	-280	1339	2180	3239

Note : All figures are inclusive of accrued interest and valuation factor.
NR(E)RA: Non-Resident (External) Rupee Accounts.
FCNR includes both Foreign Currency Non-Resident Accounts and Banks.
Others include Foreign Currency Non-Resident (Banks), Foreign Currency (Bank & Other) Deposits, Foreign Currency (Ordinary) Non-Repartiable Deposits and Non-Resident Ordinary Rupee Accounts.

Source : Handbook of Statistics on Indian Economy.

122 : Tourism Statistics

	Number of Tourist Arrivals (in million)				Foreign Exchange Earnings (in US $ billion)			
	World	India	% Share	Rank	World	India	% Share	Rank
1980	285	0.80	0.3		102.4	1.40	1.4	
1990	464	1.71	0.4		265.1	1.51	0.6	
2000	683	2.65	0.4	50	475.3	3.46	0.7	36
2001	683	2.54	0.4	51	463.8	3.20	0.7	36
2002	703	2.38	0.3	54	481.9	3.10	0.6	37
2003	691	2.73	0.4	51	529.3	4.46	0.8	37
2004	762	3.46	0.5	44	633.2	6.17	1.0	26
2005	803	3.92	0.5	43	679.6	7.49	1.1	22
2006	847	4.45	0.5	44	744.0	8.63	1.2	22
2007	904	5.08	0.6	41	857.0	10.73	1.3	20
2008	919	5.28	0.6	41	942.0	11.75	1.2	23
2009	880	5.11	0.6	41	852.0	10.61	1.2	22
2010	940	5.58	0.6	40	940.00	14.16	1.5	16

Source : Ministry of Tourism (website).

123 : India's External Debt

(US $ million)

	1991	2001	2010	2011
Multilateral Debt	20900	31105	42859	48464
Bilateral Debt	14168	15975	22593	25953
IMF	2623	0	6041	6308
Trade Credit	4301	5923	16867	18627
Commercial Borrowings	10209	24408	70800	88267
NRI & FC(BO) Deposits	10209	16568	47890	51682
Rupee Debt	12847	3719	1657	1601
Long-Term Debt	75257	97698	208707	240902
Short-Term Debt	8544	3628	52329	64990
% to Gross Debt	10.2	3.6	20.0	21.2
% to Foreign Exchange Reserves	146.5	8.6	18.8	21.3
Gross Debt	83801	101326	261036	305892
% to GDP	28.7	22.5	18.0	17.3
Concessional Debt to Total Debt	45.9	35.4	16.8	15.6
Debt Service Ratio	35.3	16.6	5.5	4.2
Ratio of Foreign Exchange Reserve to Total Debt	7.0	41.7	106.9	99.6

Source : Ministry of Finance and Reserve Bank of India.

II. SOCIAL SECTOR

- > Demography
  - Population
  - Vital Rates
- > Health & Family Welfare
- > Housing
- > Living Standard
- > Education
- > Law & Order
- > Trade Union
- > Mass Media
- > Insurance
- > Employment

124 : Growth of Population: All-India

Census Year	Population (in million)	Growth Over Decade		Density	% to Total Population	
		Total (%)	CAGR %		SCs	STs
1901	238.40			77		
1911	252.09	5.7	0.56	82		
1921	251.32	-0.3	-0.03	81		
1931	278.98	11.0	1.05	90		
1941	318.66	14.2	1.34	103		
1951	361.09	13.3	1.26	117		
1961	439.23	21.6	1.98	142	14.7	6.9
1971	548.16	24.8	2.24	177	14.6	6.9
1981	683.33	24.7	2.23	216	15.8	7.8
1991	846.42	23.9	2.16	267	16.5	8.1
2001	1028.74	21.5	1.97	325	16.2	8.2
2011	1210.19	17.6	1.64	382		

Note :
1. CAGR: Compounded Annual Growth Rate.
2. SC: Scheduled Caste, ST: Scheduled Tribe.
3. Density is the number of people per square kilometre of area.
4. Reference period of various Census is March 1 except for 1971 where it was April 1.
5. In 1981, for Assam and in 1991 for J&K, population figures were based on interpolation as Census could not be held in those states.
6. Includes estimated population of Paomata, Mao Maram and Purul sub-divisions of Senapati District of Manipur for 2001 and 2011.

Source : Office of the Registrar General of India, Ministry of Home Affairs (Census Documents).

125 : Rural-Urban Distribution of Population: All-India

Census Year	Rural			Urban		
	(in million)	CAGR (%)	% Share	(in million)	CAGR (%)	% Share
1901	212.5		89.2	25.9		10.8
1911	226.2	0.62	89.7	25.9	0.03	10.3
1921	223.2	-0.13	88.8	28.1	0.79	11.2
1931	245.5	0.96	88.0	33.5	1.76	12.0
1941	274.5	1.12	86.1	44.2	2.81	13.9
1951	298.6	0.85	82.7	62.4	3.53	17.3
1961	360.3	1.90	82.0	78.9	2.37	18.0
1971	439.1	2.00	80.1	109.1	3.29	19.9
1981	523.9	1.78	76.7	159.5	3.87	23.3
1991	628.9	1.84	74.3	217.6	3.16	25.7
2001	742.6	1.68	72.2	286.1	2.78	27.8
2011	833.1	1.16	68.8	377.1	2.80	31.2

Source : Office of the Registrar General of India, Ministry of Home Affairs (Census Documents).

126 : Gender Composition of Population: All-India

Census	Male		Female		
Year	(in million)	CAGR (%)	(in million)	CAGR (%)	Sex Ratio
1901	120.89		117.51		972
1911	128.36	0.60	123.73	0.52	964
1921	128.55	0.01	122.77	-0.08	955
1931	143.07	1.08	135.91	1.02	950
1941	163.84	1.36	154.82	1.31	945
1951	185.55	1.25	175.54	1.26	946
1961	226.29	2.00	212.94	1.95	941
1971	284.05	2.30	264.11	2.18	930
1981	353.37	2.21	329.96	2.25	934
1991	439.36	2.20	407.06	2.12	927
2001	532.22	1.94	496.51	2.01	933
2011	623.72	1.60	586.47	1.68	940

Note : Sex Ratio is defined as number of women per thousand men.
Source : Office of the Registrar General of India, Ministry of Home Affairs (Census Documents).

127 : Age Distribution of Population: All-India—Sex-wise

(in million)

Age Group	Male			Female			Sex Ratio		
	1981	1991	2001	1981	1991	2001	1981	1991	2001
Child	42.2	52.4	57.1	41.3	50.0	53.3	978	955	934
(0-4)	**12.3**	**12.0**	**10.7**	**12.8**	**12.4**	**10.7**			
Children	135.8	161.7	189.5	127.3	150.6	174.1	938	931	919
(0-14)	**39.5**	**37.2**	**35.6**	**39.6**	**37.3**	**35.1**			
Youth	110.4	144.2	179.2	104.2	136.9	168.5	944	950	940
(15-34)	**32.1**	**33.1**	**33.7**	**32.4**	**34.0**	**33.9**			
Fertile Ladies	163.7	216.3	271.5	153.3	200.7	252.7	937	928	931
(15-49)	**47.6**	**49.7**	**51.0**	**47.7**	**49.7**	**50.9**			
Worker	186.1	244.1	304.9	172.9	225.4	283.5	929	923	930
(15-59)	**54.1**	**56.1**	**57.3**	**53.8**	**55.9**	**57.1**			
Senior	22.0	29.4	37.8	21.1	27.3	38.9	960	930	1029
(60+)	**6.4**	**6.7**	**7.1**	**6.6**	**6.8**	**7.8**			
Septuagenerian	7.8	11.0	14.7	7.6	10.1	14.6	974	922	992
(70+)	**2.3**	**2.5**	**2.8**	**2.4**	**2.5**	**2.9**			
All Ages	343.9	435.2	532.2	321.4	403.4	496.5	934	927	933
	100.0	**100.0**	**100.0**	**100.0**	**100.0**	**100.0**			

Note: Figures in bold below each year are percentages to total.
Source: Office of the Registrar General of India, Ministry of Home Affairs (Census Documents).

128 : Population by Religion: All-India

Census	1951	1961	1971	1981	1991	2001
All	356.8	438.9	548.2	665.3	838.6	1028.6
% to Total	**100.0**	**100.0**	**100.0**	**100.0**	**100.0**	**100.0**
Hindus	303.6	366.4	453.4	549.7	687.6	827.6
% to Total	**85.1**	**83.5**	**82.7**	**82.6**	**82.0**	**80.5**
Muslims	35.4	46.9	61.4	75.6	101.6	138.2
% to Total	**9.9**	**10.7**	**11.2**	**11.4**	**12.1**	**13.4**
Christians	8.4	10.7	14.3	16.2	19.6	24.1
% to Total	**2.4**	**2.4**	**2.6**	**2.4**	**2.3**	**2.3**
Sikhs	6.2	7.8	10.4	13.1	16.3	19.2
% to Total	**1.7**	**1.8**	**1.9**	**2.0**	**1.9**	**1.9**
Jain	1.6	2.0	2.6	3.2	3.4	4.2
% to Total	**0.4**	**0.5**	**0.5**	**0.5**	**0.4**	**0.4**
Buddhists	0.2	3.2	3.8	4.7	6.4	8.0
% to Total	**0.1**	**0.7**	**0.7**	**0.7**	**0.8**	**0.8**

Note : Total includes others or not stated.

Source : Office of the Registrar General of India, Ministry of Home Affairs (Census Documents).

129 : Distribution of Rural Population by Size of Village

(%)

Size of Village in Terms of Population	1961	1971	1981	1991	2001
< 200	3.8	2.7	1.8	1.7	1.2
200-499	12.6	9.9	7.5	7.8	5.9
500-999	18.3	16.5	14.2	16.8	14.2
1000-1999	19.8	19.9	19.3	25.7	24.7
2000-4999	17.2	18.7	20.1	29.8	32.2
5000-9999	5.1	5.9	6.9	11.2	13.2
=>10000	2.8	4.1	4.6	7.0	8.5
Rural Population (in mn)	360.3	439.1	523.9	628.9	742.6
	82.03	80.10	76.66	74.30	72.19
Total Population (in mn)	439.2	548.2	683.3	846.4	1028.7

Note : Individual figures do not add up to total as village population are not exhaustive.

Source : Office of the Registrar General of India, Ministry of Home Affairs (Census Documents).

130 : Urbanisation by Class of Towns

Class & Size of Towns in Terms of Population	1961	1971	1981	1991	2001
		Number of Towns			
Class I	106	150	226	322	441
=> 1 lakh	**4.0**	**4.9**	**5.7**	**7.0**	**8.5**
Class II	138.0	214.0	325.0	421.0	496.0
50000-99999	**5.2**	**7.0**	**8.2**	**9.1**	**9.6**
Class III	508.0	643.0	883.0	1161.0	1388.0
20000-49999	**19.2**	**21.1**	**22.4**	**25.2**	**26.9**
Class IV	811.0	962.0	1247.0	1451.0	1561.0
10000-19999	**30.6**	**31.5**	**31.6**	**31.4**	**30.2**
Class V	827.0	797.0	920.0	971.0	1041.0
5000-9999	**31.2**	**26.1**	**23.3**	**21.0**	**20.2**
Class VI	257.0	288.0	348.0	289.0	234.0
<5000	**9.7**	**9.4**	**8.8**	**6.3**	**4.5**
All Classes	2647.0	3054.0	3949.0	4615.0	5161.0
		Population (in million)			
Class I	35.0	53.2	83.0	122.3	178.2
=> 1 lakh	**44.8**	**49.4**	**52.6**	**56.7**	**62.3**
Class II	9.5	14.4	22.0	28.8	34.5
50000-99999	**12.1**	**13.4**	**14.0**	**13.3**	**12.1**
Class III	15.5	19.7	26.9	35.3	42.1
20000-49999	**19.8**	**18.3**	**17.1**	**16.4**	**14.7**
Class IV	11.2	13.6	17.7	21.1	22.6
10000-19999	**14.3**	**12.6**	**11.2**	**9.8**	**7.9**
Class V	6.2	6.0	6.9	7.4	7.9
5000-9999	**7.9**	**5.6**	**4.4**	**3.4**	**2.8**
Class VI	0.8	0.9	1.1	0.9	0.8
<5000	**1.0**	**0.8**	**0.7**	**0.4**	**0.3**
All Classes	78.2	107.8	157.7	215.8	286.1
	100.0	**100.0**	**100.0**	**100.0**	**100.0**

Note : Figures in bold below each year are percentages to total.
Source : Office of the Registrar General of India, Ministry of Home Affairs (Census Documents).

131 : Literacy Rate by Gender/Area

(%)

	1951	1961	1971	1981	1991	2001
All	18.3	28.3	34.5	43.6	52.2	64.8
Rural	12.1	19.1	23.7	36.1	44.7	60.0
Urban	34.6	47.0	52.4	67.3	73.1	81.0
Male	27.2	40.4	46.0	56.4	64.1	75.3
Female	8.9	15.3	22.0	29.8	39.3	53.7
Male-Female Gap	18.3	25.1	24.0	26.6	24.8	21.6

Note : Literacy Rate: Literate population in population aged 7 years and above.
Source : Office of the Registrar General of India, Ministry of Home Affairs (Census Documents).

132 : Crude Birth and Death Rate

(per '000 population)

Year	Crude Birth Rate (CBR)			Crude Death Rate (CDR)		
	Total	Rural	Urban	Total	Rural	Urban
1951	41.7	na	na	22.8	na	na
1961	41.2	na	na	19.0	na	na
1971	36.9	38.9	30.1	14.9	16.4	9.7
1981	33.9	35.6	27.0	12.5	13.7	7.8
1991	29.5	30.9	34.3	9.8	10.6	7.1
2001	25.4	27.1	20.3	8.4	9.1	6.3
2002	25.0	26.6	20.0	8.1	8.7	6.1
2003	24.8	26.4	19.8	8.0	8.7	6.0
2004	24.1	25.9	19.0	7.5	8.2	5.8
2005	23.8	25.6	19.1	7.6	8.1	6.0
2006	23.5	25.2	18.8	7.5	8.1	6.0
2007	23.1	24.7	18.6	7.6	8.0	6.0
2008	22.8	24.4	18.5	7.4	8.0	5.9
2009	22.5	24.1	18.3	7.3	7.8	5.8

Note : na: not available.
Crude Birth Rate (CBR) is the number of live births during the year divided by mid-year population. Crude Death Rate (CDR) is the number of deaths during the year divided by mid-year population. The difference between the two is the Natural Growth Rate (NGR).

Source : Sample Registration System (SRS): Reports and early Bulletins, Office of the Registrar General of India.

133 : Infant Mortality Rate and Neonatal Mortality Rate

Year	Infant Mortality Rate (IMR)			Neonatal Mortality Rate (NMR)		
	Total	Rural	Urban	Total	Rural	Urban
1961	52					
1971	129	138	82	75	81	45
1981	110	119	62	70	76	39
1991	80	87	53	51	55	32
2001	66	72	42	40	44	25
2002	63	69	40	na	na	na
2003	60	66	38	37	41	22
2004	58	64	40	37	41	24
2005	58	64	40	37	41	23
2006	57	62	39	na	na	na
2007	55	61	37	na	na	na
2008	53	58	36	na	na	na
2009	50	55	34			

Note : na: not available.
Infant Mortality Rate (IMR) is the ratio of number of infant deaths during the year to number of live births during the year multiplied by thousand. Neonatal Mortality Rate (NMR) is the ratio of infant deaths of less than 29 days during the year to number of live births during the year multiplied by thousand.

Source : Sample Registration System (SRS): Reports and early Bulletins, Office of the Registrar General of India.

134 : Total Fertility Rate and General Fertility Rate

	Total Fertility Rate (TFR)			General Fertility Rate (GFR)		
Year	Total	Rural	Urban	Total	Rural	Urban
1971	5.2	5.4	4.1	161.1	168.7	130.1
1981	4.5	4.8	3.3	140.9	149.4	107.2
1991	3.6	3.9	2.7	119.2	127.2	93.3
2000	3.2	3.5	3.3	102.8	112.7	76.5
2001	3.1	3.4	2.3	99.5	108.6	74.4
2002	3.0	3.3	2.2	97.1	106.0	72.5
2003	3.0	3.3	2.1	95.3	103.5	71.9
2004	2.9	3.3	2.1	98.6	109.7	72.0
2005	2.9	3.2	2.1	95.8	106.2	70.9
2006	2.8	3.1	2.0	93.3	103.4	69.1
2007	2.7	3.0	2.0	89.5	98.6	67.3
2008	2.6	2.9	2.0	88.0	96.9	66.5

Note: Total Fertility Rate (TFR) is defined as the average number of children that would be born to a woman if she experiences the current fertility pattern throughout her reproductive span (15-49 years).
General Fertility Rate (GFR) is defined as number of live births per thousand women in the reproductive age group (15-49 years) in a given year.

Source : Sample Registration System (SRS): Reports and early Bulletins, Office of the Registrar General of India.

135 : Expectation of Life at Birth in Years

Year	Male	Female	All	Rural	Urban
1941-1951	32.4	31.7	32.1	na	na
1951-1961	41.9	40.6	41.3	na	na
1961-1971	46.4	44.7	45.6	na	na
1971-1975	50.5	49.0	49.7	48.0	58.9
1976-1980	52.5	52.1	52.3	50.6	60.1
1981-1985	55.4	55.7	55.4	53.7	63.4
1985-1990	57.7	58.1	57.7	56.1	63.8
1991-1995	59.7	58.6	60.3	58.9	65.9
1996-2000	61.0	62.7	61.9	60.7	67.3
2001-2005	62.3	63.9	63.2	na	na
2002-2006	62.6	64.2	63.6	na	na

Note : na: not available.
Expectation of Life at Birth is the average number of years expected to be lived at the time of birth if current morbidity trends were to continue.
Data from 1941-1951 to 1961-1971 are based on Census acturial reports.
Data from 1970-71 onwards on SRS estimates.
Data from 1991-1995 excludes J&K.

Source : Sample Registration System (SRS): Reports and early Bulletins, Office of the Registrar General of India.

136 : Health Infrastructure

	No. of Doctors (in thousands)	Medical Persons per Lakh of People			Medical Infrastructure	
		Doctors	Nurses	Health Visitors	No. of Hospitals (in thousands)	No. of Beds (per lakh of population)
1951	61.8	17	15	0.2	8	33
1961	83.7	19	28	0.4	7	53
1971	151.1	28	28	0.8	7	65
1981	268.7	39	31	1.4	10	84
1991	393.6	47	59	2.0	14	96
2001	577.1	56	121	3.5	18	89
2002	607.1	58	na	na	15	88
2003	625.4	59	128	3.8	5	36
2004	644.0	59	128	4.7	7	44
2005	675.4	64	138	4.7	6	43
2006	700.7	66	140	3.2	7	42
2007	731.4	68	147	3.2	8	44
2008	761.4	70	148	3.1	10	42
2009	793.3	71	148	3.0	na	na
2010	816.6	70	na	na	na	na

Note : From 2000, CHCs were excluded from the number of hospitals and beds.
na : not available.
Data for nurses includes auxiliary nurses.

Source : Director General of Health Services (CBHI).

137 : Combined Health Expenditure (Central and State Governments)

	Rs. crore	% GDP	Per Capita (Rs.)
1950-51	..	0.2	0.6
1960-61	..	0.6	2.5
1970-71	..	0.7	6.2
1980-81		0.9	19.4
1990-91	7309	1.3	87.1
2000-01	27960	1.3	274.4
2001-02	28578	1.3	274.8
2002-03	30184	1.2	285.8
2003-04	33504	1.2	312.5
2004-05	37535	1.2	344.7
2005-06	45428	1.2	410.7
2006-07	52126	1.2	464.6
2007-08	60869	1.2	534.9
2008-09(RE)	76489	1.4	662.8
2009-10(BE)	89314	1.4	763.4

Note: RE: Revised Estimates, BE: Budget Estimates.
From 2004-05, per cent to GDP worked out by using GDP figures as per 2004-05 series.

Source : Ministry of Health and Family Welfare.

138 : Percentage of Couples Protected Under Family Planning Methods

	Eligible Couples (in million)	% of Couples Protected by		
		Sterilisation	IUD	All
1965-66	1525.8	1.6	1.7	3.1
1970-71	94.5	8.0	1.4	10.4
1980-81	116.0	20.1	1.0	22.8
1990-91	145.1	30.3	6.7	44.1
2000-01	173.8	28.9	7.2	45.6
2001-02	176.7	28.7	7.1	45.7
2002-03	179.5	28.5	7	47.1
2003-04	182.4	28.4	6.9	47.2
2004-05	185.2	28.2	6.8	46.3
2005-06	187.8	27.9	6.7	46.7
2006-07	190.7	27.6	6.5	46.2
2007-08	193.5	27.5	6.4	46.5

Note: Including other methods such as pill, condom, etc., and also traditional methods.

Source : Ministry of Health and Family Welfare.

139 : Deficit in Housing

(in million)

Census Year	Number of Households			Number of Occupied Residential Houses			Deficit in Housing Stock		
	Rural	Urban	Total	Rural	Urban	Total	Rural	Urban	Total
1951	53.6	12.3	65.9	54.1	10.3	64.4	-0.5	2.0	1.5
1961	68.9	15.6	84.5	65.1	13.8	78.9	3.8	1.8	5.6
1971	79.6	20.9	100.4	72.7	18.0	90.8	6.9	2.8	9.7
1981	90.9	28.9	119.8	86.1(a)	27.6	113.7	4.8	1.3	6.1
1991(b)	111.6	40.4	152.0	107.9	39.1	147.0	3.7	1.3	5.0
2001	137.7©	55.8	193.6	135.1	52.1	187.2	2.6	3.7	6.4

Note : A household is a group of persons who commonly live together and would take their meals from a common kitchen unless the exigencies of work prevented any of them doing so. There may be a household of blood relatives, or unrelated persons or having a mix of both. Unrelated households are boarding houses, messes, hotels, rescue home, jails, asylums etc. But they are called institutional households. They are included in the number.

Deficit has been worked out on the assumption that each household requires a house and the difference between number of households and occupied residential houses indicate the apparent gap in housing.

a: excludes Assam, b: excludes J& K, c: excludes Mao Maram, Paomata & Purul and Senapati district of Manipur.

Source : Office of the Registrar General of India (NSSO Survey).

140 : Per cent Distribution of Households by Type of Housing Structure

Year	Rural			Urban		
	Pucca	Semi-*Pucca*	*Kutcha*	*Pucca*	Semi-*Pucca*	*Kutcha*
1986-87	17.2	33.1	49.6	57.2	25.7	17.0
1987-88	19.5	31.9	48.6	57.9	24.3	17.8
1988-89	27.1	33.5	59.3	71.1	18.0	10.9
1992	26.7	35.3	37.8	67.3	22.5	10.2
1993-94	29.2	38.1	32.7	70.7	19.5	9.9
1994-95	29.6	37.9	32.4	70.4	20.0	9.5
2000-01	38.4	31.6	30.0	75.2	19.4	7.4
2003	43.9	34.9	21.1	81.7	13.4	4.8
2004	48.2	32.8	17.2	85.5	10.2	3.5
2005-06	50.0	31.0	19.0	86.0	10.0	4.0
2006-07	49.0	29.0	22.0	85.0	11.0	4.0
2007-08	49.7	31.4	18.8	88.0	9.1	2.9
2008-09	55.4	27.6	17.0	91.7	6.2	2.1

Source : National Sample Survey Organisation, NSSO Surveys.

141 : Distribution of Households by Size of Dwellings

Year		No Exclusive Room	One Room	Two Rooms	Three Rooms	More than Three Rooms
		(Per cent of Total)				
1981	Total	0.65	44.72	28.62	12.22	13.79
	Rural	0.7	44.4	28.9	12.2	13.8
	Urban	0.5	45.8	27.9	12.2	13.6
1991	Total	0.0	40.5	30.6	13.9	15.1
	Rural	0.0	40.8	30.7	13.5	15.0
	Urban	0.0	39.6	30.4	14.8	15.2
2001	Total	3.1	38.5	30.0	14.4	14.1
	Rural	3.4	39.8	30.2	13.3	13.4
	Urban	2.3	35.1	29.5	17.1	15.9

Source : Census Documents.

142 : Per Capita Net Availability of Food Grains

(per day in grams)

Mid Year	Food Grains	Cereals	Pulses
1951	394.9	334.2	60.7
1961	468.7	399.7	69.0
1971	468.8	417.6	51.2
1981	454.8	417.3	37.5
1991	510.1	468.5	41.6
2001	416.2	386.2	30.0
2002	494.1	458.1	35.4
2003	437.6	408.5	29.1
2004	462.7	426.9	35.8
2005	422.4	390.9	31.5
2006	445.3	412.8	32.5
2007	442.8	407.4	35.5
2008	436.0	394.2	41.8
2009	444.0	407.0	37.0

Source : *Economic Survey.*

143 : Population Below Poverty Line, Poverty Ratio and Poverty Line

	BPL Population (in million)			Poverty Ratio (%)		
	Rural	Urban	Combined	Rural	Urban	Combined
1973-74	261.3	60.0	321.3	56.4	49.0	54.9
1977-78	264.2	64.6	328.9	53.1	45.2	51.3
1983	252.0	70.9	322.9	45.7	40.8	44.5
1987-88	231.9	75.2	307.1	39.1	38.2	38.9
1993-94	244.0	76.3	320.3	37.3	32.4	36.0
1999-00	193.2	67.0	260.3	27.1	23.6	26.1
2004-05	220.9	80.8	301.7	28.3	25.7	27.5

Note: Based on poverty line defined in terms of per capita total consumer expenditure (PCTE) in 1973-74 prices and adusjted over times and across states for change in prices. The estimate were anchored on the per capita calorie norms of 2,400 for rural and 2,100 for urban persons per day.

Source: Planning Commission.

144 : Private Final Consumption Expenditure (At Current Prices)

	PFCE (Rs. crore)	PFCE (per capita Rs.)	of which: Food (Rs.)	Clothing (Rs.)	Rent (Rs.)	Medicine (Rs.)	Education (Rs.)
1999-2000 Series							
1950-51	9643	269	164	9	55	3	2
1960-61	16312	376	193	17	91	5	3
1970-71	39493	730	408	35	127	13	8
1980-81	120094	1769	925	108	234	51	23
1990-91	392142	4674	2231	268	518	114	75
2000-01	1345583	13205	5594	569	974	538	233
2004-05	1848490	16974	5961	713	1302	790	352
2004-05 Series							
2004-05	1925592	17682	5972	996	1671	878	299
2005-06	2159434	19525	6458	1149	1793	952	332
2006-07	2488410	22178	7029	1447	2009	1033	364
2007-08	2850088	25045	7861	1466	2329	1122	391
2008-09	3266461	28306	8513	1584	2783	1218	463
2009-10	3795901	32444	8225	1479	3121	1131	445

Source : CSO, National Account Statistics.

145 : Number of Recognised Schools

As on Sep. 30	Boards of Education	Schools for General Education			
		Pre-Primary/ Nursery	Primary/ Basic	Middle/ Sr. Basic/ Upper Primary	Secondary/ Sr. Secondary/ Higher Secondary/Jr. Colleges
1951	7	303	209671	13596	7416
1961	13	1909	330399	49663	17329
1971	37	4174	408378	90621	37051
1981	49	10697	494503	118555	51573
1991	42	15877	560935	151456	79796
2001	35	37288	638738	206269	126047
2002	39	60840	664041	219626	133492
2003	39	64712	651382	245274	137207
2004	39	63167	712239	262286	145962
2005	41	63596	767520	274731	152049
2006	41	67157	772568	288493	159667
2007	39	60886	784852	305584	169568
2008	47	66165	787827	325174	172990

Note : na: not available.

Source : Department of Education, Ministry of Human Resources Development (website).

146 : Number of Institutions for Higher Education

(in numbers)

As on Sep. 30	University/Deemed University/Institution of National Importance	Total Colleges for High Level Education	of which: Arts, Science, Commerce	Enginee-ring/Tech. Colleges	Medical Colleges	Teachers' Training Colleges
1951	31	718	540	31	34	36
1961	55	1599	1161	76	80	125
1971	102	3706	2587	107	176	258
1981	133	4855	3393	149	262	331
1991	146	7532	4877	289	441	506
2001	256	13060	8640	678	1069	694
2002	266	15703	10517	1077	1255	785
2003	300	16506	10753	1172	1393	904
2004	320	17062	10796	1227	1639	1026
2005	407	16009	10377	1302	817	1082
2006	350	20769	11698	1562	2053	1669
2007	371	21108	11458	1627	2081	2019
2008	409	25987	14145	2466	2229	3283
2009	544	31324	na	na	na	na

Note : na : not available.

Deemed university includes institutes established under state legislature act.

Medical colleges include *ayurveda*, dental, pharmacy, nursing and physiotherapy.

Source : Central Statistical Office Publications.

147 : Number of Teachers and Pupil-Teacher Ratio

Year	Number of Teachers (in thousands)									Pupil-Teacher Ratio (%)		
	Primary			Upper Primary			Sec./Sr. Sec/Intermediate					
	Total	Male	Female	Total	Male	Female	Total	Male	Female	Primary (I-V)	Middle (VI-VIII)	Secondary (IX-XI)
1950-51	538	456	82	86	73	13	127	107	20	24	20	21
1960-61	742	615	127	345	262	83	296	234	62	36	31	25
1970-71	1057	832	225	638	463	175	629	474	155	39	32	25
1980-81	1363	1021	342	851	598	253	926	669	257	38	33	27
1990-91	1616	1143	473	1073	717	356	1336	919	417	43	38	32
2000-01	1896	1221	675	1326	820	506	1761	1184	577	43	38	32
2001-02	1928	1213	715	1468	921	547	1777	1157	620	43	34	34
2002-03	1913	1167	746	1581	936	645	2033	1221	812	42	34	33
2003-04	2097	1260	837	1592	944	648	2024	1250	774	45	35	33
2004-05	2161	1319	842	1589	992	597	2083	1282	801	46	35	33
2005-06	2184	1326	858	1671	998	673	2154	1333	821	46	34	33
2006-07	2323	1403	920	1717	1039	678	2248	1388	860	44	34	31
2007-08	2315	2212	1103	1780	1063	717	2127	1332	795			

Source : Department of Education, Ministry of Human Resources Development (website).

148 : Enrollment by Stages of School Education (All Students) and Gross Enrollment Ratio (GER)

(in million)

Year	Primary (I-V) Age 6-11 Years				Middle/Upper Primary (VI-VIII) Age 11-14 Years				Sec./Sr. Sec/Inter./Pre-Degree (IX-XII) Age 14-18 Years			
	Enrollment	GER (%)			Enrollment	GER (%)			Enrollment	GER (%)		
	Total (in million)	Total	Male	Female	Total (in million)	Total	Male	Female	Total (in million)	Total	Male	Female
1970-71	19.2	43.1	60.6	24.8	3.1	12.7	20.6	4.6	1.5	na	na	na
1970-71	35.0	62.4	82.6	41.4	6.7	22.5	33.2	11.3	3.4	10.6	16.7	4.1
1970-71	57.0	78.6	95.5	60.5	13.3	33.4	46.5	20.8	7.6	19.0	26.8	10.2
1980-81	73.8	80.5	95.8	64.1	20.7	41.9	54.3	28.6	11.0	17.3	23.1	11.1
1990-91	97.4	100.1	113.9	85.5	34.0	76.6	47.0	62.1	19.1	19.3	33.9	10.3
2000-01	113.8	95.7	104.9	85.9	42.8	58.6	49.9	58.6	27.6	30.1	24.6	35
2001-02	113.9	96.3	105.3	86.9	44.8	60.2	67.8	52.1	30.5	33.3	38.2	27.7
2002-03	122.4	95.3	97.5	93.1	46.9	61.0	65.3	56.2	33.2	37.5	41.3	33.2
2003-04	128.3	98.2	100.8	95.7	48.7	62.4	66.9	57.7	35.0	38.9	42.9	34.3
2004-05	130.8	107.8	110.7	104.7	51.2	69.9	74.3	65.1	37.1	39.9	44.3	35.1
2005-06	132.1	109.4	112.2	105.8	52.2	71.0	75.2	66.4	38.4	39.4	44.6	35.8
2006-07	139.1	111.4	114.6	108.0	54.5	73.8	77.6	69.6	39.9	40.4	44.6	35.8
2007-08	135.5	114.0	115.3	112.6	57.2	78.1	81.5	74.4	44.5	100.3	102.4	98.0

Note : na : not available.

Gross Enrollment Ratio (GER) : Percentage of number of population enrolled in different age groups to total population in the appropriate ages.

Source : Department of Education, Ministry of Human Resources Development (website).

149 : Dropout Ratio

(in percentages)

Year	(I-V Classes)			(I-VIII Classes)			(I-X Classes)		
	Boys	Girls	Total	Boys	Girls	Total	Boys	Girls	Total
1960-61	61.7	70.9	64.9	75.0	85.0	78.3	na	na	na
1970-71	64.5	70.9	67.0	74.6	83.4	77.9	na	na	na
1980-81	56.2	62.5	58.7	68.0	79.4	72.7	79.8	86.6	82.5
1990-91	40.1	46.0	42.6	59.1	65.1	60.9	67.5	77.0	71.3
2000-01	39.7	41.9	40.7	50.3	57.0	53.7	66.4	71.5	68.6
2001-02	38.4	39.9	39.0	52.9	56.9	54.6	64.2	68.6	66.0
2002-03	35.9	33.7	34.9	52.3	53.5	52.8	60.7	65.0	62.6
2003-04	33.7	28.6	31.5	51.9	52.9	52.3	61.0	64.9	62.7
2004-05	31.8	25.4	29.0	50.5	51.3	50.8	60.4	63.9	61.9
2005-06	48.7	21.8	25.7	48.7	49.0	48.8	60.1	63.6	61.6
2006-07	46.5	26.6	25.6	46.5	45.3	45.9	58.6	61.5	59.9
2007-08	25.7	24.4	25.1	43.7	41.3	42.7	56.6	57.3	56.7

Note: Total dropouts during a course as percentage of intake in the first year of the course (stage) has been taken.
Dropout rate is the per cent of pupils who dropped out from a given grade/cycle/level of education in a given school year. It does not include repeaters.

Source: Ministry of Human Resource Development.

150 : Public Expenditure on Education

	Expenditure		
	Rs. in billion	% to Public Expenditure	% to GDP
1951-52	0.6	7.9	0.6
1961-62	2.6	11.7	1.4
1971-72	10.1	9.5	2.0
1981-82	43.0	10.3	2.5
1991-92	223.9	13.1	3.4
2001-02	798.7	12.9	3.8
2002-03	855.1	12.6	3.8
2003-04	890.8	12.0	3.5
2004-05	966.9	12.1	3.4
2005-06	1132.3	12.7	3.5
2006-07	1373.8	13.3	3.7
2007-08	1614.2	13.3	3.7
2008-09	1865.0	13.6	3.9

Note : Public expenditure pertains to both Centre and States.
Source : Department of Secondary Education.

151 : Undergraduate Enrollment According to Faculty and Stages in Education

(in thousands)

Year	General Education				Professional Courses		
	Arts	Science	Commerce	Total	Agriculture	Engineering	Medicine
1950-51				119	3	12	15
1960-61				398	10	42	32
1970-71				1580	27	87	90
1980-81				2152	39	129	110
1990-91	2202	951	948	4101	42	258	153
2000-01	3875	1670	1500	7045	50	577	263
2001-02	4083	1598	1634	7315	54	641	273
2002-03	4159	1770	1678	7607	55	692	301
2003-04	4491	1852	1755	8098	59	717	313
2004-05	4242	1690	1587	7519	62	697	257
2005-06	4209	1809	1612	7630	na	1668	306
2006-07	4372	1875	1613	7860	na	1778	320
2007-08	5263	2057	1916	9236	68	1491	449

Source: Ministry of Human Resource Development, Statistics of Higher & Technical Education 2008-09.

152 : Gross Enrollment Ratio in Higher Education (%)

	Total	Male	Female
2001-02	8.1	9.3	6.7
2002-03	9.0	10.3	7.5
2003-04	9.2	10.6	7.7
2004-05	10.0	11.6	8.2
2005-06	11.6	13.5	9.4
2008-09	13.8	16.1	11.3

Source : Ministry of Human Resource Development.

153 : Police Strength and Cognisable Crime

End-Dec.	Police Strength			Cognisable Crimes in '000s			
	Strength of Police (in '000)	No. of Police (per 100 sq km)	No. of Police (per lakh population)	Crime (IPC)	Crime (per lakh population)	*of which:* Murder (in '000)	Theft (in '000)
1951	na	na	na	612	170	10	252
1961	na	na	na	625	144	11	233
1971	707	22	131	953	176	16	335
1981	898	27	132	1386	204	23	422
1991	1153	35	137	1678	200	39	363
2001	1308	41	130	1769	174	36	253
2002	1309	41	120	1780	171	35	247
2003	1312	41	120	1716	163	33	245
2004	1337	42	120	1832	171	34	273
2005	1343	42	120	1823	167	33	273
2006	1406	44	170	1878	170	32	274
2007	1425	45	170	1990	177	32	285
2008	1474	47	110	2093	184	33	317
2009	na	na	na	2121	184	na	na

Note : na : not available.
Source : National Crime Records Bureau, Ministry of Home Affairs.

154 : Prison Statistics

	Number of Jails		Capacity (in '000)		Inmates (in '000)		Occupancy Rate (%)	
	2001	2009	2001	2009	2001	2009	2001	2009
Central Jail	98	119	103.8	133.5	130.1	163.5	125.3	122.5
District Jail	266	321	76.4	113.1	122.2	162.5	159.8	143.7
Sub-Jail	671	832	34.5	45.3	52.2	39.9	151.1	88.1
Women Jail	13	18	2.0	3.7	2.1	2.8	103.8	75.1
BROSTAL School	12	21	2.3	2.2	1.2	1.2	54.7	53.4
Open Jail	25	32	4.3	3.5	1.6	2.5	36.8	73.2
Special Jail	25	25	4.9	5.3	3.6	4.1	73.6	78.6
Others	9	6	1.4	0.6	0.7	0.5	47.2	79.4
Total	1119	1374	229.7	307.1	313.6	377.0	136.5	122.8

Note : BROSTAL school is a school to reform criminal youths.
Source : National Crime Records, Ministry of Home Affairs.

155 : Juveniles' Delinquency Statistics

End-Dec.	Number of Cases		Deliquents Apprehended				Crime (per lakh of population)
	IPC (in '000)	SLL (in '000)	IPC (in '000)	SLL (in '000)	Total (in '000)	Girls (in '000)	
1971	268.5	142.7	36.4	67.0	103.4	5.4	4.9
1981	614.7	108.2	82.3	108.2	190.6	8.7	5.6
1991	12.6	22.1	15.9	13.7	29.6	6.4	1.5
2001	16.5	8.3	23.6	10.0	33.6	2.3	1.6
2002	18.6	9.0	25.0	10.8	35.8	2.2	1.8
2003	17.8	7.9	24.7	8.6	33.3	2.3	1.7
2004	19.2	5.8	24.7	6.2	30.9	2.1	1.8
2005	18.9	6.7	25.4	7.3	32.7	2.1	3.0
2006	21.1	5.2	26.9	5.2	32.1	1.8	2.9
2007	22.9	4.2	29.8	4.8	34.5	1.9	3.0
2008	24.5	3.2	31.0	3.5	34.5	1.7	3.0
2009	23.9	4.3	na	na	33.6	2.1	4.9

Note : na: not available.
Before 1988, Juvenile was defined as boys and girls below 21 years. Since 1988 juvenile boys are defined as boys below 16 years and girls below 18 years. As per the revised definition of Juvenile Justice Act 2000, boys in the age group 16-18 years are also included in the definition. IPC: Indian Penal Code, SLL: Special and Local Laws.

Source : National Crime Records, Ministry of Home Affairs.

156 : Incidence of Suicides by Gender

(in thousands)

	Number of Suicides				Important Causes		
	Male	Female	All	Rate	Illness	Dowry	Poverty
1961	22.6	16.2	38.8	8.9	na	na	na
1971	26.3	17.3	43.7	8.1	8.0	na	1.8
1981	23.9	16.4	40.2	5.9	5.7	na	1.2
1991	46.3	32.1	78.5	9.2	na	na	na
2001	69.3	41.1	108.5	10.6	24.1	2.4	2.5
2002	70.2	40.6	110.4	10.5	26.0	2.4	2.4
2003	72.7	41.0	110.9	10.6	24.9	2.4	2.7
2004	72.9	41.0	113.7	10.5	25.5	2.6	3.4
2005	72.9	41.0	113.9	10.3	25.1	2.4	2.5
2006	75.7	42.4	118.1	10.5	26.6	2.3	2.6
2007	79.6	43.3	122.6	10.8	21.3	3.1	2.8
2008	80.5	44.5	125.0	10.8	27.4	3.0	3.0
2009	81.5	45.7	127.2	10.9	26.7	2.9	3.0

Note : na : not available.
Rate is defined as incidence of suicides per one lakh population.

Source : *Accidental Death and Suicides in India*, National Crime Record Bureau.

157 : Profile of Suicide Victims: Number of Suicides by Gender

(in '000)

	Total Suicides					
	Male	Female	Total	*of which:*		
				Housewives	Students	Farmers/ Agri-culturists
1996	51206	37035	88241	19490	5244	13729
% to Total	58.0	42.0	100.0	22.1	5.9	15.6
2000	66032	42561	108593	22205	5352	16603
% to Total	60.8	39.2	100.0	20.4	4.9	15.3
2001	66314	42192	108506	21659	5474	16415
% to Total	61.1	38.9	100.0	20.0	5.0	15.1
2002	69332	41085	110417	22730	5355	17971
% to Total	62.8	37.2	100.0	20.6	4.8	16.3
2003	70221	40630	110851	23301	6089	17164
% to Total	63.3	36.7	100.0	21.0	5.5	15.5
2004	72651	41046	113697	23170	5610	18241
% to Total	63.9	36.1	100.0	20.4	4.9	16.0
2005	72916	40998	113914	24141	5138	17131
% to Total	64.0	36.0	100.0	21.2	4.5	15.0
2006	75702	42410	118112	25063	5857	17060
% to Total	64.1	35.9	100.0	21.2	5.0	14.4
2007	79295	43342	122637	24162	6248	16632
% to Total	64.7	35.3	100.0	19.7	5.1	13.6
2008	80544	44473	125017	24367	6060	16196
% to Total	64.4	35.6	100.0	19.5	4.8	13.0
2009	81471	45680	127151	25092	6761	17368
% to Total	64.1	35.9	100.0	19.7	5.3	13.7

Source : National Crime Records, Ministry of Home Affairs.

158: Number of Trade Unions and Membership

End-Dec.	All Union			Workers Union			Employees Union		
	Regd. Trade Union	Union Submitting Return	Member-ship	Regd. Trade Union	Unions Submitting Return	Member-ship	Regd. Trade Union	Union Submitting Return	Member-ship
1952	4623	2556	1996						
1961	11312	6813	4013						
1971	22484	9029	5470	22121	8909	5431	363	120	39
1981	37539	6682	5397	36930	6590	5377	609	92	20
1991	53535	8418	6100	52773	8351	6094	762	67	6
2001	41984	6531	5874	41568	6513	5871	416	18	3
2002	38092	7812	6974	37903	7734	6924	189	78	50
2003	46215	7258	6277	42207	7229	6272	419	29	5
2004	30391	5242	3396	30009	5217	3391	382	25	5
2005	46306	8317	8722	45842	8255	8711	464	62	12

Note : Data collected from annual returns submitted under Indian Trade Union Act 1936.
Data for years 1952 and 1961 pertains to March 31st of that year.

Source : Ministry of Labour and Employment.

159 : Industrial Disputes

Calendar Year	Number			Workers Involved (in million)	Man-Days Lost (in million)
	Strike	Lockout	Total		
1951	..	..	1071	0.7	3.8
1961	1240	117	1357	0.5	4.9
1971	2478	274	2752	1.6	16.5
1981	2245	344	2569	1.6	36.6
1991	1278	532	1810	1.3	26.4
2001	372	302	674	0.7	23.8
2002	295	284	579	1.1	26.6
2003	255	297	552	1.8	30.3
2004	236	241	477	2.1	23.9
2005	227	229	456	2.9	29.7
2006	243	187	430	1.8	20.3
2007	210	179	389	0.7	27.2
2008	240	181	421	1.6	17.4
2009	157	192	349	1.6	9.2
2010	79	20	99	0.4	1.7

Note : na : not available.
Statistics are collected on a voluntary basis by authorities of State Labour Department and regional labour commissioner's office (central) and consolidated returns are furnished to the Labour Bureau.

Source : *Indian Labour Journal*, Labour Bureau.

160 : Circulation of Newspaper in India

	Daily Newspapers		Non-Daily Newspapers and Periodicals	
	Number	Circulation per 1000 Population	Number	Circulation per 1000 Population
1961	484	12.39	6139	36.68
1971	821	16.81	11397	32.39
1981	1264	22.47	17880	52.79
1991	3229	29.00	26985	35.27
2001	5659	57.74	45974	55.83
2002-03	5966	69.07	49814	64.89
2003-04	6287	68.60	52482	54.45
2004-05	6530	72.26	53883	71.65
2005-06	6800	80.35	55683	83.07
2006-07	7131	88.09	57867	83.10
2007-08	7710	92.96	61613	89.03

Note : Newspaper means any printed or (cyclostyled), periodical work containing public news and comment on public news. Daily newspaper is one that is issued at least four times a week. Circulation is the average number of copies sold or distributed free per publishing day. Periodical is a publication appearing at an interval of a week or more.
Data upto 2001 based on registered number with Registrar of Newspapers for India (RNI). Data from 2002-03 based on Annual Statements submitted by publishers.

Source : Office of the Registrar of Newspapers for India.

161 : Life Insurance

End-March	Number of Insurance Office			New Life Policies Issued (in million)			Life Insurance Premium Collected, incl. Renewal (Rs. crore)		
	LIC	Private Players	Total	LIC	Private Players	Total	LIC	Private Players	Total
2000-01	2186	13	2199						
2001-02	2190	116	2306				49822	273	50095
2002-03	2191	254	2445	24.55	0.83	25.37	54629	1199	55748
2003-04	2196	416	2612	26.97	1.66	28.63	63534	3120	66654
2004-05	2197	804	3001	23.98	2.23	26.21	75127	7728	82855
2005-06	2220	1645	3865	31.59	3.87	35.46	90792	15084	105876
2006-07	2301	3072	5373	38.23	7.92	46.15	127823	28253	156076
2007-08	2522	6391	8913	37.61	13.26	50.87	149790	51561	201351
2008-09	3030	8785	11815	35.91	15.01	50.92	157288	64497	221785
2009-10	3250	8768	12018	38.86	14.36	53.23	186077	79373	265450

Source : Insurance Regulatory and Development Authority (IRDA).

162 : Non-Life Insurance

	New Policies Issued (in million)			Gross Direct Premium (in Rs. crore)		
	Public Sector Players	Private Sector Players	Total	Public Sector Players	Private Sector Players	Total
2001-02				11918	468	12385
2002-03	41.9	1.7	43.6	13520	1350	14870
2003-04	38.4	3.3	41.7	14285	2258	16543
2004-05	44.6	5.1	49.8	14949	3508	18457
2005-06	42.2	8.9	51.1	15976	5363	21339
2006-07	34	12.7	44.7	17286	8647	25930
2007-08	38.5	18.7	57.3	16832	10992	27824
2008-09	45.1	21.9	67.1	18031	12321	30352
2009-10	43.4	24.1	67.5	20643	13977	34620

Source : Insurance Regulatory and Development Authority (IRDA).

163 : Insurance Density and Insurance Penetration

Calendar Year	Insurance Density			Insurance Penetration		
	Total	Life	Non-Life	Total	Life	Non-Life
2001	11.5	9.1	2.4	2.7	2.2	0.6
2002	14.7	11.7	3	3.3	2.6	0.7
2003	16.4	12.9	3.5	2.9	2.3	0.6
2004	19.7	15.7	4	3.2	2.5	0.6
2005	22.7	18.3	4.4	3.1	2.5	0.6
2006	38.4	33.2	5.2	4.8	4.1	0.6
2007	46.6	40.4	6.2	4.7	4.0	0.6
2008	47.4	41.2	6.2	4.6	4.0	0.6
2009	54.3	47.7	6.7	5.2	4.6	0.6

Note : Insurance Density is ratio of premium to total population in per cent and Insurance Penetration is ratio (in per cent) of premium to GDP.

Source : Insurance Regulatory and Development Authority (IRDA).

164 : Employment in Organised Public Sector by Industry

(numbers in lakh)

As on 31-March	Total	Agriculture, Hunting etc.	Mining & Quarrying	Manufacturing	Electricity Gas & Water	Construction	Wholesale and Retail Trade	Transport, Storage & Communications	Finance/ Insurance/ Real Estate etc.	Community/ Social/ Personal Services
1961	70.50	1.80	1.29	3.69	2.24	6.03	0.94	17.24		37.27
1971	107.31	2.76	1.82	8.06	4.35	8.80	3.28	22.17		56.07
1981	154.84	4.63	8.18	15.02	6.83	10.89	1.17	27.09	7.48	73.55
1991	190.58	5.56	9.99	18.52	9.05	11.49	1.50	30.26	11.94	92.27
2001	191.39	5.02	8.75	14.30	9.35	10.81	1.63	30.42	12.81	98.30
2002	187.74	4.83	8.61	13.50	9.23	10.26	1.57	30.09	12.30	97.35
2003	185.80	5.06	8.47	12.60	9.13	9.48	1.82	29.39	13.77	96.09
2004	181.97	4.93	10.30	11.89	8.74	9.32	1.81	28.15	14.08	92.76
2005	180.07	4.96	10.14	11.30	8.60	9.11	1.84	27.51	14.08	92.52
2006	178.73	4.69	11.46	10.92	8.49	8.94	1.82	26.75	13.90	91.76
2007	176.88	4.75	11.37	10.87	8.49	8.66	1.78	26.37	13.69	90.90
2008	172.84	4.71	11.21	10.44	7.96	8.52	1.65	26.34	13.47	88.54

Source : Director General of Employment and Training as published in *Economic Survey*.

165 : Employment in Organised Private Sector by Industry

(numbers in lakh)

As on 31-March	Total	Agriculture, Hunting etc.	Mining & Quarrying	Manufacturing	Electricity, Gas & Water	Construction	Wholesale/ Retail Trade	Transport, Storage & Communication	Finance/ Insurance/ Real Estate	Community/ Social/ Personal Service
1961	50.40	6.70	5.50	30.20	0.40	2.40	1.60	0.80	..	2.80
1971	67.70	8.00	4.10	39.70	0.50	1.40	3.00	1.00	..	10.00
1981	73.95	8.58	1.30	45.45	0.35	0.72	2.77	0.60	1.96	12.22
1991	76.77	8.91	1.00	44.81	0.40	0.73	3.00	0.53	2.54	14.85
2001	86.51	9.31	0.79	50.13	0.52	0.57	3.39	0.76	3.70	17.34
2002	84.32	8.55	0.68	48.67	0.42	0.56	3.35	0.76	3.91	17.42
2003	84.20	8.95	0.66	47.44	0.50	0.44	3.60	0.79	4.26	17.56
2004	82.45	9.17	0.65	44.89	0.47	0.45	3.51	0.81	4.58	17.92
2005	84.52	9.83	0.79	44.89	0.49	0.49	3.75	0.85	5.23	18.20
2006	87.71	10.28	0.95	45.49	0.40	0.55	3.87	0.87	6.52	18.78
2007	92.40	9.50	1.00	47.50	0.50	0.70	4.10	1.00	8.60	19.50
2008	98.38	9.92	1.11	49.70	0.51	0.69	2.72	1.04	10.96	21.73

Source : Director General of Employment and Training as published in *Economic Survey*.

166 : Census Population, Workers and Non-Workers

(number in million)

Census Year	Population	Workers	% to Total Population	*of which:* Main Workers	% to Total Workers	Non-Workers	% to Total Population
Persons							
1981	683.3	244.6	(35.8)	222.5	(91.0)	420.7	(61.6)
1991	846.4	306.0	(36.2)	278.9	(91.1)	510.1	(60.3)
2001	1028.7	402.2	(39.1)	313.2	(77.9)	626.4	(60.9)
Male							
1981	353.3	181.0	(51.2)	177.5	(98.1)	162.9	(46.1)
1991	439.2	218.6	(49.8)	216.0	(98.8)	205.0	(46.7)
2001	532.2	275.0	(51.7)	240.3	(87.4)	257.1	(48.3)
Female							
1981	330.0	63.6	(19.3)	45.0	(70.8)	257.8	(78.1)
1991	407.1	87.4	(21.5)	69.9	(80.0)	305.2	(75.0)
2001	496.4	127.2	(25.6)	72.9	(57.3)	369.2	(74.4)

Note : The concept of 'main workers' was used from 1981. Total workers may include main and subsidiary workers. Workers refers to gainfully employed persons.

Source : Census Documents.

167 : Labour Force and Labour Force Participation Rate (LFPR): NSSO Reports

	Labour Force (in million)			Labour Force Participation Rate (%)		
	Rural	Urban	Total	Rural	Urban	Total
Total						
1972-73	199.6	40.6	240.2	43.9	34.5	42.0
1977-78	228.1	53.5	281.6	45.8	37.5	44.0
1983.0	247.2	63.2	310.4	45.2	36.2	43.0
1987-88	260.1	74.3	334.4	44.3	35.6	42.1
1993-94	293.0	85.7	378.7	44.9	36.3	42.7
1999-00	305.2	100.7	405.9	42.3	35.4	40.4
2004-05	348.7	120.3	469.0	44.6	38.2	43.0
2009-10	341.9	126.9	468.8	41.4	36.2	40.0
Male						
1972-73	128.7	32.9	161.6	55.1	52.1	54.5
1977-78	144.5	41.4	185.9	56.5	54.3	56.0
1983.0	155.9	50.2	206.1	55.5	54.0	55.1
1987-88	165.0	58.5	223.5	54.9	53.4	54.5
1993-94	189.3	67.3	256.6	56.1	54.3	55.6
1999-00	200.2	80.7	280.8	54.0	54.2	54.1
2004-05	222.5	93.9	316.4	55.5	57.0	55.9
2009-10	235.7	102.7	338.4	55.6	55.9	55.7
Female						
1972-73	70.9	7.7	78.6	32.1	14.2	28.6
1977-78	83.6	12.1	95.7	34.5	18.3	31.0
1983.0	91.3	13.0	104.3	34.2	15.9	29.9
1987-88	95.1	15.8	110.9	33.1	16.2	28.8
1993-94	104.7	18.4	123.1	33.0	16.5	28.7
1999-00	105.0	20.0	125.1	30.2	14.7	25.8
2004-05	126.2	26.4	152.6	33.3	17.8	29.4
2009-10	106.2	24.2	130.4	26.5	14.6	23.3

Note: Usual Status = Principal Status + Subsidiary Status.
Data relate to usual status of individuals.
Usual activity status relates to the activity status of person during the reference period of 365 days preceeding the date of survey. The activity status on which a person spent relatively longer time (i.e., major time criterion) during 365 days preceeding the date of survey is considered as the principal usual activity status of the person. If the same person simultaneously pursue another economic activity for a shorter period that is known as subsidiary activity.
Labour Force covers those involved in gainful activity regularly, those involved in gainful activity occassionaly and those unemployed.
Labour Force Participation Rate (LFPR) represents size of labour force as per cent of population.

Source: National Sample Survey Organisation (NSSO), various reports.

168 : Labour Work Force and Work Force Participation Rate (WFPR)

	Usual Status (PS+SS)					
	Work Force (in million)			Work Force Participation Rate (%)		
	Rural	Urban	Total	Rural	Urban	Total
Total						
1972-73	197.8	38.5	236.3	43.5	32.7	..
1977-78	221.5	49.2	270.7	44.4	34.1	42.3
1983.0	243.1	59.6	302.7	44.5	34.0	42.0
1987-88	252.5	69.5	322.0	43.4	33.7	41.2
1993-94	290.3	81.8	372.1	44.4	34.7	42.0
1999-00	300.8	96.0	396.8	41.7	33.7	39.7
2004-05	342.9	115.0	457.9	43.9	36.5	42.0
2009-10	336.4	122.6	459.0	40.8	35.0	39.2
Male						
1972-73	127.2	31.8	159.0	54.5	50.1	..
1977-78	141.4	38.8	180.2	55.2	50.8	54.3
1983.0	152.7	47.3	200.0	54.7	51.2	53.8
1987-88	160.5	55.0	215.5	53.9	50.6	53.1
1993-94	186.6	64.5	251.1	55.3	52.1	54.5
1999-00	196.8	77.1	273.9	53.1	51.8	52.7
2004-05	218.9	90.4	309.3	54.6	54.9	54.7
2009-10	231.9	99.8	331.7	54.7	54.3	54.6
Female						
1972-73	70.6	7.2	77.8	31.8	13.4	..
1977-78	80.1	10.4	90.5	73.1	15.6	29.7
1983.0	90.4	12.3	102.7	34.0	15.1	21.6
1987-88	92.0	14.5	106.5	32.3	15.2	28.5
1993-94	103.7	17.3	121.0	32.8	15.5	28.6
1999-00	104.0	18.9	122.9	29.9	13.9	25.9
2004-05	124.0	24.6	148.6	32.7	16.6	28.7
2009-10	104.5	22.8	127.3	26.1	13.8	22.8

Note : Usual Status = Principal Status + Subsidiary Status.
Data relate to usual status of individuals.
Work Force covers those involved in gainful activity regularly and those involved in gainful activity occassionaly.
Work Force Participation Rate (WFPR) represents size of work force as per cent of population.

Source : National Sample Survey Organisation (NSSO), various reports.

169 : Per cent Distribution of Employment by Status

	Self-Employed		Regular Employees		Casual Labour	
	Male	Female	Male	Female	Male	Female
			Total			
1972-73	60.6	63.0	19.7	6.3	19.7	30.7
1977-78	58.0	60.7	18.3	5.3	23.7	34.0
1983.0	55.9	60.0	18.2	5.6	25.9	34.4
1987-88	54.3	58.9	18.6	6.9	27.1	34.2
1993-94	52.9	56.7	17.0	6.3	30.1	37.0
1999-00	52.8	55.6	14.0	7.3	33.2	37.1
2004-05	..	..	..	..	..	..
2009-10	50	53.3	17.7	10.1	32.2	36.6
			Rural			
1972-73	65.9	64.5	12.1	4.1	22.0	31.4
1977-78	62.8	62.1	10.6	2.8	26.6	35.1
1983.0	60.5	61.9	10.3	2.8	29.2	35.3
1987-88	58.6	60.8	10.0	3.7	31.4	35.5
1993-94	57.9	58.5	8.3	2.8	33.8	38.7
1999-00	55.0	57.3	8.8	3.1	36.2	39.6
2004-05	58.1	63.7	9.0	3.7	32.9	32.6
2009-10	53.5	55.7	8.5	4.4	38.0	39.9
			Urban			
1972-73	39.2	48.4	50.7	27.9	10.1	23.7
1977-78	40.4	49.5	46.4	24.9	13.2	25.6
1983.0	40.9	45.8	43.7	25.8	15.4	28.4
1987-88	41.7	47.1	43.7	27.5	14.6	25.4
1993-94	41.7	45.4	42.1	28.6	16.2	26.2
1999-00	41.5	45.3	41.7	33.3	16.8	21.4
2004-05	44.8	47.7	40.6	35.6	14.6	16.7
2009-10	41.1	41.1	41.9	39.3	17.0	19.6

Source : National Sample Survey Organisation, various reports on *Employment and Unemployment.*

170 : Estimates of Unemployment

	Usual Status (PS+SS)					
	Unemployed (in million)			Unemployment Rate (%)		
	Rural	Urban	Total	Rural	Urban	Total
Total						
1972-73	1.8	2.1	3.9	0.9	5.2	1.6
1977-78	6.6	4.3	10.9	2.9	8.0	3.9
1983.0	4.1	3.6	7.7	1.7	5.7	2.5
1987-88	7.6	4.8	12.4	2.9	6.5	3.7
1993-94	4.7	4.8	7.5	1.6	5.6	2.5
1999-00	4.2	3.8	8.0	1.4	3.8	2.0
2004-05	5.9	5.4	11.3	1.7	4.5	2.3
2009-10	5.5	4.3	9.8	1.6	3.4	2.0
Male						
1972-73	1.5	1.6	3.1	1.2	4.8	1.9
1977-78	3.1	2.6	5.7	2.2	6.5	3.1
1983.0	3.2	2.9	6.1	2.1	5.9	3.0
1987-88	4.5	3.5	8.0	2.8	6.1	3.6
1993-94	3.7	3.6	7.3	2.0	5.4	2.8
1999-00	3.2	2.9	6.1	2.1	4.8	2.2
2004-05	3.6	3.6	7.2	1.6	3.8	2.2
2009-10	3.8	2.9	6.7	1.6	2.8	2.0
Female						
1972-73	0.3	0.5	0.8	0.5	6.0	1.0
1977-78	3.5	1.7	5.2	5.5	17.8	5.4
1983.0	0.9	0.7	1.6	1.4	6.9	1.5
1987-88	3.1	1.3	4.4	3.5	8.5	4.0
1993-94	1.0	1.2	2.2	1.4	8.3	1.8
1999-00	1.0	0.9	1.9	1.5	7.1	1.5
2004-05	2.3	1.8	5.1	1.8	6.9	2.6
2009-10	1.7	1.4	3.1	1.6	5.7	2.3

Note : Unemployment rate is the number of unemployed as percentage of labour force. PS: Principal Status, SS: Subsidiary Status.

Source : National Sample Survey Organisation, various reports on *Employment and Unemployment*.

171 : Employment in Different Sectors

	Mines (million)	Scheduled Commercial Banks (million)	Railways (million)	Insurance (LIC+GIC) (thousand)	Post & Telegraph (thousand)	Telecom-munication (thousand)	Ports (thousand)	Shops/ Establishments (thousand)	Restaurants & Theatres (thousand)
1951	549.0		0.93		194			525	117
1961	671.0		1.18	55.9	373			1737	332
1971	630.7		1.39	76.6	605		107.3	2632	480
1981	749.8		1.58	96.1	506	229	116.5	4305	689
1991	789.9		1.66	176.5	596	289	111.3	4518	622
2001	599.3	861	1.51	203.4	593	375	88.2	6058	871
2002	581.9	836	1.48	201.1	579	423	81.1	6440	923
2003	572.3	836	1.45	198.4	565	417	79.1	6168	828
2004	567.9	816	1.43	189.1	549	414	74.8	5205	689
2005	559.1	835	1.42	186.8	540	404	68.6	8638	708
2006	543.0	836	1.41	186.0	520		66.4	7055	932
2007	550.4	896	1.41	184.7	501		63.2	8523	1094
2008		906	1.39	185.0	495		61.6		
2009		937	1.39	184.9	483				
2010		950	1.37	185.1					

Note : LIC: Life Insurance Corporation of India, GIC: General Insurance Corporation of India.
Source : Directorate of Mines, RBI, *Railway Year Book*, LIC, GIC, P&T Annual Reports, Labour Bureau Publications.

III. INFRASTRUCTURE

> Land Use Pattern
> Mineral
> Electricity
> Communication
> Fuel & Energy
> Road
> Railway
> Shipping
> Aviation

172 : Pattern of Land Utilisation

(million hectares)

	Reporting Area	Forest Land	Share %	Not Available for Cultivation	Net Area Sown	Share %	Others
1950-51	284.3	40.5	14.2	47.5	118.8	41.8	77.5
1960-61	298.5	54.1	18.1	50.8	133.2	44.6	60.4
1970-71	303.8	63.9	21.0	44.6	140.9	46.4	54.4
1980-81	304.2	67.5	22.2	39.6	140.3	46.1	56.8
1990-91	304.9	67.8	22.2	40.5	143.0	46.9	53.6
2000-01	305.2	69.5	22.8	41.5	141.4	46.3	52.8
2001-02	305.1	69.6	22.8	41.6	140.7	46.1	53.2
2002-03	305.3	69.7	22.8	42.1	132.5	43.4	61.0
2003-04	305.6	69.8	22.8	42.2	140.8	46.1	52.8
2004-05	305.6	69.7	22.8	42.5	141.2	46.2	52.2
2005-06	305.4	69.8	22.9	42.6	141.5	46.3	51.5
2006-07	305.6	69.7	22.8	43.0	140.0	45.8	52.9
2007-08	305.7	69.6	22.8	43.2	140.9	46.1	52.0

Note : Total geographical area is 328.73 million hectares.
Share in percentage is with respect to total reporting area.
'Others' includes pastures, grazing land, land under trees & groves, waste & fallow land.

Source : Ministry of Agriculture.

173 : Cropped and Irrigated Area

(million hectares)

	Gross Cropped Area	Area Sown More than Once	Cropping Intensity	Net Irrigated Area	Gross Irrigated Area	% to Gross Cropped Area
1950-51	131.9	13.2	111.1	20.9	22.6	(17.1)
1960-61	152.8	19.6	114.7	24.7	28.0	(18.3)
1970-71	165.8	24.9	117.7	31.1	38.2	(23.0)
1980-81	172.6	34.6	123.1	38.7	49.8	(28.9)
1990-91	185.7	42.7	129.9	48.0	63.2	(34.0)
2000-01	185.3	44.0	131.1	55.1	76.2	(41.1)
2001-02	188.3	47.6	134.1	56.9	78.4	(41.6)
2002-03	175.6	43.1	132.4	53.9	73.4	(41.8)
2003-04	190.1	49.3	135.0	57.0	78.2	(41.1)
2004-05	191.6	50.4	135.7	59.2	81.2	(42.4)
2005-06	193.1	51.6	136.4	60.4	83.9	(43.4)
2006-07	193.2	53.3	138.1	61.7	86.5	(44.8)
2007-08	195.8	55.0	139.0	62.3	87.3	(44.6)

Note: Cropping Intensity is percentage of gross cropped area to net area sown.
Source: Ministry of Agriculture.

174 : Number of Mines

	All Minerals	Fuels		Metallic Minerals		Non-Metallic Minerals
		Coal	Lignite	Total	*of which:* Iron Ore	
1950-51	2703	893		306	34	1504
1960-61	3174	848	3	693	225	1630
1970-71	3758	779	2	871	393	2106
1980-81	3927	460	2	713	312	2503
1990-91	4075	518	4	714	279	2839
2000-01	3191	591	5	565	208	2030
2001-02	3193	564	6	574	221	2049
2002-03	3145	556	6	591	242	1992
2003-04	3132	554	8	612	266	1958
2004-05	3168	554	8	615	270	1991
2005-06	2970	563	9	589	261	1809
2006-07	3005	561	9	639	290	1796
2007-08	2854	558	11	676	300	1609
2008-09	3150	574	na	719	na	1857
2009-10	2999	574	na	700	na	1725
2010-11	2628	574	na	608	na	1446

Source : Indian Bureau of Mines.

175 : Production of Metallic Minerals

(thousand tonnes)

	Bauxite	Chromite	Gold (kgs)	Iron Ore	Manganese Ore
1951	0.67	17	7041	4152	1398
1961	0.48	49	4868	18705	1405
1971	1489	274	3656	34311	1779
1981	1955	343	2495	41618	1632
1990-91	4976	929	2208	54936	1388
2000-01	7993	1972	2615	80587	1595
2001-02	8689	1549	2810	86226	1587
2002-03	9867	3066	3153	99072	1678
2003-04	10925	2904	3457	122838	1776
2004-05	11697	3639	3526	142711	2379
2005-06	12596	3714	3047	165230	1909
2006-07	15733	5296	2488	187696	2116
2007-08	22462	4873	2969	213246	2697
2008-09	15460	4073	2438	212961	3620
2009-10	13952	3413	2106	218639	2440
2010-11E	13363	3865	2214	212613	2901

Note: E: Estimated.
Source : Indian Bureau of Mines.

176 : Electricity: Installed Capacity

	Utilities				
	Total Capacity MW	Hydro Capacity MW	Thermal Capacity MW	% to Total	Nuclear MW Capacity
31-12-47	1362	508	854	63	0
31-12-50	1713	560	1153	67	0
31-12-51	1835	575	1260	69	0
31-03-61	4653	1917	2736	59	0
31-03-71	14709	6383	7906	54	420
31-03-81	30214	11791	17562	58	860
31-03-91	66086	18753	45768	69	1565
31-03-01	101626	25153	73612	72	2860
31-03-02	105046	26269	74429	71	2720
31-03-03	107877	26767	76762	71	2720
31-03-04	112684	29507	77969	69	2720
31-03-05	118426	30942	80903	68	2770
31-03-06	124287	32326	82410	66	3360
31-03-07	132329	34654	86015	65	3900
31-03-08	143061	35909	91907	64	4120
31-03-09	147965	36878	93725	63	4120
31-03-10	159399	36863	102454	64	4560
31-03-11	153775	37467	111527	73	4780

Source : Director General, Central Electricity Authority.

177 : Electricity: Generation

(GWh)

	Utilities				
	Total Generation	Hydro Generation	Thermal Generation	% to Total	Nuclear Generation
1950	5106	2519	2587	51	0
1951	5858	2860	2999	51	0
1960-61	16937	7837	9100	54	0
1970-71	55828	25248	28162	50	2417
1980-81	110844	46541	61301	55	3001
1990-91	264329	71641	186546	71	6141
2000-01	501204	74362	409940	82	16902
2001-02	517439	73579	422300	82	19475
2002-03	532693	64014	446778	84	19390
2003-04	565102	75242	468676	83	17780
2004-05	594456	84610	488329	82	17011
2005-06	623819	101494	498358	80	17324
2006-07	670654	113502	528490	79	18802
2007-08	722625	120387	560071	78	16957
2008-09	740100	110100	585300	79	14900
2009-10	768429	103896	640537	83	18636
2010-11	811143	114257	665008	82	26266

Source : Director General, Central Electricity Authority.

178 : Electricity: Net Generation and Consumption Pattern

(billion kWh)

	Net Generation	Per Capita Consumption	Pattern of Consumption				
			Domestic	Commercial	Industrial	Agriculture	Tractions
1951	4793	18	595	332	3055	203	330
1960-61	13841	38	1492	848	9584	833	453
1970-71	43724	90	3840	2573	29579	4470	1365
1980-81	82367	132	9246	4682	48069	14489	2266
1990-91	190357	253	31982	11181	84209	50321	4112
2000-01	316600	366	75629	22545	107622	84729	8213
2001-02	374670	559	79694	24139	159507	81673	8106
2002-03	393460	567	83355	25437	168821	84486	8797
2003-04	418334	592	89736	28201	181970	87089	9210
2004-05	447993	613	95659	31381	199448	88555	9495
2005-06	474451	631	100090	35965	214121	90292	9944
2006-07	525672	672	111002	40220	241216	99023	10800
2007-08	577960	717	120918	46685	265406	104182	11108
2008-09	596943	733	124562	48047	274531	107835	11615

Note: Includes both utilities and non-utilities. Pattern of consumption is as on March 31.
Source: Director General, Central Electricity Authority.

179 : Post Offices

End-March	Number of Post Offices (thousand)	Letter Boxes (thousand)	Number of Postal Articles Handled (in crore)	Number of Inland Money Orders Issued (in crore)	Postal Revenue (Rs. crore)	Availability of Post Office (per lakh population)
1950-51	36	85	227	5.1	na	10.0
1960-61	77	143	403	7.6	na	17.5
1970-71	109	182	646	9.5	na	19.9
1980-81	139	494	973	11.2	na	20.3
1990-91	149	520	1468	10.6	841	17.6
2000-01	155	595	1420	11.0	3298	15.1
2001-02	155	589	1103	11.2	3597	14.8
2002-03	156	591	909	10.5	4010	14.6
2003-04	156	597	864	9.9	4257	14.3
2004-05	156	584	736	10.2	4432	14.1
2005-06	155	601	670	9.6	5023	13.8
2006-07	155	590	668	9.9	5322	13.8
2007-08	155	591	639	9.1	5495	13.6
2008-09	155	591	654	8.7	5862	13.4
2009-10	155	585	na	na	6267	13.2

Source : Department of Posts, Ministry of Communication.

180 : Telecommunications

End-March	Number of Telephones				
	Fixed Lines DELs (million)	Cellular Mobile Telephones (million)	Total (million)	Tele Density Per 100 Population	Per Sq Km
1950-51	0.1	..	0.1	0.0	0.0
1960-61	0.3	..	0.3	0.1	0.1
1970-71	1.0	..	1.0	0.2	0.3
1980-81	2.2	..	2.2	0.3	0.7
1990-91	5.1	..	5.1	0.6	1.5
2000-01	32.7	3.6	36.3	3.5	11.0
2001-02	38.3	6.7	45.0	4.3	13.7
2002-03	41.2	13.3	54.6	5.1	16.6
2003-04	40.9	35.6	76.5	7.8	23.2
2004-05	41.4	57.0	98.4	9.0	30.7
2005-06	40.2	101.9	142.1	12.7	32.2
2006-07	40.8	165.1	205.9	18.4	67.4
2007-08	39.4	261.1	300.5	26.0	..
2008-09	38.0	397.8	429.7	36.8	
2009-10	37.0	584.3	621.3	52.4	..

Note : Mobile telephony started only from 1997 and private fixed lines from 1999.
Source : Department of Posts, Ministry of Communication.

181 : Production and Despatch of Coal

(million tonne)

	Production of Coal				Despatch of Coal	
	Coking Coal	Non-Coking Coal	Total Coal	Lignite	Coal	Lignite
1950-51	..	..	32.3	..	..	..
1960-61	17.0	38.2	55.2	..	..	..
1970-71	17.8	55.1	72.9	3.5	..	..
1980-81	32.6	81.3	113.9	5.1	..	..
1990-91	45.3	166.4	211.7	13.8	..	..
2000-01	31.1	278.6	313.7	24.2	317.5	24.8
2001-02	28.7	299.1	327.8	24.8	329.1	24.6
2002-03	30.2	311.1	341.3	26.0	338.6	26.0
2003-04	29.4	331.9	361.3	28.0	358.0	28.5
2004-05	30.2	352.4	382.6	30.3	378.7	30.1
2005-06	31.5	375.5	407.0	30.1	395.6	30.3
2006-07	32.1	398.7	430.8	31.3	419.8	30.8
2007-08	34.5	422.6	457.1	34.0	453.6	34.7
2008-09	34.8	458.0	492.8	32.4	489.2	31.8
2009-10	44.3	487.8	532.1	34.1	513.2	34.4

Source : Office of Coal Controller, Ministry of Coal.

182 : Crude Oil Statistics

(million tonne)

	Production			Reserves		
	Production	Net Imports	Refinery Throughput	On-Shore	Off-Shore	Total
1950-51	0.3	..	0.3	..	..	..
1960-61	0.5	6.0	6.6	..	..	..
1970-71	6.8	11.7	18.4	..	..	..
1980-81	10.5	16.2	25.8	140	328	468
1990-91	33.0	20.7	51.8	314	492	806
2000-01	32.4	74.1	103.4	320	354	674
2001-02	32.0	78.7	107.3	332	409	741
2002-03	33.0	82.0	112.6	339	394	733
2003-04	33.4	90.4	121.8	357	382	739
2004-05	34.0	95.9	127.1	376	410	786
2005-06	32.2	99.4	130.1	387	369	756
2006-07	34.0	111.5	146.6	357	369	726
2007-08	34.1	121.7	156.1	..	..	..
2008-09	33.5	132.8	160.8	..	..	..
2009-10	33.7	98.9	160.0	..	..	..

Note : Reserves is as on January 1 for the year 1980-81 to 2000-01 thereafter it is as on April 1.

Source : Ministry of Petroleum and Natural Gas.

183 : Production and Consumption of Petroleum Products

(million tonne)

	Petroleum Products			of which: Naphtha		Kerosene		High Speed Diesel		Fuel Oil	
	Production*	Net Imports ($)	Consumption	Production	Consumption	Production	Consumption	Production	Consumption	Production	Consumption
1950-51	0.2	3.1	3.3	na	na	na	0.9	na	0.2	na	0.9
1960-61	5.7	2.5	7.7	na	na	0.9	2.0	1.1	1.2	1.6	1.7
1970-71	17.1	0.8	17.9	1.2	0.9	2.9	3.3	3.8	3.8	4.1	4.7
1980-81	24.1	7.3	30.9	2.1	2.3	2.4	4.2	7.4	10.3	6.1	7.5
1990-91	49.5	6.0	55.0	4.9	3.4	5.5	8.4	17.2	21.1	9.4	9.0
2000-01	95.6	0.9	100.1	9.9	11.7	8.7	11.3	39.1	37.9	11.4	12.7
2001-02	100.0	-3.1	100.4	9.2	11.7	9.7	10.4	39.8	36.5	12.2	13.0
2002-03	104.1	-3.1	104.1	9.7	11.9	10.0	10.4	40.2	36.6	12.2	12.7
2003-04	113.5	-6.6	107.8	11.3	11.9	10.2	10.2	43.3	37.1	13.4	12.9
2004-05	118.6	-9.4	111.6	14.1	14.0	9.3	9.4	45.9	39.7	15.0	13.6
2005-06	119.8	-10.1	113.2	14.5	12.2	9.1	9.5	47.6	40.2	14.3	12.8
2006-07	135.3	-15.9	120.7	16.7	13.9	8.5	9.5	53.5	42.9	15.7	12.6
2007-08	144.9	-18.3	128.9	16.4	13.3	7.8	9.4	58.4	47.7	15.8	12.7
2008-09	150.5	-20.4	133.4	14.8	13.9	8.2	9.3	62.9	51.7	17.7	12.4
2009-10	149.7	-31.3	138.2	14.8	10.2	8.5	9.3	61.1	56.3	17.5	11.6

Note: * : Exclude refining fuel consumption and import. $: Exclude LPN production from fractionator.

Source: Ministry of Petroleum and Natural Gas.

184 : Natural Gas Reserves and Production

(million tonne)

	Reserves			Life (in years)	Gross Production (billion cubic metre)	Net Production (gross flare & waste)
	On-Shore	Off-Shore	Total			
1970-71	..	..	..	..	1.4	0.8
1980-81	82.0	329.0	411.0	174	2.4	1.5
1990-91	246.0	484.0	730.0	41	18.0	12.8
2000-01	294.0	345.0	639.0	22	29.5	27.9
2001-02	315.0	436.0	751.0	24	29.7	28.0
2002-03	327.0	527.0	854.0	27	31.4	30.0
2003-04	339.0	584.0	923.0	29	32.0	30.9
2004-05	340.0	761.0	1101.0	35	31.8	30.8
2005-06	330.0	745.0	1075.0	33	32.2	31.3
2006-07	270.0	785.0	1055.0	..	31.8	30.8
2007-08	264.0	786.0	1050.0	..	32.4	31.5
2008-09	287.0	787.0	1074.0	..	32.9	31.8
2009-10	829.0	608.0	1437.0	..	42.3	46.5

Source : Ministry of Petroleum and Natural Gas.

185 : Total Road Length

(thousand kilometres)

As on 31-March	Total Road Length		Highways		Urban Roads		Project Roads@	
	Total	Surfaced	Total	Surfaced	Total	Surfaced	Total	Surfaced
1951	400	157	222	198	..	..	..	..
1961	525	263	238	210	..	..	..	..
1971	915	398	779	338	72	53	131	61
1981	1485	684	1096	577	123	86	186	21
1991	2331	1091	1931	1006	187	137	210	30
2001	2447	1415	1967	1166	252	192	224	57
2002	2483	1478	2025	1200	250	190	224	61
2003	2601	1518	2045	1209	297	215	259	69
2004	2722	1578	2107	1238	301	218	261	69
2005	2909	1612	2296	1284	287	195	260	66
2006	2981	1675	2337	1319	292	200	262	67
2007	3116	1762	2427	1365	301	207	269	69
2008	3240	1853	2473	1404	304	213	270	74

Note: @: Projects roads specifically constructed for Department of forest, navigation, electricity, Steel authority, coal mines, sugarcane development authorities.
Total length includes roads under JRY scheme.

Source: Transport Research Wing, Ministry of Road Transport and Highways.

186 : Number of Motor Vehicles Registered in India

As on 31-March	Two-Wheelers	Cars, Jeeps & Taxis	Buses*	Goods Vehicles	Others#	Total
1951	27	159	34	82	4	306
1961	88	310	57	168	42	665
1971	576	682	94	343	170	1865
1981	2618	1160	162	554	897	5391
1991	14200	2954	331	1356	2533	21374
2001	38556	7058	634	2948	5795	54991
2002	41581	7613	635	2974	6121	58924
2003	47519	8599	721	3492	6676	67007
2004	51922	9451	768	3749	6828	72718
2005	58799	10320	892	4031	7457	81502
2006	64743	11526	992	4436	7921	89618
2007	69129	12649	1350	5119	8460	96707
2008	75336	13950	1427	5601	9039	105353
2009	82402	15313	1486	6041	9710	114951

Note : * : Includes omni buses since 2001.
: Includes tractors, trailors, three-wheelers/LMV and other miscellaneous vehicles.
Source : Transport Research Wing, Ministry of Road Transport and Highways.

187 : Railway Infrastructure: Route Length and Stations

As on 31-March	Infrastructure		
	Route (kilometres)		Number of Stations
	Total	*of which:* Electrified	
1950-51	53596	388	5976
1960-61	56962	748	6523
1970-71	59997	3706	7066
1980-81	61240	5345	7035
1990-91	62231	9968	7100
2000-01	63028	14856	6853
2001-02	63140	15994	6931
2002-03	63122	16272	6906
2003-04	63221	17503	7031
2004-05	63465	17495	7133
2005-06	63332	17907	7133
2006-07	63327	17800	6909
2007-08	63300	18300	6909
2008-09	64015	18559	7030
2009-10	63974	18927	7083

Source : Railway Budget.

188 : Railway Infrastructure: Rolling Stock

As on 31-March	Locomotives*	Coaching Stock & EMU	Seating Capacity (in 1000)	Goods Wagon (in 1000)	Carrying Capacity (mn tonne)
1950-51	8209	13569	943	213	4.17
1960-61	10624	21024	1432	308	6.3
1970-71	11158	26426	1846	384	9.35
1980-81	10908	30103	2196	401	11.1
1990-91	8408	31843	2473	346	11.5
2000-01	7566	38889	3232	222	10.2
2001-02	7739	39004	3337	217	10.1
2002-03	7681	39592	3413	215	10.0
2003-04	7817	40653	3627	228	10.7
2004-05	7910	42154	3713	222	10.6
2005-06	8025	43515	3807	208	10.0
2006-07	8153	44667	4001	208	10.1
2007-08	8330	46611	4168	204	10.2
2008-09	8592	49072	5000	212	11.0
2009-10	8892	49072	5000	212	11.0

Note : Data for 2008-09 and 2009-10 are provisional.
* : Includes steam, diesel and electric.

Source : Railway Budget.

189 : Railway Traffic: Passenger

Year	Originating Passenger Traffic (million)	Passenger Kilometres (million)	Passenger Earnings (Rs. crore)	Average Lead (in Kilo-metres)	Average Rate per Passenger Kilometre (in paise)
1950-51	1284	66517	98	51.8	1.5
1960-61	1594	77665	132	48.7	1.7
1970-71	2431	118120	296	48.6	2.5
1980-81	3613	208558	828	57.7	4.0
1990-91	3858	295644	3148	76.6	10.6
2000-01	4840	457022	10515	94.4	23.0
2001-02	5093	490912	11196	96.4	22.8
2002-03	5048	515044	12575	102.0	24.4
2003-04	5203	541208	13298	104.0	24.6
2004-05	5378	575702	14114	107.0	24.5
2005-06	5818	614452	15127	105.6	24.6
2006-07	6400	682655	17225	106.7	25.2
2007-08	6524	770000	19844	118.0	25.8
2008-09	7047	839203	21931	119.1	26.1
2009-10	7383	904761	23488	122.5	26.0
2010-11RE	7831	1007181	26126	128.6	25.9
2011-12BE	8272	1084658	30456	131.1	28.1

Note: BE : Budget Estimates, RE : Revised Estimates.
Source : Railway Budget, Explanatory Memorandum and Railway Year Book.

190 : Railway Traffic: Goods

Year	Earning Freight Traffic (million)	Net Tonne Kilometre (billion)	Revenue Earnings (Rs. crore)	Average Lead in Revenue Traffic (in km)	Average Rate per Kilometre (in paise)
1950-51	73	38	139	514	3.7
1960-61	120	72	281	604	3.9
1970-71	168	111	601	659	5.4
1980-81	196	148	1551	754	10.5
1990-91	318	236	8247	741	35.0
2000-01	474	312	23045	660	73.8
2001-02	493	333	24845	677	74.6
2002-03	519	353	26505	681	75.0
2003-04	557	381	27618	684	72.5
2004-05	602	407	30489	677	74.8
2005-06	667	440	35535	660	80.8
2006-07	728	481	41073	661	85.4
2007-08	794	521	46426	656	89.1
2008-09	833	551	53433	661	97.0
2009-10	888	601	58502	677	97.3
2010-11RE	924	612	62489	662	102.1
2011-12BE	993	659	68620	664	104.1

Note: BE : Budget Estimates, RE : Revised Estimates.
Source : Railway Budget, Explanatory Memorandum and Railway Year Book.

191 : Strength of Indian Shipping

As on 31-March	Coastal Trade		Overseas Trade	
	Number of Vessels	Gross Registered Tonnage ('000)	Number of Vessels	Gross Registered Tonnage ('000)
1951	71	206	23	167
1961	97	314	75	544
1971	66	231	184	2214
1981	65	300	338	5589
1991	162	523	246	5378
2001	329	731	228	6237
2002	424	805	193	5402
2003	429	806	196	5817
2004	454	808	215	6893
2005	485	816	236	7427
2006	526	841	250	7577
2007	573	893	277	8136
2008	615	964	287	8007
2009	na	na	na	na
2010	674	997	324	8616

Note: Based on data received from ports and not on entire overseas traffic cargo handles.

Source : Ministry of Civil Aviation.

192 : Civil Aviation: Indian Scheduled Operations—Domestic Services

	Aircraft Kilometre Flown (lakh km)	Passenger			Freight & Mail		
		Numbers Flown (in '000)	Km Flown (in million)	Load Factor (%)	Freight Tonne (km million)	Mail Tonne (km million)	Load Factor (%)
1951-52	220	301	205	..	17		..
1961-62	278	745	575	71.5	18	6	75.0
1970-71	334	2123	1559	76.8	14	10	79.6
1980-81	444	4850	3917	68.5	48	15	63.4
1990-91	587	7912	7028	79.4	88	16	78.4
2000-01	1369	13719	12287	61.7	146	24	57.6
2001-02	1471	12840	11551	55.4	145	23	52.2
2002-03	1658	13951	12848	56.3	162	23	53.4
2003-04	1893	15677	14566	58.4	191	19	72.1
2004-05	2136	19445	18031	64.9	229	29	63.9
2005-06	2523	25183	23688	67.7	238	35	67.1
2006-07	3483	35792	33518	68.8	251	22	67.0
2007-08	4394	44355	41717	68.9	272	21	65.7
2008-09	4184	38819	37027	63.7	234	24	55.9
2009-10	4097	45179	43841	72.1	285	28	66.0

Source : Directorate General of Civil Aviation, Ministry of Civil Aviation.

193 : Civil Aviation: Indian Scheduled Operations—International Services

	Aircraft Kilometre Flown (lakh km)	Passenger			Freight & Mail		
		Numbers Flown (in '000)	Km Flown (in million)	Load Factor (%)	Freight Tonne (km million)	Mail Tonne (km million)	Load Factor (%)
1950-51	90	148	179				..
1960-61	170	229	698	46.7			44.5
1970-71	259	491	2031	48.7	97	8	50.8
1980-81	427	1665	6763	59.1	330	20	59.4
1990-91	511	2430	8820	66.5	553	11	62.4
2000-01	660	3769	13928	76.0	403	9	72.8
2001-02	744	3669	13284	69.1	364	11	65.7
2002-03	842	4172	15631	73.3	405	10	70.0
2003-04	977	4391	18107	72.5	399	13	66.3
2004-05	1195	5327	22272	71.6	509	12	65.8
2005-06	1534	6071	27115	68.8	555	14	60.7
2006-07	1862	7559	30374	68.1	607	12	59.7
2007-08	2408	9109	36130	66.3	769	21	55.1
2008-09	2755	9640	38905	65.3	927	23	55.2
2009-10	2697	10317	40500	71.4	1059	22	61.6

Source : Directorate General of Civil Aviation, Ministry of Civil Aviation.

IV. PROFILE OF STATES

> Population
> Vital Rates
> Education
> Employment
> Standard of Living
> Agriculture
> Factory Sector
> Establishments
> Banking
> State Finance
> Health Infrastructure
> Housing and Amenities

194 : State-wise Population of India

State	2001			2011		
	Population (million)	Share in All-India (%)	Density (per sq km)	Population (million)	Share in All-India (%)	Density (per sq km)
All-India	1028.74	100.00	325	1210.19	100.00	382
Andhra Pradesh	76.21	7.41	277	84.67	7.00	308
Arunachal Pradesh	1.10	0.11	13	1.38	0.11	17
Assam	26.66	2.59	340	31.17	2.58	397
Bihar	83.00	8.07	881	103.80	8.58	1102
Chhattisgarh	20.83	2.03	154	25.54	2.11	189
Goa	1.35	0.13	364	1.46	0.12	394
Gujarat	50.67	4.93	258	60.38	4.99	308
Haryana	21.15	2.06	478	25.35	2.09	573
Himachal Pradesh	6.08	0.59	109	6.86	0.57	123
Jammu & Kashmir*	10.14	0.99	100	12.55	1.04	124
Jharkhand	26.95	2.62	338	32.97	2.72	414
Karnataka	52.85	5.14	276	61.13	5.05	319
Kerala	31.84	3.10	819	33.39	2.76	859
Madhya Pradesh	60.35	5.87	196	72.60	6.00	236
Maharashtra	96.88	9.42	315	112.37	9.29	365
Manipur**	2.29	0.22	103	2.72	0.22	122

contd...

...contd...

State	2001			2011		
	Population (million)	Share in All-India (%)	Density (per sq km)	Population (million)	Share in All-India (%)	Density (per sq km)
Meghalaya	2.32	0.23	103	2.96	0.24	132
Mizoram	0.89	0.09	42	1.09	0.09	52
Nagaland	1.99	0.19	120	1.98	0.16	119
Orissa	36.81	3.58	236	41.95	3.47	269
Punjab	24.36	2.37	484	27.70	2.29	550
Rajasthan	56.51	5.49	165	68.62	5.67	201
Sikkim	0.54	0.05	76	0.61	0.05	86
Tamil Nadu	62.41	6.07	480	72.14	5.96	555
Tripura	3.20	0.31	305	3.67	0.30	350
Uttar Pradesh	166.20	16.16	690	199.58	16.49	828
Uttarakhand	8.49	0.83	159	10.11	0.84	189
West Bengal	80.18	7.79	903	91.35	7.55	1029
Union Territories						
A & N Islands	0.36	0.03	43	0.38	0.03	46
Chandigarh	0.90	0.09	7900	1.06	0.09	9252
D & N Haveli	0.22	0.02	449	0.34	0.03	698

contd...

...contd...

State	2001			2011		
	Population (million)	Share in All-India (%)	Density (per sq km)	Population (million)	Share in All-India (%)	Density (per sq km)
Daman & Diu	0.16	0.02	1413	0.24	0.02	2169
Delhi	13.85	1.35	9340	16.75	1.38	11297
Lakshadweep	0.06	0.01	1895	0.06	0.01	2013
Puducherry	0.97	0.09	2034	1.24	0.10	2598

Note : Density is population per square kilometre.
* : The 1991 Census not held in J&K. Total population for 1991 has been worked out by interpolation.
** : Manipur data includes estimated population for Mao Maram, Paomata and Puri Senapati district.

Source : Office of the Registrar General of India, Ministry of Home Affairs. Census of India 2011.

195 : State-wise Population of India: By Gender and Sex Ratio (Females per 1000 Males)

State	2001			2011		
	Male (million)	Female (million)	Sex Ratio (%)	Male (million)	Female (million)	Sex Ratio (%)
All-India	532.22	496.51	933	623.72	586.47	940
Andhra Pradesh	38.53	37.68	978	42.51	42.16	992
Arunachal Pradesh	0.58	0.52	893	0.72	0.66	920
Assam	13.78	12.88	935	15.96	15.21	954
Bihar	43.24	39.75	919	54.19	49.62	916
Chhattisgarh	10.47	10.36	989	12.83	12.71	991
Goa	0.69	0.66	961	0.74	0.72	968
Gujarat	26.39	24.29	920	31.48	28.90	918
Haryana	11.36	9.78	861	13.51	11.85	877
Himachal Pradesh	3.09	2.99	968	3.47	3.38	974
Jammu & Kashmir**	5.36	4.78	892	6.67	5.88	883
Jharkhand	13.89	13.06	941	16.93	16.04	947
Karnataka	26.90	25.95	965	31.06	30.07	968
Kerala	15.47	16.37	1058	16.02	17.37	1084
Madhya Pradesh	31.44	28.90	919	37.61	34.99	930
Maharashtra	50.40	46.48	922	58.36	54.01	925
Manipur***	1.16	1.13	974	1.37	1.35	987

contd...

...contd...

State	2001			2011		
	Male (million)	Female (million)	Sex Ratio (%)	Male (million)	Female (million)	Sex Ratio (%)
Meghalaya	1.18	1.14	972	1.49	1.47	986
Mizoram	0.46	0.43	935	0.55	0.54	975
Nagaland	1.05	0.94	900	1.03	0.96	931
Orissa	18.66	18.11	972	21.20	20.75	978
Punjab	12.99	11.37	876	14.64	13.07	893
Rajasthan	29.42	27.09	921	35.62	33.00	926
Sikkim	0.29	0.25	875	0.32	0.29	889
Tamil Nadu	31.40	31.00	987	36.16	35.98	995
Tripura	1.64	1.56	948	1.87	1.80	961
Uttar Pradesh	87.57	78.63	898	104.60	94.99	908
Uttarakhand	4.33	4.16	962	5.15	4.96	963
West Bengal	41.47	38.71	934	46.93	44.42	947
Union Territories						
A & N Islands	0.19	0.16	846	0.20	0.18	878
Chandigarh	0.51	0.39	777	0.58	0.47	818
D & N Haveli	0.12	0.10	812	0.19	0.15	777

contd...

...contd...

State	2001			2011		
	Male (million)	Female (million)	Sex Ratio (%)	Male (million)	Female (million)	Sex Ratio (%)
Daman & Diu	0.09	0.10	710	0.15	0.09	618
Delhi	7.61	6.24	812	8.98	7.78	775
Lakshadweep	0.03	0.03	948	0.03	0.03	946
Puducherry	0.49	0.49	1001	0.61	0.63	1038

Note : Sex Ratio : Females per 1000 of male population.
Source : Office of the Registrar General of India, Ministry of Home Affairs. Census of India 2011.

196 : State-wise Population of India: Rural and Urban

State	2001			2011		
	Rural	Urban		Rural	Urban	
	(million)	(million)	(as % of Total)	(million)	(million)	(as % of Total)
All-India	742.6	286.1	27.8	833.1	377.1	31.2
Andhra Pradesh	55.4	20.8	27.3	56.3	28.4	33.5
Arunachal Pradesh	0.9	0.2	20.8	1.1	0.3	22.6
Assam	23.2	3.4	12.9	26.8	4.4	14.1
Bihar	74.3	8.7	10.5	92.1	11.7	11.3
Chhattisgarh	16.6	4.2	20.1	19.6	5.9	23.2
Goa	0.7	0.7	49.7	0.6	0.9	62.1
Gujarat	31.7	18.9	37.4	34.7	25.7	42.6
Haryana	15.0	6.1	28.9	16.5	8.8	34.8
Himachal Pradesh	5.5	0.6	9.8	6.2	0.7	10.0
Jammu & Kashmir	7.6	2.5	24.8	9.1	3.4	27.2
Jharkhand	21.0	6.0	22.2	25.0	7.9	24.1
Karnataka	34.9	18.0	34.0	37.6	23.6	38.6
Kerala	23.6	8.3	26.0	17.5	15.9	47.7
Madhya Pradesh	44.4	16.0	26.5	52.5	20.1	27.6
Maharashtra	55.8	41.1	42.4	61.5	50.8	45.2
Manipur	1.7	0.6	25.1	1.9	0.8	30.2
Meghalaya	1.9	0.5	19.6	2.4	0.6	20.1

contd...

...contd...

State	2001			2011		
	Rural	Urban		Rural	Urban	
	(million)	(million)	(as % of Total)	(million)	(million)	(as % of Total)
Meghalaya	1.9	0.5	19.6	2.4	0.6	20.1
Mizoram	0.4	0.4	49.6	0.5	0.6	51.5
Nagaland	1.6	0.3	17.2	1.4	0.6	29.0
Orissa	31.3	5.5	15.0	35.0	7.0	16.7
Punjab	16.1	8.3	33.9	17.3	10.4	37.5
Rajasthan	43.3	13.2	23.4	51.5	17.1	24.9
Sikkim	0.5	0.1	11.1	0.5	0.2	25.0
Tamil Nadu	34.9	27.5	44.0	37.2	35.0	48.4
Tripura	2.7	0.5	17.1	2.7	1.0	26.2
Uttar Pradesh	131.7	34.5	20.8	155.1	44.5	22.3
Uttarakhand	6.3	2.2	25.7	7.0	3.1	30.6
West Bengal	57.7	22.4	28.0	62.2	29.1	31.9
Union Territories						
A & N Islands	0.2	0.1	32.6	0.2	0.1	35.8
Chandigarh	0.1	0.8	89.7	0.0	1.0	97.3
D & N Haveli	0.2	0.1	22.9	0.2	0.2	46.6

contd...

...contd...

State	2001			2011		
	Rural	Urban		Rural	Urban	
	(million)	(million)	(as % of Total)	(million)	(million)	(as % of Total)
Daman & Diu	0.1	0.1	36.3	0.1	0.2	75.3
Delhi	0.9	12.9	93.2	0.4	16.3	97.5
Lakshadweep	0.0	0.0	44.2	0.0	0.1	78.1
Puducherry	0.3	0.6	66.6	0.4	0.9	68.3

Source : Office of the Registrar General of India, Ministry of Home Affairs. Census of India 2011.

197 : Crude Birth Rate

State	Crude Birth Rate 1981	1991	2001	2009
All-India	33.9	29.5	25.4	22.5
Andhra Pradesh	31.7	26.0	20.8	18.3
Arunachal Pradesh#	na	30.9	22.0	21.1
Assam	33.0	30.9	26.8	23.6
Bihar	39.1	30.7	31.2	28.5
Chhattisgarh	na	na	26.3	25.7
Goa#	15.5	16.8	13.9	13.6
Gujarat	34.5	27.5	24.9	22.3
Haryana	36.6	33.1	26.7	22.7
Himachal Pradesh#	31.5	28.5	21.0	17.2
Jammu & Kashmir	31.6	na	20.1	18.6
Jharkhand	na	na	26.3	25.6
Karnataka	28.3	26.9	22.2	19.5
Kerala	25.6	18.3	17.2	14.7
Madhya Pradesh	37.6	35.8	30.8	27.7
Maharashtra	28.5	26.2	20.6	17.6
Manipur#	26.6	20.1	18.2	15.4
Meghalaya#	32.6	32.4	28.3	24.4
Mizoram	na	na	15.7	17.6
Nagaland#	na	18.5	na	17.2
Orissa	33.1	28.8	23.4	21.0
Punjab	30.3	27.7	21.2	17.0
Rajasthan	37.1	35.0	31.0	27.2
Sikkim	31.0	22.5	21.6	18.1
Tamil Nadu	28.0	20.8	19.0	16.3
Tripura#	26.4	24.4	16.1	14.8
Uttar Pradesh	39.6	35.7	32.1	28.7
Uttarakhand	na	na	18.5	19.7
West Bengal	33.2	27.0	20.5	17.2
Union Territories				
A & N Islands#	34.7	20.0	16.8	16.3
Chandigarh#	24.6	13.9	16.1	15.9
D & N Haveli#	na	na	29.3	27.0
Daman & Diu#	na	27.9	22.3	19.2
Delhi#	26.9	24.7	18.7	18.1
Lakshadweep#	na	27.1	20.4	15.0
Puducherry#	21.7	19.2	17.9	16.5

Note : na : not available.

Crude Birth Rate is number of live births during the year divided by mid-year population and multiplied by 1000.

Data for small states and union territories are based on three-year moving averages.

Source : Sample Registration System, (*www.censusindia.gov.in*).

198 : Crude Death Rate

State	1981	1991	2001	2009
All-India	12.5	9.8	8.4	7.3
Andhra Pradesh	11.1	9.7	8.1	7.6
Arunachal Pradesh#	na	13.5	5.5	6.1
Assam	12.6	11.5	9.5	8.4
Bihar	13.9	9.8	8.2	7.0
Chhattisgarh	na	na	8.8	8.1
Goa#	6.8	7.5	7.5	6.7
Gujarat	12.0	8.5	7.8	6.9
Haryana	11.3	8.2	7.6	6.6
Himachal Pradesh#	11.1	8.9	7.0	7.2
Jammu & Kashmir	9.0	na	6.1	5.7
Jharkhand	na	na	8.8	7.0
Karnataka	9.1	9.0	7.6	7.2
Kerala	6.6	6.0	6.6	6.8
Madhya Pradesh	16.6	13.8	10.0	8.5
Maharashtra	9.6	8.2	7.5	6.7
Manipur#	6.6	5.4	5.1	4.7
Meghalaya#	8.2	8.8	9.0	8.1
Mizoram	na	na	4.4	4.5
Nagaland#	na	3.8	na	3.6
Orissa	13.1	12.8	10.2	8.8
Punjab	9.4	7.8	7.0	7.0
Rajasthan	14.3	10.1	7.9	6.6
Sikkim	8.9	7.5	5.1	5.7
Tamil Nadu	11.8	8.8	7.6	7.6
Tripura#	8.0	7.6	5.6	5.1
Uttar Pradesh	16.3	11.3	10.1	8.2
Uttarakhand	na	na	7.8	6.5
West Bengal	11.0	8.3	6.8	6.2
Union Territories				
A & N Islands#	8.4	5.8	4.7	4.1
Chandigarh#	2.4	4.6	3.5	3.9
D & N Haveli#	na	na	6.5	4.8
Daman & Diu#	na	9.0	6.7	5.1
Delhi#	7.1	6.3	5.0	4.4
Lakshadweep#	na	4.7	5.0	5.8
Puducherry#	7.3	6.6	7.0	7.0

Note : na : not available.

Crude Death Rate is number of deaths during the year divided by mid-year population and multiplied by 1000.

Data for small states and UTs are based on three-year moving averages.

Source : Sample Registration System, (*www.censusindia.gov.in*).

199 : Fertility Rate

State	Total Fertility Rate (15-49 years)			
	1992-93	1998-99	2005-06	2008
All-India	3.4	2.9	2.7	2.6
Andhra Pradesh	2.6	2.3	1.8	1.8
Arunachal Pradesh#	4.3	2.5	3.0	na
Assam	3.5	2.3	2.4	2.6
Bihar	na	3.7	4.0	3.9
Chhattisgarh	na	2.8	2.6	3.0
Goa#	1.9	1.8	1.8	na
Gujarat	3.0	2.7	2.4	2.5
Haryana	4.0	2.9	2.7	2.5
Himachal Pradesh#	3.0	2.1	1.9	1.9
Jharkhand	na	2.8	3.3	3.2
Jammu & Kashmir*	0.0	2.7	2.4	2.2
Karnataka	2.9	2.1	2.1	2.0
Kerala	2.0	2.0	1.9	1.7
Madhya Pradesh	na	3.4	3.1	3.3
Maharashtra	2.9	2.5	2.1	2.0
Manipur#	2.8	3.0	2.8	na
Meghalaya#	3.7	4.6	3.8	na
Mizoram	2.3	2.9	2.9	na
Nagaland#	3.3	3.8	3.7	na
Orissa	2.9	2.5	2.4	2.4
Punjab	2.9	2.2	2.0	1.9
Rajasthan*	3.6	3.8	3.2	3.3
Sikkim	na	2.8	2.0	na
Tamil Nadu	2.5	2.2	1.8	1.7
Tripura#	2.7	1.9	2.2	na
Uttar Pradesh	na	4.1	3.8	3.8
Uttarakhand	na	2.6	2.6	na
West Bengal	2.9	2.3	2.3	1.9
Delhi#	3.0	2.4	2.1	2.0

Note : na : not available.
Fertility Rate is the number of live births during a year per 1000 female population aged 15-49 years at the mid-point of the same year.

Source : National Health Profile 2010.

200 : Infant Mortality Rate

	Infant Mortality Rate				
	1971	1981	1991	2001	2009
All-India	129	110	80	66	50
Andhra Pradesh	106	86	73	66	49
Arunachal Pradesh#	na	na	65	39	32
Assam	139	106	81	74	61
Bihar	na	118	69	62	52
Chhattisgarh	na	na	na	na	54
Goa#	na	na	21	19	na
Gujarat	144	116	69	60	48
Haryana	72	108	68	66	51
Himachal Pradesh#	na	na	na	54	45
Jharkhand	na	na	na	na	44
Jammu & Kashmir*	na	na	na	48	45
Karnataka	95	69	77	58	41
Kerala	58	37	16	11	12
Madhya Pradesh	135	142	117	86	67
Maharashtra	105	79	60	45	31
Manipur#	na	na	22	20	16
Meghalaya#	na	na	57	56	59
Mizoram	na	na	0	19	36
Nagaland#	na	na	7	0	26
Orissa	127	135	124	91	65
Punjab	102	81	53	52	38
Rajasthan*	123	108	79	80	59
Sikkim	na	na	51	42	34
Tamil Nadu	113	91	57	49	28
Tripura#	na	na	56	39	31
Uttar Pradesh	167	150	97	83	63
Uttarakhand	na	na	na	48	41
West Bengal	na	91	71	51	33
Union Territories					
A & N Islands#	na	na	30	18	27
Chandigarh*#	na	na	35	24	25
D & N Haveli#	na	na	68	58	37
Daman & Diu#	na	na	52	40	24
Delhi#	na	na	43	29	33
Lakshadweep#	na	na	44	33	25
Puducherry#	na	na	21	22	22

Note : IMR is the ratio of infant deaths to live births during the year multiplied by 1000.

* : Data for 1971 pertains to 1972.

: Data for small states and union territories are based on three-year moving averages.

Source : Sample Registration System.

201 : Maternal Mortality Rate

State	1999-2001	2001-2003	2004-2006	2007-2009
All-India	327	301	254	212
Andhra Pradesh	220	195	154	134
Assam	398	490	480	390
Bihar/Jharkhand	400	371	312	261
Gujarat	202	172	160	148
Haryana	176	162	186	153
Karnataka	266	228	213	178
Kerala	149	110	95	81
Madhya Pradesh/ Chhattisgarh	407	379	335	269
Maharashtra	169	149	130	104
Orissa	424	358	303	258
Punjab	177	178	192	172
Rajasthan	501	445	388	318
Tamil Nadu	167	134	111	97
Uttar Pradesh/Uttarakhand	539	517	440	359
West Bengal	218	194	141	145

Note: Maternal Mortality Rate is the number of maternal deaths in the age group 15-49 years per one lakh live births.

There is a major data gap in India with regard to this estimates.

Quality of data suffers due to a small sample size and the various difficulties associated with ascertaining the cause of death. This data gives a broad idea of MMR in big states and at the national level. Estimates for small states and union territories have not been presented due to small size of the sample.

Source: Sample Registration System, (*www.censusindia.gov.in*).

202 : Literacy Rate

(in percentage)

State	Female Literacy Rate			All Persons		
	1991	2001	2011	1991	2001	2011
All-India	39	54	65	52	65	74
Andhra Pradesh	33	50	60	44	60	68
Arunachal Pradesh	30	44	60	42	54	67
Assam	43	55	67	53	63	73
Bihar	22	33	53	37	47	64
Chhattisgarh	28	52	61	43	65	71
Goa	67	75	82	76	82	87
Gujarat	49	58	71	61	69	79
Haryana	40	56	67	56	68	77
Himachal Pradesh	52	67	77	64	76	84
Jammu & Kashmir	..	43	58	..	56	69
Jharkhand	..	39	56	..	54	68
Karnataka	44	57	68	56	67	76
Kerala	86	88	92	90	91	94
Madhya Pradesh	29	50	60	45	64	71
Maharashtra	52	67	75	65	77	83
Manipur	48	60	73	60	70	80
Meghalaya	45	60	74	49	63	75
Mizoram	79	87	89	82	89	92
Nagaland	55	61	77	62	67	80
Orissa	35	51	64	49	63	73
Punjab	50	63	71	59	70	77
Rajasthan	20	44	53	39	60	67
Sikkim	47	60	76	57	69	82
Tamil Nadu	51	64	74	63	73	80
Tripura	50	65	83	60	73	88
Uttar Pradesh	24	42	59	41	56	70
Uttarakhand	42	60	71	58	72	80
West Bengal	47	60	71	58	69	77
Union Territories						
A & N Islands	65	75	82	73	81	86
Chandigarh	72	76	81	78	82	86
D & N Haveli	27	40	66	41	58	78
Daman & Diu	59	66	80	71	78	87
Delhi	67	75	81	75	82	86
Lakshadweep	73	80	88	82	87	92
Puducherry	66	74	81	75	81	87

Note : Literacy Rates estimated on the basis of population aged seven years and above.

Literacy rates for 1991 exclude states of Assam and J&K.

Data for Manipur includes estimated population for Mao Maram, Paomata and Puri Senapati districts.

Source : Registrar General of India for relevant years.

203 : Number of Schools

(in numbers)

State	2001-02			2007-08		
	Pre-Primary +Primary (I-V)	Upper Primary (VI-VIII)	Secondary (IX-XII)	Pre-Primary +Primary (I-V)	Upper Primary (VI-VIII)	Secondary (IX-XII)
All-India	664041	219626	133492	787827	325174	172990
Andhra Pradesh	14255	14472	58249	62464	17957	20969
Arunachal Pradesh	191	347	1315	1561	664	260
Assam	4832	8019	33236	31042	13023	5820
Bihar	3575	9691	39299	45980	16245	3746
Chhattisgarh	2532	6358	31023	34034	14066	4226
Goa	442	84	1033	1253	442	457
Gujarat	6734	21205	15545	17443	23927	8328
Haryana	4579	1847	11208	13602	3196	6095
Himachal Pradesh	1954	1768	10877	11517	5009	2964
Jammu & Kashmir	1504	3728	10926	13369	5202	1498
Jharkhand	1157	4187	16643	19818	9996	1654
Karnataka	10796	27712	22404	28871	27570	15261
Kerala	4296	2983	6754	6802	3042	5525
Madhya Pradesh	8471	25090	62530	98463	38107	9672
Maharashtra	16059	24574	45971	42467	26863	20337
Manipur	659	796	2573	2563	769	804
Meghalaya	643	1041	5646	6618	2259	774
Mizoram	403	851	1377	1752	1090	590
Nagaland	344	479	1499	1662	465	406
Orissa	7313	11510	42104	49765	20013	8522
Punjab	3901	2512	13074	13238	2477	4110
Rajasthan	7434	16736	38342	55361	34211	13667
Sikkim	110	129	501	772	221	164
Tamil Nadu	8511	5809	31488	29364	8629	7572
Tripura	636	432	2095	2151	1021	713
Uttar Pradesh	9073	20429	88927	127247	42201	15518
Uttarakhand	1593	3487	13795	15356	4263	2362
West Bengal	9463	2384	52426	49913	1283	8640
Union Territories						
A & N Islands	92	55	208	226	64	96
Chandigarh	107	16	29	30	11	126
D & N Haveli	19	58	137	174	108	44
Daman & Diu	26	22	53	50	24	28
Delhi	1578	680	2415	2569	640	1768
Lakshadweep	13	3	20	21	4	13
Puducherry	197	132	319	309	112	261

Source : Ministry of Higher Education. Statistics of School Education 2007-08.

204 : Enrollment in Classes

(number of pupils in thousands)

State	2001-02			2007-08		
	Primary (I-V)	Upper Primary (VI-VIII)	Secondary (IX-XII)	Primary (I-V)	Upper Primary (VI-VIII)	Secondary (IX-XII)
All-India	113883	44828	30507	139086	54476	39938
Andhra Pradesh	8626	3090	2445	8072	3789	3381
Arunachal Pradesh	162	54	35	227	66	47
Assam	4081	1519	923	3935	1327	826
Bihar	7809	1914	1133	11510	2773	1562
Chhattisgarh	2973	1062	570	3243	1346	670
Goa	120	73	62	115	69	63
Gujarat	6495	2381	1712	6661	2533	1852
Haryana	1970	989	877	2359	1244	968
Himachal Pradesh	718	402	341	742	406	414
Jammu & Kashmir	1059	476	344	1241	479	363
Jharkhand	2854	776	326	4066	1142	413
Karnataka	6517	2756	1871	5725	2997	2420
Kerala	2524	1766	1458	2524	1595	1619
Madhya Pradesh	8265	2687	1516	11813	4506	2529
Maharashtra	11528	5725	4250	14236	6326	4778
Manipur	298	127	84	489	147	103
Meghalaya	327	96	57	746	180	89
Mizoram	135	50	36	151	54	40
Nagaland	212	66	39	329	92	55
Orissa	4769	1505	1177	4485	1854	1371
Punjab	2073	993	856	1960	1074	869
Rajasthan	7932	3307	1434	9672	3667	2066
Sikkim	77	25	13	114	31	18
Tamil Nadu	5674	3524	2485	6146	3662	3153
Tripura	461	166	104	497	204	128
Uttar Pradesh	13378	4672	3318	25867	7453	6222
Uttarakhand	1048	489	380	1202	571	514
West Bengal	10151	3211	1965	8862	3845	2500
Union Territories						
A & N Islands	40	22	17	44	23	20
Chandigarh	58	37	40	90	41	48
D & N Haveli	29	10	5	38	13	7
Daman & Diu	16	8	6	19	9	7
Delhi	1394	783	575	1750	888	756
Lakshadweep	8	5	3	8	4	5
Puducherry	101	66	50	148	68	65

Source : Ministry of Higher Education. Statistics of School Education 2007-08.

205 : Dropout Rates from Classes

(in per cent)

State	2001-02			2007-08		
	I-V	I-VIII	I-X	I-V	I-VIII	I-X
All-India				25.1	42.7	56.7
Andhra Pradesh	43.0	63.1	70.1	18.8	48.8	63.1
Arunachal Pradesh	49.8	60.6	76.0	41.0	48.0	63.0
Assam	48.6	69.2	75.6	5.3	69.3	75.7
Bihar	61.6	74.8	82.9	46.9	70.7	83.9
Chhattisgarh	na	na	na	31.7	na	na
Goa	5.7	4.2	42.2	0.0	1.2	38.9
Gujarat	25.1	52.5	70.2	27.0	48.2	59.1
Haryana	30.5	12.4	35.9	0.0	6.5	36.4
Himachal Pradesh	16.7	21.9	31.8	2.9	0.0	30.2
Jammu & Kashmir	29.3	30.1	48.9	0.0	40.5	64.0
Jharkhand	na	na	na	9.4	na	na
Karnataka	23.9	51.0	61.7	8.7	33.9	49.4
Kerala	0.0	0.0	16.6	0.0	0.0	(0.5)
Madhya Pradesh	29.6	50.1	69.9	0.0	46.1	69.4
Maharashtra	7.4	37.0	52.3	18.9	30.5	46.2
Manipur	27.1	37.8	53.9	37.5	41.9	44.6
Meghalaya	57.0	77.0	83.4	36.4	60.4	76.1
Mizoram	59.3	59.9	69.7	47.8	62.8	70.2
Nagaland	41.5	53.4	64.9	38.0	46.7	74.0
Orissa	39.4	60.7	73.1	23.2	61.3	64.7
Punjab	20.3	37.0	38.6	(0.7)	26.0	50.0
Rajasthan	63.2	53.6	75.4	46.6	62.3	71.5
Sikkim	61.8	63.4	88.4	19.7	64.9	80.0
Tamil Nadu	27.2	40.1	57.7	8.5	9.1	37.7
Tripura	50.5	69.0	76.9	22.6	54.8	73.4
Uttar Pradesh	49.4	60.1	59.0	33.9	28.6	30.2
Uttarakhand	na	na	na	19.8	na	na
West Bengal	39.9	70.9	78.5	35.9	63.9	72.8
Union Territories						
A & N Islands	0.0	27.0	54.9	10.5	15.9	31.4
Chandigarh	12.7	-1.2	12.0	0.0	0.0	38.5
D & N Haveli	35.4	55.4	71.6	18.5	34.9	57.0
Daman & Diu	0.0	16.7	36.6	16.5	14.3	30.7
Delhi	27.7	16.3	42.4	0.0	0.0	36.0
Lakshadweep	17.2	23.4	54.2	2.6	0.0	30.7
Puducherry	0.0	2.9	25.3	0.0	0.0	2.2

Source : Ministry of Higher Education. Statistics of School Education 2007-08.

206 : State-wise Classification and Occupational Distribution of Workers

(numbers in million)

State/Region	1991		2001		2001			
					Occupational Distribution of Workers (%)			
	Total Number of Workers	Share in Total Population (%)	Total Number of Workers	Share in Total Population (%)	Cultivators	Agricultural Labourers	Household Industry Workers	Others
All-India	314.12	37.5	402.51	39.1	31.7	26.7	4.1	37.5
Andhra Pradesh	29.96	45.1	34.87	45.7	22.7	39.6	4.5	33.2
Arunachal Pradesh	0.40	46.1	0.48	43.7	58.4	3.9	0.9	36.8
Assam	8.09	36.1	9.56	35.9	39.2	13.5	3.4	43.9
Bihar	27.78	32.2	28.08	33.8	29.2	48.2	3.9	18.8
Chhattisgarh		0.0	9.69	46.5	44.6	31.9	2.1	21.5
Goa	0.41	35.3	0.52	38.8	9.7	6.9	2.7	80.7
Gujarat	16.62	40.2	20.37	40.2	27.6	24.5	1.9	46.1
Haryana	5.10	31.0	8.38	39.6	36.3	15.2	2.5	46.0
Himachal Pradesh	2.21	42.8	2.99	49.2	65.5	3.1	1.7	29.7
Jammu & Kashmir		0.0	3.69	36.4	43.4	6.7	6.2	43.7
Jharkhand		0.0	10.13	37.6	38.6	28.3	4.1	29.0
Karnataka	18.89	42.0	23.52	44.5	29.5	26.4	4.0	40.1
Kerala	9.15	31.4	10.29	32.3	7.2	16.1	3.5	73.2
Madhya Pradesh	28.34	42.8	25.76	42.7	42.9	28.7	3.9	24.5
Maharashtra	33.91	43.0	42.05	43.4	28.6	26.8	2.5	42.1
Manipur	0.77	42.1	1.07	46.6	46.1	11.3	9.2	33.5

contd...

...contd...

State/Region	1991		2001		2001			
					Occupational Distribution of Workers (%)			
	Total Number of Workers	Share in Total Population (%)	Total Number of Workers	Share in Total Population (%)	Cultivators	Agricultural Labourers	Household Industry Workers	Others
Meghalaya	0.76	42.6	0.96	41.4	47.8	18.1	1.9	32.2
Mizoram	0.34	48.8	0.47	52.9	53.9	5.9	1.4	38.8
Nagaland	0.52	42.6	0.85	42.7	64.1	4.0	2.1	29.8
Orissa	11.88	37.5	14.27	38.8	29.7	35.0	4.8	30.4
Punjab	6.26	30.9	9.14	37.5	23.0	16.4	3.4	57.3
Rajasthan	17.10	38.9	23.78	42.1	55.4	10.6	2.7	31.3
Sikkim	0.17	41.4	0.26	48.6	49.9	6.4	1.2	42.4
Tamil Nadu	24.19	43.3	27.81	44.6	18.4	31.2	5.2	45.2
Tripura	0.86	31.1	1.16	36.2	26.9	24.0	2.9	46.2
Uttar Pradesh	44.80	32.2	54.18	32.6	40.9	25.1	5.3	28.6
Uttarakhand		0.0	3.13	36.9	49.8	8.3	2.2	39.7
West Bengal	21.91	32.2	29.50	36.8	19.0	24.9	7.3	48.8

contd...

...contd...

State/Region	1991		2001		2001			
					Occupational Distribution of Workers (%)			
	Total Number of Workers	Share in Total Population (%)	Total Number of Workers	Share in Total Population (%)	Cultivators	Agricultural Labourers	Household Industry Workers	Others
Union Territories								
A & N Islands	0.10	35.2	0.14	38.2	15.5	3.7	5.1	75.6
Chandigarh	0.22	34.9	0.34	37.7	0.5	0.1	1.0	98.4
D & N Haveli	0.07	53.4	0.11	51.8	34.6	12.9	0.7	51.7
Daman & Diu	0.04	37.3	0.07	45.9	5.4	1.8	1.6	91.3
Delhi	2.98	31.6	4.53	32.7	0.8	0.3	3.0	95.9
Lakshadweep	0.01	26.3	0.02	25.2	0.0	0.0	5.9	94.1
Puducherry	0.27	33.0	0.34	35.1	3.3	21.1	1.8	73.8

Note: * : 1981 Census not held in Assam, total population for the year worked out by interpolation.
** : 1991 Census not held in J&K, total population for the year worked out by interpolation.
*** : Data for India and Manipur includes estimated population for Mao Maram, Paomata and Puri Senapati district of Manipur.

Source: Office of the Registrar General of India, Ministry of Home Affairs, Census data.

207 : Labour Force and Work Force Participation Rate

(in percentage)

State/Region	Labour Force Participation Rate (LFPR)				Work Force Participation Rate (WFPR)			
	Rural		Urban		Rural		Urban	
	1999-2000	2009-10	1999-2000	2004-05	1999-2000	2004-05	1999-2000	2004-05
All-India	42.3	44.6	35.4	38.2	41.7	43.9	33.7	36.5
Andhra Pradesh	54.6	54.8	36.2	40.6	54.2	54.4	34.8	39.2
Arunachal Pradesh	37.1	46.2	27.5	32.3	36.9	45.8	26.7	31.9
Assam	36.4	40.1	36.8	36.2	34.9	39.1	33.2	33.6
Bihar	34.4	32.0	28.7	29.0	33.8	31.6	26.6	27.2
Chhattisgarh		51.2		37.7		50.9		36.4
Goa	39.5	38.5	37.9	39.8	35.9	34.2	30.9	36.3
Gujarat	50.1	51.6	35.2	38.7	49.9	51.3	34.5	37.7
Haryana	34.9	43.4	32.3	35.3	34.6	42.4	31.4	33.9
Himachal Pradesh	50.9	54.0	34.4	47.4	50.3	53.0	32.2	45.6
Jammu & Kashmir	44.7	42.2	29.6	34.8	44.2	41.6	28.1	33.1
Jharkhand		43.3		33.3		42.7		31.1
Karnataka	49.1	54.6	37.8	39.7	48.7	54.2	36.6	38.6
Kerala	42.2	44.8	41.5	44.0	38.7	40.0	37.3	37.1
Madhya Pradesh	46.4	46.1	33.1	35.7	46.2	45.9	31.9	34.7
Maharashtra	49.0	52.7	36.7	39.9	48.4	52.1	34.6	38.4
Manipur	38.7	44.5	35.3	35.8	38.0	44.0	33.0	33.8

contd...

...contd...

State/Region	Labour Force Participation Rate (LFPR)				Work Force Participation Rate (WFPR)			
	Rural		Urban		Rural		Urban	
	1999-2000	2009-10	1999-2000	2004-05	1999-2000	2004-05	1999-2000	2004-05
Meghalaya	48.8	52.7	31.0	38.7	48.6	52.5	29.6	37.3
Mizoram	50.3	52.3	37.4	39.0	49.9	52.1	36.3	38.3
Nagaland	49.4	53.7	33.5	38.5	48.2	52.7	30.5	36.4
Orissa	43.2	47.6	33.9	38.6	42.3	45.2	31.7	33.4
Punjab	41.7	45.8	36.3	38.5	41.0	44.0	35.3	36.5
Rajasthan	44.8	46.3	33.2	35.9	44.6	45.9	32.3	34.9
Sikkim	39.1	45.3	40.7	38.3	38.0	44.3	37.5	36.9
Tamil Nadu	52.3	53.4	41.0	43.4	51.3	52.8	39.3	41.8
Tripura	30.7	37.3	31.3	41.4	30.3	32.3	29.5	29.8
Uttar Pradesh	34.8	37.3	31.7	34.2	34.5	37.1	30.4	33.1
Uttarakhand		48.0		35.1		47.4		33.2
West Bengal	35.9	38.9	37.8	41.0	34.9	37.9	35.0	38.4

contd...

...contd...

	Labour Force Participation Rate (LFPR)				Work Force Participation Rate (WFPR)			
	Rural		Urban		Rural		Urban	
State/Region	1999-2000	2009-10	1999-2000	2004-05	1999-2000	2004-05	1999-2000	2004-05
Union Territories								
A & N Islands	38.4	47.1	45.4	41.6	37.1	44.2	42.2	37.9
Chandigarh	63.9	39.9	36.9	35.8	63.5	38.8	35.1	34.3
D & N Haveli	47.5	53.3	40.9	46.6	47.0	51.6	40.4	45.2
Daman & Diu	50.9	40.3	38.7	42.8	50.3	40.2	37.6	41.5
Delhi	32.4	31.7	34.3	35.1	30.8	31.1	33.2	33.4
Lakshadweep	35.6	40.8	34.3	36.3	28.5	37.9	30.8	27.4
Puducherry	44.3	49.5	36.8	37.3	42.5	46.1	35.2	34.3

Note : Based on 'usual status' of individuals.
Labour Force defined as those involved in gainful activity regularly, those involved in gainful activity occasionally and also the unemployed. LFPR represents size of the labour force as a per cent of the population.
Work Force defined as those involved in gainful activity regularly and those involved in gainful activity occasionally. WFPR represents the size of the work force as a per cent of population.

Source : NSSO Report No. 455, 458 and 515 on *Employment and Unemployment Situation in India*.

208 : Unemployment Rates According to Usual Status (PS+SS) (or Usual Status Adjusted)

State/Region	Rural (%)		Urban (%)	
	1999-2000	2004-05	1999-2000	2004-05
All-India	1.5	1.7	4.8	4.5
Andhra Pradesh	0.8	0.7	3.9	3.6
Arunachal Pradesh	0.5	0.9	2.9	1.2
Assam	3.9	2.6	9.7	7.2
Bihar	1.8	1.5	7.4	6.4
Chhattisgarh	..	0.6	..	3.5
Goa	9.3	11.1	18.5	8.7
Gujarat	0.4	0.5	2.0	2.4
Haryana	0.8	2.2	2.7	4.0
Himachal Pradesh	1.2	1.8	6.6	3.8
Jammu & Kashmir	1.1	1.5	5.0	4.9
Jharkhand	..	1.4	..	6.5
Karnataka	0.7	0.7	3.3	2.8
Kerala	8.2	10.7	10.2	15.6
Madhya Pradesh	0.5	0.5	3.5	2.8
Maharashtra	1.4	1.0	5.8	3.6
Manipur	1.9	1.1	6.7	5.5
Meghalaya	0.4	0.3	4.6	3.5
Mizoram	0.9	0.3	3.0	1.9
Nagaland	2.4	1.8	9.1	5.5
Orissa	1.9	5.0	6.7	13.4
Punjab	1.8	3.8	2.7	5.0
Rajasthan	0.4	0.7	2.5	2.9
Sikkim	2.8	2.4	7.5	3.7
Tamil Nadu	2.0	1.2	4.0	3.5
Tripura	1.2	13.3	5.8	28.0
Uttar Pradesh	0.8	0.6	4.1	3.3
Uttarakhand	..	1.3	..	5.4
West Bengal	2.8	2.5	7.6	6.2
Union Territories				
A & N Islands	3.4	6.2	6.9	8.8
Chandigarh	0.7	2.6	4.8	4.0
D & N Haveli	1.0	3.3	1.4	3.0
Daman & Diu	1.0	0.3	3.0	3.0
Delhi	4.7	1.9	3.3	4.8
Lakshadweep	19.4	7.5	10.0	25.0
Puducherry	4.0	7.0	4.1	8.1

Note: Unemployment Rate is the percentage of unemployed persons to total number of persons in the labour force.

Source: NSSO Report No. 458 and 515 on *Employment and Unemployment Situation in India.*

209 : Employment in Organised Sector

(numbers in lakh)

State/Region	Public Sector			Private Sector		
	1997	2008	CAGR (%)	1997	2008	CAGR (%)
All-India	195.66	176.77	(0.9)	87.55	98.77	1.10
Andhra Pradesh	15.11	13.66	(0.9)	5.42	7.25	2.68
Assam	5.49	5.25	(0.4)	5.57	6.47	1.37
Bihar	14.42	3.70	(11.6)	2.55	0.24	(19,33)
Chhattisgarh	..	3.07		..	0.35	..
Goa	0.70	0.80	1.2	0.39	0.53	2.83
Gujarat	9.55	7.86	(1.8)	8.34	10.53	2.14
Haryana	4.24	3.81	(1.0)	2.33	2.86	1.88
Himachal Pradesh	2.46	2.61	0.5	0.43	1.05	8.45
Jammu & Kashmir	2.00	2.00	0.0	0.11	0.11	0.00
Jharkhand	..	12.43		..	3.12	
Karnataka	10.84	10.53	(0.3)	7.57	10.94	3.40
Kerala	6.25	6.10	(0.2)	5.60	5.08	(0.88)
Madhya Pradesh	14.19	8.56	(4.5)	2.48	1.38	(5.19)
Maharashtra	23.46	19.80	(1.5)	15.17	17.03	1.06
Manipur	0.78	0.76	(0.2)	0.02	0.03	3.75
Meghalaya	0.69	0.73	0.5	0.08	0.09	1.08
Mizoram	0.40	0.40	0.0	0.01	0.01	0.00
Nagaland	0.69	0.71	0.3	0.03	0.06	6.50
Orissa	7.09	5.77	(1.9)	0.94	0.88	(0.60)
Punjab	5.93	5.20	(1.2)	2.48	3.25	2.49
Rajasthan	10.24	9.48	(0.7)	2.64	2.73	0.31
Tamil Nadu	16.45	15.01	(0.8)	9.32	8.40	(0.94)
Tripura	1.00	1.47	3.6	0.11	0.13	1.53
Uttar Pradesh	21.12	16.19	(2.4)	5.36	4.95	(0.72)
Uttarakhand	..	2.17		..	0.49	
West Bengal	14.93	11.80	(2.1)	7.98	7.58	(0.47)
Union Territories						
A & N Islands	0.32	0.35	0.8	0.04	0.02	(6.11)
Chandigarh	0.63	0.58	(0.7)	0.19	0.43	7.71
Daman & Diu	0.02	0.02	0.0	0.09	0.13	3.40
Delhi	6.26	5.55	(1.1)	2.21	2.36	0.60
Puducherry	0.40	0.40	0.0	0.09	0.29	11.22

Note : Data for Arunachal Pradesh, Dadra & Nagar Haveli and Lakshadweep are not covered under EMI programme. CAGR refers to Compounded Annual Growth Rate between the two years.

Source : Directorate of General Employment and Training, Ministry of Labour & Employment.

210 : Human Development Index

State	1981	Rank	1991	Rank	2001
All-India	0.302		0.381		0.472
Andhra Pradesh	0.298	23	0.377	23	0.416
Arunachal Pradesh	0.242	31	0.328	29	
Assam	0.272	26	0.348	26	0.386
Bihar	0.237	32	0.308	32	0.367
Goa	0.445	5	0.575	4	
Gujarat	0.360	14	0.431	17	0.479
Haryana	0.360	15	0.443	16	0.509
Himachal Pradesh	0.398	10	0.469	13	
Jammu & Kashmir	0.337	19	0.402	21	
Karnataka	0.346	16	0.412	19	0.478
Kerala	0.500	2	0.591	3	0.638
Madhya Pradesh	0.245	30	0.328	30	0.394
Maharashtra	0.363	13	0.452	15	0.523
Manipur	0.461	4	0.536	9	
Meghalaya	0.317	21	0.365	24	
Mizoram	0.411	9	0.548	7	
Nagaland	0.328	20	0.486	11	
Orissa	0.267	27	0.345	28	0.404
Punjab	0.411	9	0.475	12	0.537
Rajasthan	0.256	28	0.347	27	0.424
Sikkim	0.342	18	0.425	18	
Tamil Nadu	0.343	17	0.466	14	0.531
Tripura	0.287	24	0.389	22	
Uttar Pradesh	0.255	29	0.314	31	0.388
West Bengal	0.305	22	0.404	20	0.472
Union Territories					
A & N Islands	0.394	11	0.574	5	
Chandigarh	0.550	1	0.674	1	
Dadra & Nagar Haveli	0.276	25	0.361	25	
Daman & Diu	0.438	6	0.544	8	
Delhi	0.495	3	0.624	2	
Lakshadweep	0.434	7	0.532	10	
Puducherry	0.386	12	0.571	6	

Note: Human Development Index is a composite of variables capturing attainments in three dimensions of human development *viz.*, economic situation, education and health. These have been captured by per capita monthly expenditure adjusted for inequality, a combination of literacy rate and intensity of formal education and a combination of life expectancy at age one and infant mortality rate. 2001 data are for major states only.

Source : Planning Commission.

211 : State-wise Poverty Ratio

(in percentage)

State	Rural			Urban		
	1983	1993-94	2004-05	1983-84	1993-94	2004-05
NSSO Round	38	50	61	38	50	61
All-India	45.7	37.3	28.3	40.8	32.4	25.7
Andhra Pradesh	26.5	15.9	11.2	36.3	38.3	28.0
Arunachal Pradesh	42.6	45.0	22.3	21.7	7.7	3.3
Assam	42.6	45.0	22.3	21.7	7.7	3.3
Bihar	64.4	58.2	42.1	47.3	34.5	34.6
Chhattisgarh	..	..	40.8	..	..	41.2
Goa	14.8	5.3	5.4	27.0	27.0	21.3
Gujarat	29.8	22.2	19.1	39.1	27.9	13.0
Haryana	20.6	28.0	13.6	24.2	16.4	15.1
Himachal Pradesh	17.0	30.3	10.7	9.4	9.2	3.4
Jammu & Kashmir	26.0	30.3	4.6	17.8	9.2	7.9
Jharkhand	..	..	46.3	..	..	20.2
Karnataka	36.3	29.9	20.8	42.8	40.1	32.6
Kerala	39.0	25.8	13.2	45.7	24.6	20.2
Madhya Pradesh	48.9	40.6	36.9	53.1	48.4	42.1
Maharashtra	45.2	37.9	29.6	40.3	35.2	32.2
Manipur	42.6	45.0	22.3	21.7	7.7	3.3
Meghalaya	42.6	45.0	22.3	21.7	7.7	3.3
Mizoram	42.6	45.0	22.3	21.7	7.7	3.3
Nagaland	42.6	45.0	22.3	21.7	7.7	3.3
Orissa	67.5	49.7	46.8	49.2	41.6	44.3
Punjab	13.2	12.0	9.1	23.8	11.4	7.1
Rajasthan	33.5	26.5	18.7	37.9	30.5	32.9
Sikkim	42.6	45.0	22.3	21.7	7.7	3.3
Tamil Nadu	54.0	32.5	22.8	47.0	39.8	22.2
Tripura	42.6	45.0	22.3	21.7	7.7	3.3
Uttar Pradesh	46.5	42.3	33.4	49.8	35.4	30.6
Uttarakhand	..	..	40.8	..	..	36.5
West Bengal	63.1	40.8	28.6	32.3	22.4	15.8
Union Territories						
A & N Islands	54.0	32.5	22.9	47.0	39.8	22.2
Chandigarh	23.8	12.0	7.1	23.8	11.4	7.1
Dadra & Nagar Haveli	14.8	52.0	39.8	27.0	39.9	19.1
Daman & Diu	..	5.3	5.4	..	27.0	21.2
Delhi	7.7	1.9	6.9	27.9	16.0	15.2
Lakshadweep	39.0	25.8	13.3	45.7	24.6	20.2
Puducherry	54.0	32.5	22.8	47.0	39.8	22.2

Source : Planning Commission.

212 : Gross State Domestic Product

State	2004-05		Constant (2004-05) Prices 2009-10		Current Prices 2009-10	
	GSDP (Rs. crore)	Per Capita (Rs.)	GSDP (Rs. crore)	Per Capita (Rs.)	GSDP (Rs. crore)	Per Capita (Rs.)
All-India						
Andhra Pradesh	224713	28265	340712	40731	475267	56817
Arunachal Pradesh	3488	30355	5535	45332	7241	59306
Assam	53398	18993	69924	23279	92472	30786
Bihar	76574	8637	121567	12683	168603	17590
Chhattisgarh	47862	21463	76078	31052	109823	44826
Goa	12636	88424	19525	116287	25882	154152
Gujarat	203373	37803	331633	57267	429356	74142
Haryana	95319	41978	151692	61045	216287	87041
Himachal Pradesh	24077	37001	35888	50783	43281	61244
Jammu & Kashmir	27005	25198	35538	30886	43236	37577
Jharkhand	59766	20850	79663	25810	106358	34459
Karnataka	166306	30059	249006	42527	335747	57342
Kerala	119264	36278	181289	52984	230316	67312
Madhya Pradesh	112927	17449	159075	22538	216958	30738
Maharashtra	413826	40347	701550	63497	901330	81579

contd...

...contd...

State			Constant (2004-05) Prices		Current Prices	
	2004-05		2009-10		2009-10	
	GSDP (Rs. crore)	Per Capita (Rs.)	GSDP (Rs. crore)	Per Capita (Rs.)	GSDP (Rs. crore)	Per Capita (Rs.)
Manipur	5131	20775	na	na	8687	31927
Meghalaya	6526	26887	8796	34118	12502	48494
Mizoram	2682	27564	4330	39206	5633	51009
Nagaland*	5204	21919	6227	22569	6751	24470
Orissa	76579	19980	120057	29716	162327	40178
Punjab	96694	37173	140976	49453	199459	69968
Rajasthan	127745	21056	177953	26836	255440	38522
Sikkim	1739	30730	2586	42888	3476	57637
Tamil Nadu	219234	34034	348297	52112	464009	69425
Tripura	8904	26586	12248	34433	14604	41058
Uttar Pradesh	258653	14498	363560	18564	519899	26547
Uttarakhand	24821	27536	45580	46787	62214	63861
West Bengal	208857	24893	295022	33398	400561	45346

contd...

...contd...

State	Constant (2004-05) Prices				Current Prices	
	2004-05		2009-10		2009-10	
	GSDP (Rs. crore)	Per Capita (Rs.)	GSDP (Rs. crore)	Per Capita (Rs.)	GSDP (Rs. crore)	Per Capita (Rs.)
Union Territories						
A & N Islands	1813	45429	2877	60700	3841	81030
Chandigarh	8504	82887	13711	99427	18341	133001
Delhi	100325	65205	165796	93538	217851	122906
Puducherry	5754	55218	9691	84685	11255	98350

Note : na : not available.

* : Data for 2009-10 pertains to 2007-08.

Source : Directorate of Economics & Statistics of respective state governments, Central Statistical Organisation.

213 : Per Capita Consumption Expenditure

State	2000-01				2009-10			
	Rural		Urban		Rural		Urban	
	Total (Rs.)	Share of Food (%)	Total (Rs.)	Share of Food (%)	Total (Rs.)	Share of Food (%)	Total (Rs.)	Share of Food (%)
All-India	494.9	56.3	914.6	43.8	1054.0	57.0	1984.0	44.4
Andhra Pradesh	490.2	55.7	928.4	41.3	1234.0	58.1	2238.0	44.8
Assam	457.3	65.6	789.4	52.8	1003.0	64.4	1755.0	52.9
Bihar	396.3	61.6	595.4	51.4	780.0	64.7	1238.0	52.9
Chhattisgarh	394.8	58.3	740.0	46.2	784.0	58.2	1647.0	43.7
Gujarat	591.2	58.6	953.2	45.4	1110.0	57.7	1909.0	46.2
Haryana	682.3	52.8	897.9	45.3	1510.0	54.0	2321.0	43.1
Himachal Pradesh	700.8	56.8	1178.5	45.9				
Jammu & Kashmir	679.8	60.5	1047.6	50.4				
Jharkhand	385.1	0.0	690.6	52.8	825.0	60.9	1584.0	51.5
Karnataka	531.0	54.3	900.5	43.3	1020.0	56.5	2053.0	42.3
Kerala	841.3	49.6	1203.7	43.2	1835.0	45.9	2413.0	40.2
Madhya Pradesh	390.0	53.1	727.4	42.9	903.0	55.8	1666.0	41.7
Maharashtra	506.8	53.5	1033.9	42.3	1153.0	54.0	2437.0	41.0
Orissa	392.5	62.8	772.7	48.2	818.0	61.9	1548.0	48.4

contd...

...contd...

State	2000-01				2009-10			
	Rural		Urban		Rural		Urban	
	Total (Rs.)	Share of Food (%)	Total (Rs.)	Share of Food (%)	Total (Rs.)	Share of Food (%)	Total (Rs.)	Share of Food (%)
Punjab	771.2	48.7	973.2	43.0	1649.0	48.2	2109.0	44.3
Rajasthan	538.3	56.7	793.4	46.8	1179.0	54.8	1663.0	48.0
Tamil Nadu	525.7	55.3	969.5	42.9	1160.0	54.7	1948.0	45.0
Uttar Pradesh	452.7	54.1	737.8	44.8	899.0	57.9	1574.0	46.3
West Bengal	473.1	61.6	902.2	47.3	952.0	63.5	1965.0	46.2
N-Eastern States	619.9	59.2	988.4	49.3				
Delhi			1308.7	36.5				
Union Territories	791.1	54.7	1054.6	46.4				

Notes: Data for all states/UTs taken for All-India estimates. Separate estimates have been presented for rural/urban consumers of major states (20 million or more population as per Census 2001). Combines estimates for NE states and UTs are given. Northeastern states include Arunachal Pradesh, Manipur, Meghalaya, Mizoram, Nagaland, Sikkim and Tripura and UTs include A&N Islands, Chandigarh, D&N Haveli, Daman and Diu, Lakshadweep and Puducherry.

Source: NSSO Reports.

214 : Agriculture Input

State	Irrigated Area under All Crops (%) (% to cropped area)		Fertiliser Use Per Hectare (kgs/hectare of cropped area)		Consumption of Electricity in GWH Agriculture (% share)	
	2000-01	2007-08	2000-01	2008-09	2007-08	
All-India	40.2	44.6	86.7	128.6	104182	20.8
Andhra Pradesh	43.7	46.3	159.6	239.7	15241	31.2
Arunachal Pradesh	16.4	19.9	2.4	3.0	0	0.0
Assam	5.6	2.4	35.7	62.1	20	0.8
Bihar	47.8	60.6	98.2	179.0	659	15.0
Chhattisgarh	19.6	26.5		80.7	1459	13.8
Goa	20.9	20.8	34.2	47.3	39	1.5
Gujarat	33.9	41.7	70.1	140.7	10946	24.8
Haryana	85.4	86.0	147.2	201.6	7335	40.2
Himachal Pradesh	19.1	19.2	36.7	60.6	27	0.5
Jammu & Kashmir	40.3	40.8	60.1	93.3	271	6.7
Jharkhand		10.1		55.7	67	0.6
Karnataka	26.6	29.4	109.5	147.3	10844	31.7
Kerala	15.2	16.5	59.4	89.4	241	2.0
Madhya Pradesh	24.0	32.2	36.9	70.8	7536	31.9
Maharashtra	17.4	19.6	74.3	113.7	12676	18.7
Manipur	36.0	21.7	102.0	57.5	0	0.1
Meghalaya	22.6	25.8	14.5	13.9	1	0.1
Mizoram	14.0	10.0	12.4	47.3	0	0.0
Nagaland	24.9	29.1	1.4	2.2	0	0.0
Orissa	27.0	36.7	37.9	61.6	172	1.5
Punjab	96.0	97.7	161.8	221.4	10022	33.5
Rajasthan	31.9	36.4	31.1	48.9	8145	34.4
Sikkim	14.3	8.8	8.5	0.0	0	0.0
Tamil Nadu	55.1	55.9	145.3	216.5	10717	20.2
Tripura	13.9	35.1	20.7	47.2	24	6.0
Uttar Pradesh	67.3	75.5	115.3	156.3	6200	16.5
Uttarakhand		45.6		123.3	300	6.3
West Bengal	37.0	56.9	116.8	157.7	1110	4.2
Union Territories						
A & N Islands			9.1	42.9	0	0.0
Chandigarh			25.5	0.0	1	0.1
D & N Haveli			34.2	39.3	2	0.2
Daman & Diu			52.0	130.0	9	0.3
Delhi			85.5	14.9	37	0.2
Lakshadweep			0.0	0.0	82	0.9
Puducherry			550.6	776.1	0	0.0

Source: *Agricultural Statistics at a Glance 2010*, Ministry of Agriculture.

215 : Production of Food Grains

(mn tonnes)

State/Region	1990-91	Growth (%)	2000-01	Growth (%)	2008-09	Growth (%)
1. Food Grains - Top 10 States						
All-India	176.1	3.1	196.6	1.1	234.5	2.2
Uttar Pradesh	35.7	3.6	42.7	1.8	46.7	1.1
Punjab	19.2	4.9	25.3	2.8	27.3	1.0
Andhra Pradesh	12.3	2.1	16.0	2.7	20.4	3.1
Rajasthan	10.9	5.3	10.0	(0.8)	16.7	6.6
West Bengal	11.3	3.1	13.8	2.1	16.3	2.1
Haryana	9.6	4.7	13.3	3.4	15.6	2.0
Madhya Pradesh	18.0	3.8	10.2	(5.5)	13.9	4.0
Bihar	12.3	2.1	12.1	(0.2)	12.2	0.2
Maharashtra	12.2	2.2	10.1	(1.8)	11.4	1.5
Karnataka	6.4	0.9	11.0	5.6	11.3	0.3
2. Rice - Top 5 States						
All-India	74.2	3.3	84.8	1.4	99.2	2.0
West Bengal	10.4	3.4	12.4	1.8	15.0	2.4
Andhra Pradesh	9.7	3.3	12.5	2.6	14.2	1.7
Uttar Pradesh	10.3	6.3	11.7	1.3	13.1	1.4
Punjab	6.5	7.3	9.2	3.4	11.0	2.3
Orissa	5.3	2.1	4.6	(1.3)	6.8	5.0
3. Wheat - Top 5 States						
All-India	55.0	4.3	69.6	2.4	80.7	2.5
Uttar Pradesh	18.6	3.3	25.2	3.1	28.6	2.1
Punjab	12.2	4.7	15.6	2.5	15.7	0.1
Haryana	6.4	6.2	9.7	4.2	10.8	1.8
Rajasthan	4.3	6.0	5.5	2.5	7.3	4.8
Madhya Pradesh	5.8	6.5	5	(1.7)	6.5	4.9
4. Pulses - Top 5 States						
All-India	14.3	3.0	11.1	(2.5)	14.6	4.6
Madhya Pradesh	3.1	4.4	2.3	(3.1)	3.7	8.1
Uttar Pradesh	2.8	0.9	2.2	(2.5)	2.0	(1.6)
Rajasthan	1.7	3.9	0.7	(8.2)	1.8	17.4
Maharashtra	1.4	5.7	1.6	1.3	1.7	0.6
Andhra Pradesh	0.7	5.3	1.0	4.2	1.5	6.4

Note : Growth (%) refers to compounded annual growth rates between the two years, negative values in brackets.

Source : Ministry of Agriculture.

216 : Production of Commercial Crops

State/Region	1991	2001	2009	Growth (CAGR%) 1991-2001	Growth (CAGR%) 2001-2007
1. Nine Oilseeds - Top 5 States (mn tonnes)					
All-India	18.6	18.4	27.7	(0.1)	5.2
Madhya Pradesh	3.2	4.1	7.0	2.5	6.9
Rajasthan	2.4	2.0	5.2	(1.5)	12.4
Gujarat	2.1	1.7	4.0	(2.3)	11.7
Maharashtra	1.9	2.1	3.4	1.0	6.3
Andhra Pradesh	2.5	2.5	2.2	(0.1)	(1.7)
2. Cotton - Top 5 States (in mn bales of 170 kgs each)					
All-India	9.8	9.5	22.3	(0.3)	11.2
Gujarat	1.3	1.2	7.0	(1.3)	25.2
Maharashtra	1.9	1.8	4.8	(0.4)	12.9
Andhra Pradesh	1.1	1.7	3.6	4.1	10.0
Punjab	1.9	1.2	2.3	(4.5)	8.4
Haryana	1.2	1.4	1.9	1.8	3.8
3. Sugarcane - Top 5 States (mn tonnes)					
All-India	240.8	295.8	285.0	2.1	(0.5)
Uttar Pradesh	103.6	106.1	109.1	0.2	0.3
Maharashtra	38.4	49.6	60.7	2.6	2.5
Tamil Nadu	23.5	33.2	32.8	3.5	(0.1)
Karnataka	21.0	42.9	23.3	7.4	(7.3)
Gujarat	10.6	12.7	15.5	1.8	2.5

Source: Ministry of Agriculture.

217 : Number of Factories

(number)

State	Number of Factories					
	1990-91	Share in %	2000-01	Share in %	2008-09	Share in %
All-India	110179	100.0	131270	100.0	155321	100.0
Andhra Pradesh	15205	13.8	14029	10.7	16903	10.9
Assam	1548	1.4	1435	1.1	2211	1.4
Bihar	3409	3.1	1535	1.2	1775	1.1
Chhattisgarh			1275	1.0	1919	1.2
Goa	220	0.2	524	0.4	519	0.3
Gujarat	10943	9.9	14090	10.7	14863	9.6
Haryana	3070	2.8	4448	3.4	4450	2.9
Himachal Pradesh	282	0.3	507	0.4	1294	0.8
Jammu & Kashmir	235	0.2	356	0.3	649	0.4
Jharkhand			1500	1.1	1846	1.2
Karnataka	5911	5.4	7010	5.3	8451	5.4
Kerala	3484	3.2	4853	3.7	5867	3.8
Madhya Pradesh	3962	3.6	3221	2.5	3345	2.2
Maharashtra	15595	14.2	18528	14.1	20450	13.2
Manipur	60	0.1	59	0.0	72	0.0
Meghalaya	32	0.0	30	0.0	95	0.1
Nagaland	50	0.0	129	0.1	91	0.1
Orissa	1465	1.3	1665	1.3	1930	1.2
Punjab	6255	5.7	7137	5.4	10065	6.5
Rajasthan	3358	3.0	5112	3.9	6352	4.1
Tamil Nadu	14617	13.3	20601	15.7	26122	16.8
Tripura	242	0.2	239	0.2	363	0.2
Uttar Pradesh	10417	9.5	9635	7.3	10935	7.0
Uttarakhand			744	0.6	1907	1.2
West Bengal	5606	5.1	6091	4.6	6260	4.0
Union Territories						
A & N Islands	52	0.0	23	0.0	12	0.0
Chandigarh	295	0.3	295	0.2	278	0.2
D & N Haveli	127	0.1	902	0.7	1151	0.7
Daman & Diu	53	0.0	1275	1.0	1443	0.9
Delhi	3453	3.1	3498	2.7	3026	1.9
Puducherry	233	0.2	524	0.4	675	0.4

Note : Share in % represents the percentage share from each individual state in the total.

Source : *Annual Survey of Industries* (Factory Sector).

218 : Factories: Invested Capital

(Rs. crore)

State	Number of Factories					
	1990-91	Share in %	2000-01	Share in %	2008-09	Share in %
All-India	194913	100.0	571799	100.0	1535178	100.0
Andhra Pradesh	20362	10.4	39121	6.8	109607	7.1
Assam	1523	0.8	7309	1.3	13619	0.9
Bihar	10228	5.2	2920	0.5	5849	0.4
Chhattisgarh		0.0	9053	1.6	38018	2.5
Goa	453	0.2	4076	0.7	9493	0.6
Gujarat	18696	9.6	93001	16.3	246911	16.1
Haryana	6106	3.1	21874	3.8	61334	4.0
Himachal Pradesh	1308	0.7	4577	0.8	28743	1.9
Jammu & Kashmir	146	0.1	564	0.1	3989	0.3
Jharkhand		0.0	20325	3.6	39920	2.6
Karnataka	7863	4.0	35685	6.2	115587	7.5
Kerala	3809	2.0	10378	1.8	19281	1.3
Madhya Pradesh	13652	7.0	19733	3.5	40364	2.6
Maharashtra	35399	18.2	103631	18.1	261095	17.0
Manipur	15	0.0	7	0.0	24	0.0
Meghalaya	263	0.1	49	0.0	886	0.1
Nagaland	34	0.0	50	0.0	61	0.0
Orissa	6209	3.2	14809	2.6	66810	4.4
Punjab	8133	4.2	15008	2.6	46123	3.0
Rajasthan	6898	3.5	18553	3.2	46636	3.0
Tamil Nadu	17700	9.1	55785	9.8	146993	9.6
Tripura	84	0.0	76	0.0	563	0.0
Uttar Pradesh	20953	10.7	49010	8.6	94232	6.1
Uttarakhand		0.0	3546	0.6	34693	2.3
West Bengal	12518	6.4	25221	4.4	61963	4.0
Union Territories						
A & N Islands	44	0.0	36	0.0	66	0.0
Chandigarh	118	0.1	404	0.1	1110	0.1
D & N Haveli	243	0.1	7332	1.3	19760	1.3
Daman & Diu	42	0.0	2941	0.5	8658	0.6
Delhi	1757	0.9	4289	0.8	7408	0.5
Puducherry	358	0.2	2436	0.4	5382	0.4

Note : Share in % represents the percentage share from each individual state in the total.

Source : *Annual Survey of Industries* (Factory Sector).

219 : Number of Factory Workers

(number)

State/Region	1990-91	Share in %	2000-01	Share in %	2008-09	Share in %
All-India	6307143	100.0	6135235	100.0	8776745	100.0
Andhra Pradesh	699885	11.1	763892	12.5	909828	10.4
Assam	90878	1.4	92474	1.5	126338	1.4
Bihar	280420	4.4	49190	0.8	62864	0.7
Chhattisgarh		0.0	65894	1.1	126890	1.4
Goa	12520	0.2	21255	0.3	40545	0.5
Gujarat	523929	8.3	553704	9.0	871459	9.9
Haryana	189469	3.0	217532	3.5	377322	4.3
Himachal Pradesh	36202	0.6	29788	0.5	84497	1.0
Jammu & Kashmir	10632	0.2	18371	0.3	45033	0.5
Jharkhand			134317	2.2	122524	1.4
Karnataka	307929	4.9	359199	5.9	598070	6.8
Kerala	228353	3.6	262981	4.3	331043	3.8
Madhya Pradesh	287899	4.6	191131	3.1	202428	2.3
Maharashtra	908457	14.4	817305	13.3	1034201	11.8
Manipur	815	0.0	695	0.0	2313	0.0
Meghalaya	3434	0.1	870	0.0	4571	0.1
Nagaland	1908	0.0	2440	0.0	2468	0.0
Orissa	116918	1.9	99127	1.6	174774	2.0
Punjab	311670	4.9	278303	4.5	431568	4.9
Rajasthan	181076	2.9	175566	2.9	275950	3.1
Tamil Nadu	766377	12.2	925389	15.1	1456155	16.6
Tripura	9869	0.2	7839	0.1	23643	0.3
Uttar Pradesh	619864	9.8	401674	6.5	574874	6.5
Uttarakhand			28704	0.5	172861	2.0
West Bengal	578651	9.2	455812	7.4	449887	5.1
Union Territories						
A & N Islands	4589	0.1	2159	0.0	299	0.0
Chandigarh	8871	0.1	6503	0.1	7068	0.1
D & N Haveli	4297	0.1	29545	0.5	71327	0.8
Daman & Diu	2205	0.0	30987	0.5	69038	0.8
Delhi	102701	1.6	82174	1.3	87552	1.0
Puducherry	17325	0.3	30415	0.5	39356	0.4

Note : Share in % represents the percentage share from each individual state in the all-India total.

Source : *Annual Survey of Industries* (Factory Sector).

220 : Wages to Workers

(Rs. crore)

State	1990-91	Share in %	2000-01	Share in %	2008-09	Share in %
All-India	13192	100.0	29348	100.0	59772	100.0
Andhra Pradesh	823	6.2	2268	7.7	4875	8.2
Assam	81	0.6	274	0.9	544	0.9
Bihar	859	6.5	180	0.6	290	0.5
Chhattisgarh			455		911	
Goa	29	0.2	128	0.4	365	0.6
Gujarat	963	7.3	2611	8.9	5934	9.9
Haryana	390	3.0	1068	3.6	2738	4.6
Himachal Pradesh	62	0.5	118	0.4	512	0.9
Jammu & Kashmir	14	0.1	72	0.2	215	0.4
Jharkhand			1397		1710	
Karnataka	680	5.2	1679	5.7	4254	7.1
Kerala	362	2.7	1002	3.4	1576	2.6
Madhya Pradesh	601	4.6	992	3.4	1447	2.4
Maharashtra	2859	21.7	5735	19.5	9727	16.3
Manipur	1	0.0	3	0.0	6	0.0
Meghalaya	11	0.1	2	0.0	31	0.1
Nagaland	4	0.0	4	0.0	5	0.0
Orissa	253	1.9	587	2.0	1737	2.9
Punjab	556	4.2	1041	3.5	2316	3.9
Rajasthan	381	2.9	770	2.6	1609	2.7
Tamil Nadu	1387	10.5	3615	12.3	8506	14.2
Tripura	10	0.1	14	0.0	45	0.1
Uttar Pradesh	1246	9.4	1694	5.8	3591	6.0
Uttarakhand			251		1793	
West Bengal	1345	10.2	2640	9.0	3432	5.7
Union Territories						
A & N Islands	8	0.1	5	0.0	2	0.0
Chandigarh	20	0.2	40	0.1	60	0.1
D & N Haveli	5	0.0	110	0.4	414	0.7
Daman & Diu	2	0.0	94	0.3	350	0.6
Delhi	203	1.5	375	1.3	525	0.9
Puducherry	34	0.3	127	0.4	254	0.4

Note: Share in % represents the percentage share from each individual state in the all-India total.

Source: *Annual Survey of Industries* (Factory Sector).

221 : Factories: Value of Output

(in Rs. crore)

State	1993-94	Share in %	2000-01	Share in %	2008-09	Share in %
All-India	252757	100.0	926902	100.0	3272798	100.0
Andhra Pradesh	15654	6.2	61347	6.6	212403	6.2
Assam	2839	1.1	8741	0.9	36768	1.3
Bihar	11437	4.5	7255	0.8	29540	0.9
Chhattisgarh	..		12743	1.4	76405	1.6
Goa	880	0.3	8089	0.9	27526	0.8
Gujarat	25379	10.0	127977	13.8	508088	16.1
Haryana	9438	3.7	44675	4.8	144336	4.5
Himachal Pradesh	1079	0.4	6482	0.7	42279	0.9
Jammu & Kashmir	439	0.2	1343	0.1	13494	0.4
Jharkhand	..		19278	2.1	59108	2.2
Karnataka	11543	4.6	46259	5.0	225813	6.9
Kerala	5823	2.3	26711	2.9	70905	2.3
Madhya Pradesh	13614	5.4	36712	4.0	90402	2.6
Maharashtra	57649	22.8	184971	20.0	600174	19.6
Manipur	9	0.0	18	0.0	67	0.0
Meghalaya	38	0.0	101	0.0	1922	0.0
Nagaland	24	0.0	92	0.0	128	0.0
Orissa	4630	1.8	13243	1.4	69532	1.5
Punjab	11953	4.7	35019	3.8	105514	3.1
Rajasthan	7929	3.1	30784	3.3	90665	2.8
Tamil Nadu	25667	10.2	103540	11.2	300802	10.0
Tripura	41	0.0	311	0.0	756	0.0
Uttar Pradesh	24510	9.7	64854	7.0	200463	6.2
Uttarakhand	..		4884	0.5	82924	0.8
West Bengal	15291	6.0	39183	4.2	141796	4.3
Union Territories						
A & N Islands	48	0.0	36	0.0	153	0.0
Chandigarh	414	0.2	980	0.1	3526	0.1
D & N Haveli	874	0.3	13665	1.5	64965	1.8
Daman & Diu	93	0.0	7305	0.8	30313	1.4
Delhi	4925	1.9	14298	1.5	27476	1.1
Puducherry	538	0.2	6008	(0.6)	14558	(0.6)

Note : Share in % represents the percentage share from each individual state in the all-India total.

Source : *Annual Survey of Industries* (Factory Sector).

222 : Factories: Net Value Added

(in Rs. crore)

State	1990-91	Share in %	2000-01	Share in %	2005-06	Share in %
All-India	51515	100.0	143621	100.0	527766	100.0
Andhra Pradesh	2981	5.8	8879	6.2	35471	6.7
Assam	734	1.4	1284	0.9	3014	0.6
Bihar	2598	5.0	729	0.5	3184	0.6
Chhattisgarh			2493	1.7	16614	3.1
Goa	158	0.3	1470	1.0	4902	0.9
Gujarat	4468	8.7	16856	11.7	60417	11.4
Haryana	1636	3.2	5571	3.9	20354	3.9
Himachal Pradesh	378	0.7	1308	0.9	13332	2.5
Jammu & Kashmir	76	0.1	159	0.1	3208	0.6
Jharkhand			4044	2.8	14300	2.7
Karnataka	2769	5.4	8302	5.8	42533	8.1
Kerala	1222	2.4	3554	2.5	7705	1.5
Madhya Pradesh	3007	5.8	6208	4.3	15021	2.8
Maharashtra	12004	23.3	31261	21.8	112878	21.4
Manipur	0	0.0	2	0.0	12	0.0
Meghalaya	11	0.0	8	0.0	524	0.1
Nagaland	-1	0.0	7	0.0	28	0.0
Orissa	1153	2.2	2352	1.6	16674	3.2
Punjab	1857	3.6	4301	3.0	12568	2.4
Rajasthan	1556	3.0	5258	3.7	16884	3.2
Tamil Nadu	5793	11.2	16536	11.5	39714	7.5
Tripura	8	0.0	130	0.1	155	0.0
Uttar Pradesh	4625	9.0	9577	6.7	24139	4.6
Uttarakhand			961	0.7	28433	5.4
West Bengal	3198	6.2	5699	4.0	16600	3.1
Union Territories						
A & N Islands	14	0.0	6	0.0	8	0.0
Chandigarh	70	0.1	145	0.1	442	0.1
D & N Haveli	73	0.1	1861	1.3	7785	1.5
Daman & Diu	14	0.0	1370	1.0	4398	0.8
Delhi	1016	2.0	2009	1.4	3480	0.7
Puducherry	97	0.2	1281	0.9	2992	0.6

Note: Share in % represents the percentage share from each individual state in the all-India total.

Source: *Annual Survey of Industries* (Factory Sector).

223 : Factories: Gross Capital Formation

(in Rs. crore)

State	1990-91	Share in %	2000-01	Share in %	2008-09	Share in %
All-India	24292	100.0	61415	100.0	261585	100.0
Andhra Pradesh	2235	9.2	3451	5.6	22700	8.7
Assam	198	0.8	2380	3.9	1254	0.5
Bihar	1180	4.9	526	0.9	447	0.2
Chhattisgarh		0.0	824	1.3	8957	3.4
Goa	33	0.1	608	1.0	1915	0.7
Gujarat	2703	11.1	7302	11.9	40353	15.4
Haryana	410	1.7	2655	4.3	10851	4.1
Himachal Pradesh	113	0.5	566	0.9	3336	1.3
Jammu & Kashmir	17	0.1	92	0.2	551	0.2
Jharkhand		0.0	3486	5.7	10908	4.2
Karnataka	867	3.6	4343	7.1	25261	9.7
Kerala	429	1.8	309	0.5	1468	0.6
Madhya Pradesh	1796	7.4	1919	3.1	5330	2.0
Maharashtra	4700	19.3	12320	20.1	37112	14.2
Manipur	8	0.0	0	0.0	1	0.0
Meghalaya	42	0.2	12	0.0	169	0.1
Nagaland		0.0	4	0.0	0	0.0
Orissa	767	3.2	904	1.5	16306	6.2
Punjab	897	3.7	1360	2.2	5576	2.1
Rajasthan	833	3.4	1556	2.5	12013	4.6
Tamil Nadu	2661	11.0	7112	11.6	23727	9.1
Tripura	13	0.1	16	0.0	264	0.1
Uttar Pradesh	2242	9.2	4849	7.9	11334	4.3
Uttarakhand		0.0	255	0.4	10238	3.9
West Bengal	1843	7.6	2374	3.9	5599	2.1
Union Territories						
A & N Islands	19	0.1	-19	0.0	6	0.0
Chandigarh	16	0.1	58	0.1	128	0.0
D & N Haveli	25	0.1	814	1.3	3125	1.2
Daman & Diu	13	0.1	651	1.1	557	0.2
Delhi	195	0.8	483	0.8	996	0.4
Puducherry	35	0.1	204	0.3	1102	0.4

Note: Share in % represents the percentage share from each individual state in the all-India total.

Source: *Annual Survey of Industries* (Factory Sector).

224 : Number of Factories Engaged in All (Agricultural & Non-Agricultural) Activities

State/UTs	Rural + Urban Enterprises (OAE+Estt.) (in thousand)					
	1990	Share in %	1998	Share in %	2005	Share in %
All-India	25002	100.0	30349	100.0	41827	100.0
Andhra Pradesh	2487	9.9	2903	9.6	3997	9.6
Arunachal Pradesh	21	0.1	21	0.1	29	0.1
Assam	495	2.0	593	2.0	984	2.4
Bihar	1228	4.9	1443	4.8	1225	2.9
Chhattisgarh	0	0.0	0	0.0	637	1.5
Goa	61	0.2	72	0.2	74	0.2
Gujarat	1498	6.0	1915	6.3	2426	5.8
Haryana	457	1.8	533	1.8	834	2.0
Himachal Pradesh	183	0.7	225	0.7	268	0.6
Jammu & Kashmir	0	0.0	216	0.7	325	0.8
Jharkhand	0	0.0	0	0.0	491	1.2
Karnataka	1694	6.8	1912	6.3	2539	6.1
Kerala	1229	4.9	1565	5.2	2804	6.7
Madhya Pradesh	1873	7.5	2124	7.0	1735	4.1
Maharashtra	2624	10.5	3234	10.7	4225	10.1
Manipur	61	0.2	80	0.3	105	0.3
Meghalaya	50	0.2	56	0.2	83	0.2
Mizoram	23	0.1	25	0.1	48	0.1
Nagaland	24	0.1	30	0.1	36	0.1
Orissa	1094	4.4	1450	4.8	1830	4.4
Punjab	599	2.4	717	2.4	1072	2.6
Rajasthan	1169	4.7	1531	5.0	1961	4.7
Sikkim	11	0.0	13	0.0	19	0.0
Tamil Nadu	2111	8.4	2514	8.3	4433	10.6
Tripura	85	0.3	104	0.3	189	0.5
Uttar Pradesh	2633	10.5	3043	10.0	4021	9.6
Uttarakhand	0	0.0	0	0.0	325	0.8
West Bengal	2750	11.0	3234	10.7	4205	10.1
Union Territories						
A & N Islands	12	0.0	14	0.0	13	0.0
Chandigarh	33	0.1	40	0.1	65	0.2
Dadra & Nagar Haveli	3	0.0	4	0.0	9	0.0
Daman & Diu	5	0.0	6	0.0	10	0.0
Delhi	455	1.8	686	2.3	758	1.8
Lakshadweep	5	0.0	5	0.0	3	0.0
Puducherry	31	0.1	43	0.1	50	0.1

Note : OAE: Own Account Enterprises: Enterprise owned and operated with the help of household labour only.
Estt: Establishment is an enterprise engaged in economic activities with the assistance of at least one hired worker on a regular basis.
Share in % represents percentage of individual states to total.

Source : CSO (2007), Economic Census (2005) and earlier issues.

225 : Economic Census: Total Employment in Thousand Numbers

State/Region	1990	CAGR (%)	1998	CAGR (%)	2005	CAGR (%)
All-India	72073	**3.0**	83299	**1.8**	100904	**2.8**
Northern Region	8717	**2.1**	11970	**4.0**	14466	**2.7**
Haryana	1353	3.3	1559	1.8	2245	5.3
Himachal Pradesh	469	3.1	577	2.6	659	1.9
Jammu & Kashmir	0		474		752	6.8
Punjab	1770	2.9	2100	2.2	2702	3.7
Rajasthan	2838	2.1	3542	2.8	4301	2.8
Chandigarh	203	5.3	218	0.9	251	2.0
Delhi	2085	3.6	3501	6.7	3556	0.2
N-Eastern Region	2533	**17.3**	3181	**2.9**	3465	**1.2**
Arunachal Pradesh	93	7.8	81	(1.8)	110	4.6
Assam	1689	0.0	2195	3.3	2208	0.1
Manipur	157	4.1	201	3.1	236	2.3
Meghalaya	170	4.6	184	1.0	242	4.0
Mizoram	72	4.7	77	0.9	107	4.7
Nagaland	130	5.7	175	3.8	175	0.0
Tripura	220	5.1	268	2.5	386	5.3
Eastern Region	13613	**3.0**	15405	**1.6**	17282	**1.7**
Bihar	3454	2.2	3429	(0.1)	2270	(5.7)
Jharkhand	0		0		1152	
Orissa	2612	3.0	3095	2.1	3706	2.6
Sikkim	47	4.5	48	0.1	68	5.3
West Bengal	7448	3.4	8771	2.1	10032	1.9
A & N Islands	52	3.3	63	2.3	53	(2.3)
Central Region	11794	**2.7**	12736	**1.0**	14377	**1.7**
Chhattisgarh	0		0		1515	
Madhya Pradesh	4886	4.0	5256	0.9	3979	(3.9)
Uttar Pradesh	6909	1.9	7480	1.0	8145	1.2
Uttarakhand	0		0		738	
Western Region	13940	**2.7**	16005	**1.7**	17766	**1.5**
Goa	219	(0.9)	216	(0.2)	228	0.8
Gujarat	4726	2.6	5280	1.4	6100	2.1
Maharashtra	8960	2.9	10445	1.9	11309	1.1
D & N Haveli	14	7.2	33	10.8	67	10.7
Daman & Diu	21	4.8	32	5.5	62	10.2
Southern Region	21476	**2.8**	24003	**1.4**	33550	**4.9**
Andhra Pradesh	6734	3.6	7512	1.4	11202	5.9
Karnataka	5080	2.8	5253	0.4	6346	2.7
Kerala	3289	3.0	3849	2.0	5733	5.9
Tamil Nadu	6236	1.9	7191	1.8	10063	4.9
Lakshadweep	16	1.4	16	(0.2)	12	(3.9)
Puducherry	120	4.0	182	5.3	195	1.0

Source : CSO (2007), Economic Census (2005) and earlier issues.

226 : Number of Scheduled Commercial Bank Offices

Region/State/ Union Territories	End-Dec.		End-Mar.		End-Mar.		C-D Ratio (%)
	1969	Share (%)	2001	Share (%)	2010	Share (%)	2009
All-India	**9007**	**100.0**	**35724**	**100.0**	**86960**	**100.0**	**73.3**
Northern Region	**1416**	**15.7**	**5080**	**14.2**	**15087**	**17.3**	**74.4**
Haryana	191	2.1	749	2.1	2438	2.8	63.3
Himachal Pradesh	48	0.5	619	1.7	1017	1.2	42.2
Jammu & Kashmir	48	0.5	502	1.4	1013	1.2	46.4
Punjab	415	4.6	1135	3.2	3595	4.1	71.5
Rajasthan	393	4.4	1994	5.6	4242	4.9	88.4
Chandigarh	25	0.3	12	0.0	326	0.4	131.1
Delhi	296	3.3	69	0.2	2456	2.8	74.6
North-Eastern Region	**99**	**1.1**	**1303**	**3.6**	**2268**	**2.6**	**35.5**
Arunachal Pradesh	..	0.0	59	0.2	80	0.1	27.6
Assam	89	1.0	831	2.3	1477	1.7	37.8
Manipur	..	0.0	53	0.1	81	0.1	42.1
Meghalaya	..	0.0	130	0.4	213	0.2	25.6
Mizoram	..	0.0	66	0.2	98	0.1	53.2
Nagaland	4	0.0	42	0.1	90	0.1	30.3
Tripura	6	0.1	122	0.3	229	0.3	30.8
Eastern Region	**953**	**10.6**	**7830**	**21.9**	**14359**	**16.5**	**50.8**
Bihar	309	3.4	2678	7.5	4142	4.8	29.0
Jharkhand	0	0.0	998	2.8	1862	2.1	35.1
Orissa	111	1.2	1634	4.6	2876	3.3	54.4
Sikkim	..	0.0	33	0.1	74	0.1	37.2
West Bengal	533	5.9	2470	6.9	5368	6.2	61.5
Andaman & Nicobar Islands	..	0.0	17	0.0	37	0.0	36.5
Central Region	**1179**	**13.1**	**8258**	**23.1**	**17280**	**19.9**	**47.3**
Chhattisgarh	0	0.0	710	2.0	1331	1.5	52.3
Madhya Pradesh	361	4.0	1951	5.5	4270	4.9	60.6
Uttar Pradesh	818	9.1	5059	14.2	10475	12.0	43.3
Uttarakhand	0	0.0	538	1.5	1204	1.4	33.7
Western Region	**2128**	**23.6**	**4508**	**12.6**	**13543**	**15.6**	**79.1**
Goa	96	1.1	153	0.4	443	0.5	26.5
Gujarat	833	9.2	1727	4.8	4733	5.4	65.3
Maharashtra	1199	13.3	2619	7.3	8321	9.6	82.9
Dadra & Nagar Haveli	..	0.0	6	0.0	27	0.0	60.0
Daman & Diu	..	0.0	3	0.0	19	0.0	20.1
Southern Region	**3227**	**35.8**	**8745**	**24.5**	**24423**	**28.1**	**92.7**
Andhra Pradesh	618	6.9	2794	7.8	7132	8.2	105.1
Karnataka	851	9.4	2364	6.6	6271	7.2	77.6
Kerala	642	7.1	1351	3.8	4390	5.0	63.1
Tamil Nadu	1104	12.3	2199	6.2	6474	7.4	113.8
Lakshadweep	..	0.0	9	0.0	11	0.0	7.2
Puducherry	12	0.1	28	0.1	145	0.2	57.2

Note : C-D Ratio: Credit Deposit Ratio.
Total Includes A&N Islands, D&N Haveli and Manipur for 1969.
1969 data is for Commercial Banks
The data is based on the Master Office Files of bank branches, which are regularly updated. The information presented in this table is the latest available and may not match with the data published earlier.

Source : RBI Basic Statistical Returns and RBI Statistical Table 1969.

227 : Scheduled Commercial Bank: Deposits (Rs. crore)

Region/State/ Union Territories	End-Dec.		End-Mar.		End-Mar.	
	1969	Share (%)	2001	Share (%)	2010	Share (%)
All-India	**5172**	**100.0**	**949434**	**100.0**	**4561029**	**100.0**
Northern Region	**976**	**18.9**	**223032**	**23.5**	**1006497**	**22.1**
Haryana	64	1.2	19887	2.1	109172	2.4
Himachal Pradesh	18	0.3	7413	0.8	26885	0.6
Jammu & Kashmir	35	0.7	9892	1.0	34003	0.7
Punjab	231	4.5	44298	4.7	133200	2.9
Rajasthan	94	1.8	27539	2.9	106736	2.3
Chandigarh	41	0.8	7565	0.8	31488	0.7
Delhi	493	9.5	106438	11.2	565013	12.4
North-Eastern Region	**54**	**1.0**	**15409**	**1.6**	**76948**	**1.7**
Arunachal Pradesh	0	0.0	614	0.1	4126	0.1
Assam	48	0.9	9858	1.0	48594	1.1
Manipur	0	0.0	432	0.0	2699	0.1
Meghalaya	0	0.0	1646	0.2	7643	0.2
Mizoram	0	0.0	396	0.0	2239	0.0
Nagaland	1	0.0	897	0.1	4188	0.1
Tripura	5	0.1	1565	0.2	7459	0.2
Eastern Region	**934**	**18.1**	**126263**	**13.3**	**527261**	**11.6**
Bihar	186	3.6	26801	2.8	100367	2.2
Jharkhand	0	0.0	15464	1.6	63583	1.4
Orissa	36	0.7	15072	1.6	82425	1.8
Sikkim	0	0.0	609	0.1	3134	0.1
West Bengal	712	13.8	67931	7.2	276140	6.1
Andaman & Nicobar Islands	0	0.0	386	0.0	1613	0.0
Central Region	**553**	**10.7**	**131331**	**13.8**	**520191**	**11.4**
Chhattisgarh	0	0.0	7518	0.8	47777	1.0
Madhya Pradesh	126	2.4	29084	3.1	118183	2.6
Uttar Pradesh	427	8.3	85373	9.0	312233	6.8
Uttarakhand	0	0.0	9356	1.0	41998	0.9
Western Region	**1742**	**33.7**	**235306**	**24.8**	**1448817**	**31.8**
Goa	52	1.0	7142	0.8	29199	0.6
Gujarat	460	8.9	55049	5.8	215217	4.7
Maharashtra	1230	23.8	172489	18.2	1201991	26.4
Dadra & Nagar Haveli	0	0.0	222	0.0	964	0.0
Daman & Diu	0	0.0	404	0.0	1445	0.0
Southern Region	**913**	**17.7**	**218093**	**23.0**	**981315**	**21.5**
Andhra Pradesh	173	3.3	54446	5.7	249264	5.5
Karnataka	255	4.9	54743	5.8	289775	6.4
Kerala	166	3.2	44178	4.7	152097	3.3
Tamil Nadu	313	6.1	63065	6.6	283637	6.2
Lakshadweep	0	0.0	55	0.0	428	0.0
Puducherry	6	0.1	1607	0.2	6115	0.1

Note : Share % indicates share of each individual state in the total.
Total Includes A&N Islands, D&N Haveli and Manipur for 1969.
1969 data is for commercial banks.
The data is based on the Master Office Files of bank branches, which are regularly updated. The information presented in this table is the latest available and may not match with the data published earlier.

Source : RBI Basic Statistical Returns and RBI Statistical Table 1969.

228 : Scheduled Commercial Bank: Credit

(Rs. crore)

Region/State/Uts	End-Dec. 1969	Share (%)	End-Mar. 2001	Share (%)	End-Mar. 2010	Share (%)
All-India	**3729**	**100.0**	**538434**	**100.0**	**3345169**	**100.0**
Northern Region	**388**	**10.4**	**122036**	**22.7**	**748658**	**22.4**
Haryana	30	0.8	8155	1.5	69138	2.1
Himachal Pradesh	4	0.1	1576	0.3	11355	0.3
Jammu & Kashmir	4	0.1	3410	0.6	15769	0.5
Punjab	77	2.1	18186	3.4	95256	2.8
Rajasthan	47	1.3	12841	2.4	94307	2.8
Chandigarh	26	0.7	7520	1.4	41279	1.2
Delhi	200	5.4	70349	13.1	421554	12.6
North-Eastern Region	**21**	**0.6**	**4250**	**0.8**	**27350**	**0.8**
Arunachal Pradesh	0	0.0	89	0.0	1137	0.0
Assam	21	0.6	3160	0.6	18367	0.5
Manipur	0	0.0	173	0.0	1135	0.0
Meghalaya	0	0.0	281	0.1	1958	0.1
Mizoram	0	0.0	95	0.0	1191	0.0
Nagaland	0	0.0	112	0.0	1269	0.0
Tripura	0	0.0	340	0.1	2294	0.1
Eastern Region	**786**	**21.1**	**46351**	**8.6**	**267976**	**8.0**
Bihar	51	1.4	5542	1.0	29125	0.9
Jharkhand	0	0.0	4335	0.8	22324	0.7
Orissa	18	0.5	6065	1.1	44820	1.3
Sikkim	0	0.0	88	0.0	1167	0.0
West Bengal	717	19.2	30257	5.6	169951	5.1
Andaman & Nicobar Islands	0	0.0	63	0.0	589	0.0
Central Region	**262**	**7.0**	**42888**	**8.0**	**245884**	**7.4**
Chhattisgarh	0	0.0	2895	0.5	24976	0.7
Madhya Pradesh	71	1.9	13847	2.6	71617	2.1
Uttar Pradesh	191	5.1	24121	4.5	135129	4.0
Uttarakhand	0	0.0	2026	0.4	14163	0.4
Western Region	**1389**	**37.2**	**177641**	**33.0**	**1145957**	**34.3**
Goa	24	0.6	1865	0.3	7729	0.2
Gujarat	232	6.2	26702	5.0	140498	4.2
Maharashtra	1133	30.4	148989	27.7	996860	29.8
Dadra & Nagar Haveli	0	0.0	32	0.0	578	0.0
Daman & Diu	0	0.0	54	0.0	291	0.0
Southern Region	**886**	**23.8**	**145268**	**27.0**	**909346**	**27.2**
Andhra Pradesh	163	4.4	35128	6.5	262085	7.8
Karnataka	186	5.0	33369	6.2	224825	6.7
Kerala	114	3.1	19108	3.5	96011	2.9
Tamil Nadu	418	11.2	57120	10.6	322894	9.7
Lakshadweep	0	0.0	6	0.0	31	0.0
Puducherry	5	0.1	538	0.1	3499	0.1

Note : Share % indicates share of each individual state in the total.
Total Includes A&N Islands, D&N Haveli and Manipur for 1969.
1969 data is for commercial banks.
The data is based on the Master Office Files of bank branches, which are regularly updated. The information presented in this table is the latest available and may not match with the data published earlier.

Source : RBI Statistical Table 1969 and Basic Statistical Returns 2010.

229 : Gross Fiscal Deficit (Rs. crore)

State/Region	1990-91	% to GSDP	2000-01*	% to GSDP	2010-11** (BE)
All-India	18787	3.9#	87923	5.0#	198539
Andhra Pradesh	967	2.9	7306	5.0	12983
Arunachal Pradesh	26	5.1	210	11.8	113
Assam	568	5.3	1540	4.2	9315
Bihar	1595	6.0	4884	8.5	4594
Chhattisgarh	0		(48)	(0.2)	3180
Goa	96	7.6	413	6.1	1428
Gujarat	1798	6.4	7988	7.2	15143
Haryana	386	2.8	2265	3.9	8816
Himachal Pradesh	279	9.9	1845	11.8	2438
Jammu & Kashmir	661	18.3	2166	13.0	1965
Jharkhand					674
Karnataka	559	2.4	4219	4.1	9708
Kerala	799	5.7	3878	5.4	8543
Madhya Pradesh	1019	3.3	2712	3.4	8003
Maharashtra	1611	2.5	8976	3.6	24294
Manipur	40	4.8	234	7.5	282
Meghalaya	41	4.6	250	6.3	376
Mizoram	(94)	(27.7)	375	21.6	42
Nagaland	102	15.6	359	10.1	296
Orissa	616	5.7	3325	7.6	5798
Punjab	1242	6.6	3904	5.2	7706
Rajasthan	545	2.6	4313	5.2	8461
Sikkim	20	8.6	51	5.0	361
Tamil Nadu	1126	3.6	5076	3.5	16222
Tripura	86	8.3	445	8.1	986
Uttar Pradesh	3068	5.5	10180	5.6	22742
Uttarakhand			136	0.9	1747
West Bengal	1634	4.7	10920	7.6	22323
Delhi			1610	2.7	3116
Puducherry					1010

Note : Negative values in brackets and it indicates surplus in deficit indicator.
* : Includes NCT Delhi.
** : Includes NCT Delhi and Puducherry.
# : Data calculated as % to GDP at current prices (1989-2000 Series).

Source : RBI (2011), *State Finances-A Study of Budgets of 2010-11.*

230 : Outstanding Liabilities of State Governments

(Rs. crore)

State	As at End-March					
	1991	% to GSDP	2001	% to GSDP	2011	% to GSDP
All-India	128155	22.5	594150	28.3	1820155	23.1
Andhra Pradesh	8150	24.4	41809	28.9	136666	31.3
Arunachal Pradesh	280	55.0	739	41.4	4724	77.8
Assam	4341	40.9	10227	27.8	27385	27.8
Bihar	10633	40.2	29942	33.5	66514	39.5
Chhattisgarh			6967	27.0	19036	18.0
Goa	903	71.8	2822	41.8	8627	33.6
Gujarat	8076	28.8	42781	38.5	136552	31.4
Haryana	3076	22.6	14650	25.2	46526	18.9
Himachal Pradesh	1329	47.2	8705	55.6	29867	53.2
Jammu & Kashmir	3358	92.9	9101	54.5	25534	67.1
Jharkhand			8448	26.3	29867	32.9
Karnataka	5898	25.3	25301	23.3	82337	25.1
Kerala	4983	35.3	26259	36.1	81742	33.4
Madhya Pradesh	7777	25.5	22127	27.9	74574	37.2
Maharashtra	12878	20.0	67601	26.8	236526	26.7
Manipur	390	47.5	1870	60.1	5379	66.3
Meghalaya	218	24.5	1388	35.0	4550	36.2
Mizoram	330	96.7	1375	79.2	4688	98.1
Nagaland	409	62.5	1604	47.2	4843	58.0
Orissa	5156	47.3	24220	55.9	50937	30.0
Punjab	7071	37.4	30763	41.2	73794	34.1
Rajasthan	6580	31.8	35541	43.1	98881	40.9
Sikkim	142	60.5	852	84.0	2731	82.2
Tamil Nadu	7044	22.5	34541	23.5	109381	25.1
Tripura	517	50.1	2384	43.4	5931	43.2
Uttar Pradesh	19760	35.6	83098	45.8	234581	45.8
Uttarakhand			4106	28.3	21154	39.5
West Bengal	8857	25.5	54929	38.2	198195	40.8
Delhi			7924	13.2	26744	12.0
Puducherry					3938	25.9

Note : All-India includes Puducherry and Delhi also.

Source : RBI (2011), *State Finances-A Study of Budgets of 2010-11.*

231 : Social Sector Expenditure

(Rs. crore)

State/Region	1990-2001	% to Total	2000-01	% to Total	2010-11 BE	% to Total
All-India	35132	38.6	124919	36.8	460607	39.2
Andhra Pradesh	2741	41.7	10006	35.6	39648	35.8
Arunachal Pradesh	128	32.1	325	26.9	1116	16.1
Assam	932	34.7	3077	40.3	13756	37.4
Bihar	2381	38.3	7408	43.7	22990	42.8
Chhattisgarh	–	–	968	50.5	13500	53.1
Goa	162	40.9	518	26.4	2223	33.4
Gujarat	1993	36.4	9681	35.6	26536	38.6
Haryana	776	32.4	3387	37.0	13697	39.2
Himachal Pradesh	444	39.7	1963	36.9	5241	34.8
Jammu & Kashmir	600	29.7	2044	26.1	7880	30.8
Jharkhand	–	–	–	–	9962	44.7
Karnataka	1842	37.0	7541	38.3	28319	41.2
Kerala	1477	43.7	5242	39.9	14671	34.8
Madhya Pradesh	2439	41.3	7153	42.3	21128	39.5
Maharashtra	3792	35.2	15429	36.6	56085	4.3
Manipur	151	33.4	449	32.5	1883	31.7
Meghalaya	160	39.3	578	40.6	1967	39.9
Mizoram	153	30.6	505	39.2	1331	37.2
Nagaland	182	33.0	585	31.9	1813	30.5
Orissa	1113	36.5	4065	36.8	15789	40.5
Punjab	957	28.1	3887	27.6	9898	25.8
Rajasthan	1866	39.5	7224	41.3	23018	42.4
Sikkim	61	33.3	259	27.3	1250	31.1
Tamil Nadu	2985	45.1	9618	39.4	32602	39.3
Tripura	264	43.1	896	42.0	2285	34.1
Uttar Pradesh	4711	38.5	12135	33.1	53256	37.9
Uttarakhand	–	–	355	32.0	6232	42.2
West Bengal	2824	46.9	9623	36.0	32531	42.9
Delhi	–	–	3000	40.8	10979	42.2
Puducherry	–	–	–	–	2026	46.0

Note: Includes expenditure on social services, rural development, food storage and warehousing under revenue expenditure and capital outlays including education and loans and advances by state governments.

Source: RBI (2011), *State Finances-A Study of Budgets of 2010-11.*

232 : Number of Government Hospitals and Beds

State As on 1.1.2010	Number of		Population Served per Government	
	Hospitals	Beds	Hospitals	Beds
All-India	12760	576793	90972	2012
Andhra Pradesh	475	38050	176766	2207
Arunachal Pradesh	161	2218	5920	533
Assam	153	7622	19486	3911
Bihar	1717	22494	54533	4163
Chhattisgarh	218	9428	105202	2433
Goa	20	2686	85700	638
Gujarat	373	28958	153979	1983
Haryana	154	7879	159721	3122
Himachal Pradesh	142	7961	4692	837
Jammu & Kashmir	92	3945	120641	2813
Jharkhand	500	5414	59490	5494
Karnataka	919	63741	63309	913
Kerala	386	31285	88246	1089
Madhya Pradesh	457	28533	155470	2490
Maharashtra	1772	50003	62708	2222
Manipur	31	2318	78097	1044
Meghalaya	39	2837	66436	913
Mizoram	25	1511	39240	649
Nagaland	48	2150	45771	1022
Orissa	1709	15880	23633	2543
Punjab	231	10620	114247	2485
Rajasthan	475	32067	133491	1977
Sikkim	33	1560	18333	388
Tripura	32	3032	111687	1179
Tamil Nadu	581	47198	112959	1391
Uttar Pradesh	861	56384	229118	3499
Uttarakhand	695	7965	13685	1194
West Bengal	294	54759	298772	1604
Union Territories				
A & N Islands	8	835	60000	575
Chandigarh	4	620	342000	2206
D & N Haveli	2	281	168500	1199
Daman & Diu	4	200	64750	1295
Delhi	130	23858	130423	711
Lakshadweep	5	160	15000	469
Puducherry	14	2341	95071	569

Note : Government Hospitals includes those run by Central, state and local bodies.
Source : National Health Profile 2010.

233 : Number of Doctors Registered with State Medical Council

State	1991	2001	2010	Population/ Doctor
All-India	393640	577095	816629	1413
Andhra Pradesh	33367	44575	62349	1295
Arunachal Pradesh			325	3686
Assam	10499	14586	19116	1579
Bihar	26376	33070	37233	2477
Chhattisgarh			3156	7267
Goa		2030	2818	608
Gujarat	22392	33653	46439	1237
Haryana	644	1146	4132	5953
Himachal Pradesh			847	7070
Jammu & Kashmir	4407	6875	11240	1002
Jharkhand			3081	9654
Karnataka	32813	61163	87320	673
Travancore-Cochin	19465	30173	39180	876
Madhya Pradesh	11187	19021	26589	2541
Maharashtra	49365	80764	137824	806
Orissa	11087	14315	16786	2406
Punjab	26636	32558	38434	669
Rajasthan	14041	20438	28513	2263
Sikkim			603	1003
Tamil Nadu	46419	65771	86822	772
Uttar Pradesh	33178	43492	57944	3405
Uttarakhand			3334	2939
West Bengal	41722	49941	58872	1506
MCI Delhi			36999	
Delhi	10042	23523	9829	1452

Note: Figures in last column denote population served by doctors.
Source: Medical Council of India. National Health Profile 2010.

234 : Number of Health Centres (Mainly in Rural Areas)

State	Public Health Centres (PHCs)		Sub-Centres		Community Health Centres (CHCs)	
	1996	2009	1996	2009	1996	2009
All-India	21855	23391	132778	145894	2420	4510
Andhra Pradesh	1283	1570	7894	12522	46	167
Arunachal Pradesh	47	116	223	592	9	44
Assam	619	844	5280	4592	105	108
Bihar	2209	1776	14799	8858	148	70
Chhattisgarh		715		4776		144
Goa	21	19	175	171	5	5
Gujarat	957	1084	7284	7274	185	281
Haryana	397	437	2299	2465	63	93
Himachal Pradesh	245	449	1954	2071	47	73
Jammu & Kashmir	335	375	1700	1907	45	85
Jharkhand		321		3947		194
Karnataka	1459	2193	7793	8143	224	324
Kerala	959	697	5094	4575	54	226
Madhya Pradesh	1376	1155	11937	8869	190	333
Maharashtra	1695	1816	9725	10579	295	376
Manipur	72	72	420	420	16	16
Meghalaya	88	105	337	401	9	28
Mizoram	38	57	261	370	6	9
Nagaland	33	123	244	397	5	21
Orissa	1056	1279	5927	6688	157	231
Punjab	484	394	2852	2950	105	129
Rajasthan	1572	1503	8692	10951	256	367
Sikkim	24	24	147	147	2	0
Tamil Nadu	1436	1277	8681	8706	72	256
Tripura	63	76	536	579	11	11
Uttar Pradesh	3761	3690	20153	20521	262	515
Uttarakhand		239		1765		55
West Bengal	1558	922	7873	10356	89	334
Union Territories						
A & N Islands	17	19	96	114	4	4
Chandigarh	0	0	12	16	1	2
D & N Haveli	6	6	34	38	0	1
Daman & Diu	4	2	21	26	2	2
Delhi	8	8	42	41	0	0
Lakshadweep	7	4	14	14	3	3
Puducherry	26	24	79	53	4	3

Source : National Health Profile 2010.

235 : Expenditure on Public Health and Family Welfare

(Rs. crore)

	1990-91	% to Total	2000-01	% to Total	2010-11 (BE)	% to Total
All-India	4822	5.3	16140	4.6	50297	4.3
Andhra Pradesh	330	5.0	1334	4.7	4232	3.8
Arunachal Pradesh	18	4.5	60	5.0	157	2.3
Assam	128	4.8	356	4.7	1767	4.8
Bihar	325	5.2	996	5.9	2105	3.9
Chhattisgarh	0	0.0	79	4.1	1080	4.3
Goa	33	8.2	86	4.4	377	5.7
Gujarat	252	4.6	919	3.4	2949	4.3
Haryana	87	3.6	298	3.3	1125	3.2
Himachal Pradesh	77	6.9	300	5.6	719	4.8
Jammu & Kashmir	100	5.0	383	4.9	1398	5.5
Jharkhand	0	0.0	0	0.0	1033	4.6
Karnataka	250	5.0	1005	5.1	2757	4.0
Kerala	222	6.6	691	5.3	2089	5.0
Madhya Pradesh	282	4.8	862	5.1	1879	3.5
Maharashtra	498	4.6	1634	3.9	4384	3.5
Manipur	20	4.3	67	4.8	286	4.8
Meghalaya	24	5.9	80	5.6	231	4.7
Mizoram	16	3.1	64	5.0	160	4.5
Nagaland	28	5.2	89	4.8	240	4.0
Orissa	141	4.6	459	4.2	1587	4.1
Punjab	170	5.0	640	4.5	1354	3.5
Rajasthan	258	5.5	903	5.2	2928	5.4
Sikkim	10	5.5	35	3.7	156	3.9
Tamil Nadu	390	5.9	1187	4.9	3998	4.8
Tripura	30	4.9	86	4.0	278	4.2
Uttar Pradesh	676	5.5	1459	4.0	6757	4.8
Uttarakhand	0	0.0	34	3.1	828	5.6
West Bengal	460	7.6	1506	5.6	3442	4.5
Delhi	0	0.0	527	7.2	2102	8.1
Puducherry	0	0	0	0.0	400	6.2

Note : % to Total denotes percentage to total disbursements (revenue + capital).
Source : RBI (2011), *State Finances-A Study of Budgets of 2010-11.*

236 : Percentage Distribution of Type of Households

State	1991			2001		
	Pucca	Semi-*Pucca*	*Kutcha*	*Pucca*	Semi-*Pucca*	*Kutcha*
All-India	41.61	30.95	27.44	51.62	30.13	18.24
Andhra Pradesh	38.41	22.58	39.01	54.69	21.31	24.00
Arunachal Pradesh	14.94	11.72	73.34	20.68	18.16	61.16
Assam	14.62	15.16	70.22	19.47	31.23	49.12
Bihar	30.18	36.00	33.82	40.21	25.51	34.28
Chhattisgarh				25.43	72.00	2.57
Goa	50.70	44.47	4.82	70.15	27.84	2.01
Gujarat	56.93	39.01	4.06	63.37	31.83	5.45
Haryana	50.14	35.73	14.13	65.75	28.29	5.96
Himachal Pradesh	53.03	40.99	5.99	64.55	32.57	2.87
Jammu & Kashmir				54.14	32.84	13.01
Jharkhand				31.46	57.57	10.97
Karnataka	42.55	40.90	16.55	54.94	35.52	9.54
Kerala	55.97	19.13	24.90	68.16	21.60	10.24
Madhya Pradesh	30.47	64.87	4.66	41.54	55.78	2.68
Maharashtra	52.20	36.14	11.67	57.85	34.33	7.82
Manipur	5.40	40.65	53.95	8.39	55.13	36.47
Meghalaya	13.30	33.72	52.98	22.14	37.49	40.37
Mizoram	19.10	42.52	38.38	52.84	25.69	21.47
Nagaland	12.62	36.47	50.91	16.19	50.50	33.30
Orissa	18.71	22.06	59.23	27.78	25.02	47.20
Punjab	76.97	11.07	11.96	86.11	8.86	5.02
Rajasthan	56.13	22.94	20.93	64.86	21.03	14.11
Sikkim	26.95	39.11	33.94	37.87	46.26	16.07
Tamil Nadu	45.54	18.03	36.44	58.41	18.19	23.41
Tripura	5.50	20.71	73.79	9.81	45.99	44.19
Uttar Pradesh	41.03	30.34	28.63	53.38	25.56	21.06
Uttarakhand				86.32	6.60	7.08
West Bengal	32.61	29.38	38.01	40.44	37.27	22.30
Union Territories						
A & N Islands	10.40	47.25	42.35	28.40	38.56	33.05
Chandigarh	82.49	8.42	9.10	89.87	6.94	3.18
D & N Haveli	20.80	22.54	56.66	45.74	51.65	2.60
Daman & Diu	79.80	17.33	2.87	92.50	6.34	1.63
Delhi	85.60	4.61	9.79	91.67	4.87	3.50
Lakshadweep	88.84	9.04	2.12	95.29	2.93	1.78
Puducherry	44.48	12.16	42.96	60.43	13.89	25.68

Note: All-India figures for 1991 exclude Jammu and Kashmir.
Source: *Statistical Abstract of India*, CSO.

237 : Percentage Distribution of Households Having Electricity

State	1991			2001		
	Rural	Urban	Total	Rural	Urban	Total
All-India	30.54	75.78	42.37	43.53	87.58	55.85
Andhra Pradesh	37.50	73.31	46.30	59.65	89.99	67.17
Arunachal Pradesh	33.88	80.96	40.85	44.53	89.42	54.69
Assam	12.44	63.21	18.74	16.54	74.29	24.90
Bihar	5.57	58.77	12.57	5.13	59.28	10.25
Chhattisgarh				46.11	82.85	53.10
Goa	81.82	88.77	84.69	92.43	94.73	93.57
Gujarat	58.43	82.96	65.93	72.17	93.39	80.40
Haryana	63.20	89.31	70.35	78.50	92.94	82.89
Himachal Pradesh	85.86	96.24	87.01	94.48	97.38	94.81
Jammu & Kashmir				74.77	97.94	80.66
Jharkhand				9.99	75.61	24.30
Karnataka	43.75	76.27	52.47	72.16	90.53	78.55
Kerala	41.95	67.65	48.43	65.53	84.34	70.24
Madhya Pradesh	34.49	72.52	43.30	92.26	62.32	69.98
Maharashtra	53.45	86.07	69.40	65.17	94.28	77.49
Manipur	41.73	75.45	50.92	52.53	81.99	60.04
Meghalaya	16.34	83.04	29.16	30.26	88.14	42.74
Mizoram	35.47	85.50	59.20	44.14	94.42	69.63
Nagaland	47.16	75.58	53.42	56.88	90.33	63.60
Orissa	17.45	62.11	23.54	19.35	74.08	26.91
Punjab	76.98	94.60	82.31	89.46	96.48	91.91
Rajasthan	32.44	76.67	35.03	44.02	89.61	54.69
Sikkim	57.12	92.37	60.66	75.02	97.09	77.76
Tamil Nadu	44.49	76.80	54.74	71.18	88.00	78.18
Tripura	28.50	80.43	36.93	31.75	86.36	41.84
Uttar Pradesh	10.96	67.76	21.91	19.84	79.92	31.90
Uttarakhand				50.35	90.92	60.32
West Bengal	17.75	70.19	32.90	20.27	79.56	37.45
Union Territories						
A & N Islands	53.62	90.55	63.52	68.09	95.22	76.78
Chandigarh	65.25	85.48	83.12	97.41	96.70	96.79
D & N Haveli	51.20	87.57	54.42	82.63	95.84	85.99
Daman & Diu	92.87	95.46	94.13	97.46	98.31	97.76
Delhi	59.85	81.38	79.48	85.50	93.38	92.86
Lakshadweep	97.65	99.11	98.46	99.73	99.67	99.70
Puducherry	51.20	71.71	63.58	81.00	91.40	87.81

Note: All-India figures for 1991 exclude Jammu and Kashmir.

Source: *Housing and Amenities*, Paper 2 of 1993; Census India and Central Electricity Authority. *Statistical Abstract of India*, CSO.

238 : Percentage Distribution of Households Having Safe Drinking Water Facilities

State	1991			2001		
	Rural	Urban	Total	Rural	Urban	Total
All-India	55.54	81.38	62.30	73.20	90.00	77.90
Andhra Pradesh	48.98	73.82	55.08	76.90	90.20	80.10
Arunachal Pradesh	66.87	88.20	70.02	73.70	90.70	77.50
Assam	43.28	64.07	45.86	56.80	70.40	58.80
Bihar	56.55	73.39	58.76	86.10	91.20	86.60
Chhattisgarh				66.20	88.80	70.50
Goa	30.54	61.71	43.41	58.30	82.10	70.10
Gujarat	60.04	87.23	69.78	76.90	95.40	84.10
Haryana	67.14	93.18	74.32	81.10	97.30	86.10
Himachal Pradesh	75.51	91.93	77.34	87.50	97.30	88.60
Jammu & Kashmir				54.90	95.70	65.20
Jharkhand				35.50	68.20	42.60
Karnataka	67.31	81.38	71.68	80.50	92.10	84.60
Kerala	12.22	38.68	18.89	16.90	42.80	23.40
Madhya Pradesh	45.56	79.45	53.41	61.50	88.60	68.40
Maharashtra	54.02	90.50	68.49	68.40	95.40	79.80
Manipur	33.72	52.10	38.72	29.30	59.40	37.00
Meghalaya	26.82	75.42	36.16	29.50	73.50	39.00
Mizoram	12.89	19.88	16.21	23.80	47.80	36.00
Nagaland	55.60	45.47	53.37	47.50	42.30	46.50
Orissa	35.32	62.83	39.07	62.90	72.30	64.20
Punjab	92.09	94.24	92.74	96.90	98.90	97.60
Rajasthan	50.62	86.51	58.96	60.40	93.50	68.20
Sikkim	70.80	92.95	73.19	67.00	97.10	70.70
Tamil Nadu	64.28	74.17	67.42	85.30	85.90	85.60
Tripura	30.60	71.12	37.18	45.00	85.80	52.50
Uttar Pradesh	56.62	85.78	62.24	85.50	97.20	87.80
Uttarakhand				83.00	97.80	86.70
West Bengal	80.26	86.23	81.98	87.00	92.30	88.50
Union Territories						
A & N Islands	59.43	90.91	67.87	66.80	97.80	76.70
Chandigarh	98.11	97.68	97.73	99.90	99.80	99.80
D & N Haveli	41.17	90.97	45.57	70.50	96.10	77.00
Daman & Diu	56.90	86.76	71.42	94.90	98.90	96.30
Delhi	91.01	96.24	95.78	90.10	97.70	97.20
Lakshadweep	3.41	18.79	11.90	4.60	4.60	4.60
Puducherry	92.86	86,05	88.75	96.60	95.50	95.90

Note : All-India figures for 1991 exclude Jammu and Kashmir.

Source : *Statistical Abstract of India*, CSO.

V. INTERNATIONAL COMPARISONS

> People
> Environment
> Economy
> External Sector

239 : Total Population

(in million)

Countries	1990	2010	2030*	CAGR (%) 1990-2010	CAGR (%) 2010-2030	CAGR (%) 1990-2030
World	**5291**	**6909**	**8309**	**1.3**	**0.9**	**1.1**
Russia	148	140	129	(0.3)	(0.4)	(0.3)
Japan	123	127	117	0.2	(0.4)	(0.1)
Germany	79	82	78	0.2	(0.3)	(0.0)
Italy	57	60	60	0.3	(0.0)	0.1
Korea, Rep. of	43	49	49	0.7	0.0	0.3
France	57	63	67	0.5	0.3	0.4
UK	57	62	68	0.4	0.5	0.4
China	1142	1354	1463	0.9	0.4	0.6
Sri Lanka	17	20	22	0.8	0.4	0.6
Spain	39	45	50	0.8	0.5	0.6
Argentina	33	40	42	1.0	0.2	0.6
Thailand	57	68	74	0.9	0.4	0.7
Mexico	83	107	113	1.3	0.3	0.8
Canada	28	34	40	1.0	0.8	0.9
Brazil	150	195	217	1.3	0.5	0.9
USA	255	318	370	1.1	0.8	0.9
South Africa	37	51	55	1.6	0.4	1.0
Chile	13	17	20	1.3	0.8	1.0
Australia	17	22	26	1.2	0.9	1.0
Indonesia	177	233	272	1.4	0.8	1.1
Turkey	56	76	90	1.5	0.9	1.2
Peru	22	30	36	1.5	1.0	1.3
India	**862**	**1215**	**1485**	**1.7**	**1.0**	**1.4**
Bangladesh	116	164	203	1.8	1.1	1.4
Egypt	58	85	111	1.9	1.4	1.6
Malaysia	18	28	35	2.2	1.2	1.7
Philippines	62	94	124	2.0	1.4	1.7
Nepal	19	30	41	2.3	1.5	1.9
Saudi Arabia	16	26	37	2.4	1.7	2.0
Pakistan	116	185	266	2.4	1.8	2.1

Note : Countries arranged according to ascending CAGR for 1990-2030.
Negative values in brackets.
CAGR : Compounded Annual Growth Rate.
* : Projected.

Source : Human Development Index Data Base 2011.

240 : Density of Population and Urban Share

Countries	Density of Population (people per sq km)		Urban Population as % to Total Population	
	2005	2009	1990	2010
World	**50**	**52**	**43.0**	**50.0**
Australia	3	3	85.4	89.1
Canada	4	4	76.6	80.6
Russia	9	9	73.4	72.8
Saudi Arabia	12	13	76.6	82.1
Argentina	14	15	87.0	92.4
Chile	22	23	83.3	89.0
Brazil	22	23	74.8	86.5
Peru		23	68.9	71.6
USA	32	34	75.3	82.3
South Africa	39	41	52.0	61.7
Mexico	54	55	71.4	77.8
Egypt	74	83	43.5	42.8
Malaysia	77	84	49.8	72.2
Spain	87	92	75.4	77.4
Turkey	94	97	59.2	69.6
France	111	114	74.1	77.8
Indonesia	122	127	30.6	53.7
Thailand	126	133	29.4	34.0
China	140	143	27.4	44.9
Nepal		205	8.9	18.2
Italy	199	205	66.7	68.4
Pakistan	202	220	30.6	37.0
Germany	236	235	73.1	73.8
UK	249	256	88.7	90.1
Philippines	279	308	48.8	66.4
Sri Lanka	304	324	17.2	15.1
Japan	351	350	63.1	66.8
India	**368**	**389**	**25.5**	**30.1**
Korea, Rep. of	489	503	73.8	81.9
Bangladesh	1090	1246	19.8	28.1

Note: Countries arranged in ascending order of density in 2009.
Source: Human Development Index Data Base 2011.

241 : Dependency Ratio

	Child Dependency Ratio			Old Age Dependency Ratio		
Countries	1990	2005	2010	1990	2005	2010
World	**53.8**	**43.6**	**41.2**	**10.0**	**11.5**	**11.6**
Saudi Arabia	75.1	62.4	49.1	4.1	4.8	4.6
Bangladesh	79.8	58.3	47.4	5.6	5.9	6.1
Nepal	78.1	68.0	59.8	5.9	6.5	6.8
Pakistan	82.1	66.1	61.7	7.0	6.6	6.9
Philippines	72.6	57.5	53.8	5.8	6.4	6.9
South Africa	67.2	51.7	46.6	5.5	6.7	7.1
Egypt	78.4	54.5	50.8	6.9	7.8	7.3
Malaysia	63.5	51.4	44.0	6.2	7.3	7.3
India	**64.9**	**51.2**	**47.9**	**5.6**	**8.5**	**7.7**
Turkey	60.5	43.2	39.0	6.8	9.0	8.8
Indonesia	59.3	42.7	39.7	6.3	8.3	9.0
Peru	66.3	50.8	46.7	6.9	8.9	9.3
Mexico	67.4	48.7	42.7	7.6	8.3	10.0
Brazil	58.5	42.3	37.7	7.4	9.2	10.2
Thailand	45.9	34.4	30.3	7.1	10.3	10.9
China	42.9	30.1	27.7	8.3	10.7	11.4
Sri Lanka	51.1	35.1	35.7	8.9	10.6	11.4
Chile	46.7	37.2	32.5	9.6	12.1	13.5
UK	36.9	27.1	22.3	7.2	24.2	15.2
Korea, Rep. of	36.9	25.8	22.3	7.2	13.1	15.2
Argentina	50.2	41.6	38.6	15.3	11.5	16.6
Russia	34.3	21.6	20.8	15.1	19.5	17.9
USA	33.0	31.1	30.3	18.7	18.4	19.4
Canada	30.4	25.4	23.5	16.6	18.9	20.3
Australia	32.9	29.0	28.1	16.8	18.8	20.7
Spain	29.8	20.7	22.0	20.5	23.8	25.3
France	30.5	27.9	28.4	21.6	25.5	26.2
Italy	27.0	21.2	25.4	22.3	30.3	26.4
Germany	23.3	21.4	20.2	21.7	28.1	30.9
Japan	26.3	21.1	20.5	17.2	29.7	35.1

Note : Countries are arranged in an ascending order of old age dependency ratio in 2010.
Child Dependency Ratio : Population aged under 15 years expressed as percentage of the proportion of working age (15-64 years of age). Old Age Dependency Ratio : Population aged 65 years and above expressed as percentage of the population of working age (15-64 years of age).

Source : *World Development Indicators 2011.*

242 : Crude Death Rate, Crude Birth Rate and Life Expectancy at Birth

Countries	Crude Death Rate (CDR)		Crude Birth Rate (CBR)		Life Expectancy at Birth: Years	
	1991	2009	1991	2009	1990	2010
World	**9**	**8**	**26**	**20**	**65**	**69**
South Africa	9	15	31	22	61	52
India	**10**	**7**	**38**	**22**	**58**	**64**
Bangladesh	13	6	34	21	54	67
Pakistan	11	7	41	30	61	67
Russia	11	14	12	12	68	67
Nepal		6		25	54	67
Thailand	6	9	21	14	69	69
Egypt	9	6	32	24	63	71
Indonesia	9	6	25	18	62	71
Turkey	7	6	28	18	65	72
Philippines	7	5	28	24	65	72
Brazil	7	6	24	16	66	73
Saudi Arabia	5	4	37	24	68	73
China	7	7	22	12	68	73
Peru		5		21	66	74
Sri Lanka	6	5	21	19	69	74
Malaysia	5	5	29	20	70	75
Argentina	9	8	21	17	72	76
Mexico	5	5	28	18	71	77
Chile	6	5	23	15	74	79
USA	9	8	16	14	75	80
UK	11	9	14	13	76	80
Korea, Rep. of	6	5	16	10	71	80
Germany	11	10	10	8	75	80
Canada	7	7	15	11	77	81
Spain	9	8	10	11	77	81
Italy	9	10	10	10	77	81
France	9	9	13	13	77	82
Australia	7	6	15	14	77	82
Japan	7	9	10	9	79	83

Note : Countries are arranged in an ascending order of life expectancy in 2009.
Crude Death Rate and Birth Rate indicate the number of deaths and live births occuring per thousand population in a year.
Life Expectancy at Birth is the number of years a newborn infant could expect to live if patterns of age-specific mortality rates at the time of birth were to stay the same throughout the child's life.

Source : Human Development Index Data Base 2011.

243 : Infant & Maternal Mortality and Fertility Rate

Countries	Infant Mortality Rate (IMR)		Maternal Mortality Rate (modelled estimates)		Total Fertility Rate (TFR)	
	1990	2009	1990	2008	1990	2010
World	**64**	**43**	**400**	**260**	**3.3**	**2.5**
Italy	8	3	10	5	1.3	1.4
Japan	5	2	12	6	1.5	1.4
Spain	8	4	7	6	1.3	1.4
Germany	7	4	13	7	1.5	1.4
Russia	23	11	74	39	1.9	1.6
Canada	7	5	6	12	1.8	1.6
China	37	17	110	38	2.3	1.8
Thailand	27	12	50	48	2.1	1.8
Brazil	46	17	120	58	2.8	1.8
Australia	8	4	10	8	1.9	1.9
Chile	18	7	56	26	2.6	1.9
Korea, Rep. of	8	5	18	18	2.4	1.9
UK	8	5	10	12	1.8	2.0
France	7	3	13	8	1.8	2.0
Mexico	36	15	93	85	3.4	2.1
USA	9	7	12	24	2.1	2.1
Turkey	69	19	68	23	3.1	2.1
Indonesia	56	30	620	240	3.1	2.1
Argentina	25	13	72	70	3.0	2.2
Sri Lanka	23	13	91	39	2.5	2.3
Bangladesh	102	41	870	340	4.4	2.3
Malaysia	16	6	56	31	3.7	2.5
South Africa	48	43	230	410	3.7	2.5
Peru	62	19	250	98	3.8	2.5
India	**84**	**50**	**570**	**230**	**4.0**	**2.7**
Egypt	66	18	220	82	4.6	2.8
Nepal	99	39	870	380	5.2	2.8
Philippines	41	26	180	94	4.3	3.0
Saudi Arabia	35	18	41	24	5.8	3.0
Pakistan	101	71	490	290	6.1	3.9

Note: Countries are arranged in ascending order of fertility rate in 2009.
IMR is number of infants per 1000 live births in a year, who die before reaching the age of one. TFR is number of children that would be born to a woman if she were to live to the end of her childbearing years and bear children in accordance with current age-specific rates.
Maternal Mortality Rate (MMR) is the number of women who die from pregnancy related causes during pregnancy and childbirth per 100000 live births.

Source: *World Development Indicators 2011.*

244 : Adult Literacy Rate and Gross Enrollment Ratio

Countries	Gross Enrollment Ratio (GER) 1990	2000	2010	Dropout Rate (2005-2008)	Adult Literacy Rate (2005-2009)
World				**18.0**	**84**
Pakistan	30.9	..	39.3	30.3	56
Bangladesh	34.7	54.0	52.1	45.2	56
Nepal	54.8	56.0	60.8	38.4	59
India	**50.1**	**52.2**	**61.0**	**34.2**	**63**
Indonesia	61.4	62.1	68.2	19.9	92
Sri Lanka	66.0	70.8	68.7	2.0	91
China	53.6	67.0	68.7	0.4	94
Turkey	55.0	67.9	71.1	5.8	91
Malaysia	59.1	68.0	71.5	7.8	92
Egypt	65.3	80.9	76.4	3.2	66
South Africa	72.6	76.4	76.8	23.0	89
Thailand	49.7	71.3	78.0	-	94
Saudi Arabia	48.1	..	78.5	3.6	86
Philippines	75.0	78.8	79.6	26.8	95
Mexico	65.3	71.8	80.2	8.5	93
Russia	83.7	..	81.9	4.8	100
Chile	71.3	77.7	82.5	5.1	99
Japan	76.9	83.1	86.6	-	..
Brazil	66.8	90.2	87.2	24.4	90
Peru	77.7	88.1	88.1	17	90
Argentina	79.5	..	88.6	5.1	98
UK	74.4	90.0	89.2	-	..
Italy	70.8	80.9	91.8	13.5	99
USA	90.1	91.5	92.4	1.5	..
France	82.9	92.2	95.4	2	..
Spain	83.9	92.4	96.5	0.1	98
Korea, Rep. of	78.9	91.2	98.5	1.6	..
Canada	99.6	94.9	99.3	-	..
Australia	77.8	115.2	114.2		..
Germany	75.8	..	..	4.4	..

Note : .. : not available.
Countries arranged as per ascending enrollment rate in 2010.
Gross Enrollment Ratio (GER) is the ratio to total enrollment, regardless of age, to the population of the age group that officially corresponds to the level of education shown.
Adult Literacy Rate is % of population aged 15 and older that can with understanding, both read and write a short sentence in their everyday life.
Dropout rate is n % of primary school cohort.

Source : Human Development Index Data Base 2011.

245 : Education Inputs

Countries	Public Expenditure on Education % of GDP 1991	% of GDP 2009	% of Government Expenditure 1991	% of Government Expenditure 2009	Pupils per Teacher (primary) 1991	Pupils per Teacher (primary) 2009
World	**..**	**4.5**	**..**	**..**	**33**	**29**
Argentina	3.3	4.9	..	13.5	18	17
Australia	4.9	4.5	14.8	..	17	..
Bangladesh	1.5	2.4	10.3	14.0	63	51
Brazil	..	5.1	..	16.1	23	22
Canada	6.5	4.9	14.2	..	15	..
Chile	2.4	4.0	10.0	18.2	25	27
China	..	..	..	..	22	21
Egypt	3.9	3.8	..	11.9	..	22
France	5.5	5.6	..	10.7	12	19
Germany	..	4.5	..	10.3	17	14
India	**3.7**	**..**	**12.2**	**..**	**60**	**40**
Indonesia	1.0	2.8	..	17.9	23	20
Italy	3.0	4.3	..	9.0	12	11
Jamaica	4.5	5.8	12.8	0.0	37	28
Japan	..	3.5	..	9.4	21	19
Korea, Rep. of	3.8	4.2	25.6	14.8	34	29
Malaysia	5.1	4.1	18.0	17.2	20	18
Mexico	3.8	4.8	15.3	0.0	30	28
New Zealand	6.1	6.1	..	0.0	19	16
Pakistan	2.6	2.7	7.4	11.2	41	38
Philippines	3.0	2.8	10.5	16.9	33	35
Russia	3.6	0.0	..	0.0	..	17
Saudi Arabia	5.8	5.6	17.8	19.3	16	..
South Africa	5.9	5.4	..	16.9	..	36
Spain	4.1	4.3	..	11.1	21	14
Sri Lanka	3.2	..	8.4	..	12	22
Thailand	3.1	4.1	20.0	20.3	18	21
Turkey	2.4	0.0	..	0.0	29	..
UK	4.8	5.5	..	11.7	20	18
USA	5.1	5.5	12.3	14.1	..	14

Source : *World Development Indicators 2011.*

246 : Health Infrastructure

Countries	Health Expenditure		Physicians per 1000 People		Hospital Beds per 1000 People	
	% to GDP 2008	Per Capita PPP $ 2008	1990	2004-2009	1990	2004-2009
World	**9.4**	**901**	**1.4**	**1.4**	**3.7**	**2.9**
Bangladesh	3.3	44	0.2	0.3	0.3	0.4
Pakistan	2.6	62	1.9	0.8	8.5	0.6
Nepal	6.0	66	..	0.2	..	5.0
Indonesia	2.3	91	0.1	0.3	0.7	..
India	**4.2**	**122**	**0.5**	**0.6**	**0.8**	**0.9**
Philippines	3.7	129	0.1	1.2	1.4	0.5
Sri Lanka	4.1	187	..	0.5	1.1	3.1
Egypt	4.8	261	0.8	2.8	2.1	1.7
China	4.3	265	1.5	1.4	2.6	4.1
Thailand	4.1	328	0.2	0.3	1.6	..
Peru	4.5	381	..	0.9	..	1.5
Malaysia	4.3	621	0.4	0.9	2.1	1.8
Saudi Arabia	3.6	831	1.4	0.9	2.5	2.2
Mexico	5.9	837	1.0	2.9	1.0	1.6
South Africa	8.2	843	0.6	0.8	..	2.8
Turkey	6.1	845	0.9	1.6	2.4	2.4
Brazil	8.4	875	1.4	1.7	3.3	2.4
Russia	4.8	985	4.1	4.3	13.1	9.7
Argentina	8.4	1062	2.7	3.2	4.6	4.0
Chile	7.5	1088	1.1	1.3	3.2	2.1
Korea, Rep. of	6.5	1806	0.8	2.0	3.1	12.3
Japan	8.3	2817	1.7	2.1	..	13.8
Italy	8.7	2836	..	4.2	7.2	3.7
Spain	9.0	2941	..	3.7	4.6	3.2
UK	8.7	3222	1.6	2.7	5.9	3.4
Australia	8.5	3365	2.2	3.0	9.2	3.8
France	11.2	3851	3.1	3.5	9.7	7.1
Canada	9.8	3867	2.1	1.9	6.0	3.4
Germany	10.5	3922	2.8	3.5	10.4	8.2
USA	15.2	7164	1.8	2.7	4.9	3.1

Note: Countries arranged according to per capita ppp US$.
Source: *World Development Indicators 2011.*

247 : Labour Force and Labour Force Participation Rate

Countries	Labour Force Total (million)		Labour Force Participation Rate (%)			
			Male		Female	
	1990	2009	1990	2009	1990	2009
World	**2342.6**	**3175.8**	**81**	**78**	**52**	**52**
Argentina	13.5	19.6	78	78	43	52
Australia	8.5	11.5	76	72	52	58
Bangladesh	49.5	78.6	89	83	61	59
Brazil	62.6	101.5	85	82	45	60
Canada	14.7	19.1	76	73	58	63
Chile	5.0	7.5	77	73	32	42
China	643.9	783.2	85	80	73	67
Egypt	16.8	27.4	74	75	27	22
France	25.0	28.7	65	62	46	51
Germany	38.8	42.3	73	67	45	53
India	**317.8**	**457.5**	**84**	**81**	**34**	**33**
Indonesia	74.9	115.6	81	86	50	52
Italy	23.7	25.4	66	61	35	38
Jamaica	1.1	1.2	80	74	65	56
Japan	63.9	65.8	77	72	50	48
Korea, Rep. of	19.2	24.7	73	72	47	50
Malaysia	7.0	12.0	80	79	43	44
Mexico	29.9	47.2	84	81	34	43
New Zealand	1.7	2.4	74	76	54	62
Pakistan	31.0	58.1	85	85	14	22
Peru	8.3	13.6	75	76	49	58
Philippines	24.1	38.8	83	79	48	49
Russia	76.8	75.9	76	69	60	58
Saudi Arabia	5.0	8.6	80	74	15	17
South Africa	10.4	18.8	62	63	36	47
Spain	15.6	22.9	67	69	34	49
Sri Lanka	6.8	8.3	79	75	37	34
Thailand	32.1	38.7	87	81	75	66
Turkey	20.7	25.6	81	70	34	24
UK	29.0	31.8	74	70	52	55
USA	129.2	159.0	76	72	57	58

Note : Labour Force Participation Rate is the proportion of the population between ages 15 and 64 that is economically active. Total Labour Force comprises people of ages 15 years and above who meet the ILO definition of economically active population and includes both employed and unemployed.

Source : *World Development Indicators 2011.*

248 : Unemployment

Countries	Unemployment: Total (% of total labour force) 1990-1992	2006-2009	Male (% of male labour force) 1990-1992	2006-2009	Female (% of female labour force) 1990-1992	2006-2009
World						
Argentina	6.7	8.6	6.4	7.8	7.0	9.8
Australia	10.8	5.6	11.4	5.7	10.0	5.4
Bangladesh	1.9		2.0		1.9	
Brazil	6.4	8.3	5.4	6.1	7.9	11.0
Canada	11.2	8.3	12.0	9.4	10.2	7.0
Chile	4.4	9.7	3.9	9.1	5.3	10.7
China	2.3	4.3	na	na	na	na
Egypt	na	9.4	na	5.2	..	22.9
France	10.2	9.1	8.1	8.9	12.8	9.3
Germany	6.6	7.7	5.3	8.1	8.4	7.3
India	**na**	**na**	**na**	**na**	**na**	**na**
Indonesia	2.8	7.9	2.7	7.5	3.0	8.5
Italy	9.3	7.8	6.7	6.8	13.9	9.3
Jamaica	15.4	11.4	9.4	8.5	22.2	14.8
Japan	2.2	5.0	2.1	5.3	2.2	4.7
Korea, Rep. of	2.5	3.6	2.8	4.1	2.1	3.0
Malaysia	3.7	3.7	na	3.2	na	3.7
Mexico	3.1	5.2	2.7	5.4	4.0	4.8
New Zealand	10.6	6.1	11.4	6.1	9.7	6.1
Pakistan	5.2	5.0	3.8	4.0	14.0	8.7
Peru	9.4	6.8	7.5	5.4	12.5	8.3
Philippines	8.6	7.5	7.9	7.5	9.9	7.4
Russia	5.2	8.2	5.2	8.4	5.2	7.9
Saudi Arabia	na	5.4	na	3.5	na	15.9
South Africa	na	23.8	na	22.0	na	25.9
Spain	18.1	18.0	13.9	17.7	25.8	18.4
Sri Lanka	14.2	7.6	na	7.2	na	8.1
Thailand	1.4	1.2	1.3	1.2	1.5	1.1
Turkey	8.5	14.0	8.8	13.9	7.8	14.3
UK	9.7	7.7	11.5	8.8	7.3	6.4
USA	7.5	9.3	7.9	10.3	7.0	8.1

Note : na : not available.
Source : World Development Indicators 2011.

249 : Human Development Index (HDI)

Countries	1980	1990	2000	2010	Rank
Australia	0.791	0.819	0.914	0.937	1
USA	0.810	0.857	0.893	0.902	4
Canada	0.789	0.845	0.867	0.888	8
Germany	0.000	0.782	0.000	0.885	10
Japan	0.768	0.814	0.855	0.884	11
Korea, Rep. of	0.616	0.725	0.815	0.877	12
France	0.711	0.766	0.834	0.872	14
Spain	0.680	0.729	0.828	0.863	20
Italy	0.703	0.764	0.825	0.854	23
UK	0.737	0.770	0.823	0.849	26
Chile	0.607	0.675	0.734	0.783	45
Argentina	0.656	0.682	0.734	0.775	46
Saudi Arabia	0.556	0.620	0.690	0.752	55
Mexico	0.591	0.635	0.698	0.750	56
Malaysia	0.541	0.616	0.691	0.744	57
Peru	0.560	0.608	0.675	0.723	63
Russia	0.000	0.692	0.662	0.719	64
Brazil	0.000	0.000	0.649	0.699	73
Turkey	0.467	0.552	0.629	0.679	83
China	0.368	0.460	0.567	0.663	89
Sri Lanka	0.513	0.558	0.000	0.658	91
Thailand	0.483	0.546	0.600	0.654	92
Philippines	0.523	0.552	0.597	0.638	97
Egypt	0.393	0.484	0.566	0.620	101
Indonesia	0.390	0.458	0.500	0.600	108
South Africa	0.000	0.601	0.000	0.597	110
India	**0.320**	**0.389**	**0.440**	**0.519**	**119**
Pakistan	0.311	0.359	0.416	0.490	125
Bangladesh	0.259	0.313	0.390	0.469	129
Nepal	0.210	0.316	0.375	0.428	138

Note: HDI is an index which measures the country's attainments in longevity, knowledge and income. Ranking is for 169 countries in 2010, with a lower number signifying a better HDI.

Source: *World Development Indicators 2011.*

250 : Multidimensional Poverty Index

Countries	Multidimensional Poverty Index: 2000-2008	Population in Multidimensional Poverty: 2000-2008		Population Below Poverty Line (% in 2000-2008)	
		Headcount (%)	Intensity of Deprivation (%)	PPP < $ 1.25 a day (%)	National Poverty Line (%)
Argentina	0.011	3	37.7	3.4	
Bangladesh	0.291	58	50.4	49.6	40.0
Brazil	0.039	9	46.0	5.2	21.5
China	0.056	13	44.9	15.9	2.8
Egypt	0.026	6	40	<2	16.7
India	**0.296**	**55**	**53.5**	**41.6**	**28.6**
Indonesia	0.095	21	46	29.4	16.7
Mexico	0.015	4	39	4.0	47.0
Nepal	0.350	65	54.1	55.1	30.9
Pakistan	0.275	51	54.0	22.6	..
Peru	0.085	20	43.1	7.7	51.6
Philippines	0.067	13	53.5	22.6	..
Russia	0.005	1	39	<2	19.6
South Africa	0.014	3	46.7	26.2	22.0
Sri Lanka	0.021	5	38.7	14.0	22.7
Thailand	0.006	2	39	<2	..
Turkey	0.039	9	45.9	2.6	27.0

Source : Human Development Report 2011.

251 : Carbon Dioxide Emissions: Top 30 Countries

Rank	Country	Carbon Dioxide Emissions 1990 (million metric tonnes)	Carbon Dioxide Emissions 2007 (million metric tonnes)	Growth (%) 1990-2005	Share in World Total (%) 1990	Share in World Total (%) 2007	Per Capita Emissions 1990 (metric tonnes)	Per Capita Emissions 2007 (metric tonnes)
	World	**22530**	**30649**	**36.0**	**100.0**	**100.0**	**4.3**	**4.6**
1	UAR	55	135	145.5	0.2	0.4	29.3	31.0
2	USA	4861	5832	20.0	21.6	19.0	19.5	19.3
3	Australia	293	374	27.6	1.3	1.2	17.2	17.7
4	Canada	450	557	23.8	2.0	1.8	16.2	16.9
5	Saudi Arabia	215	402	87.0	1.0	1.3	13.2	16.6
6	Kazakhstan	261	227	(13.0)	1.2	0.7	18.0	14.7
7	Russia	2074	1536	(25.9)	9.2	5.0	15.8	10.8
8	Netherlands	164	173	5.5	0.7	0.6	11.0	10.6
9	Korea, Rep. of	242	503	107.9	1.1	1.6	5.6	10.4
10	Japan	1152	1254	8.9	5.1	4.1	9.3	9.8
11	Germany	960	787	(18.0)	4.3	2.6	12.0	9.6
12	South Africa	333	4333	1201.2	1.5	14.1	9.5	9.0
13	UK	570	539	(5.4)	2.5	1.8	10.0	8.8
14	Poland	348	317	(8.9)	1.5	1.0	9.1	8.3
15	Spain	227	359	58.1	1.0	1.2	5.9	8.0
16	Italy	425	456	7.3	1.9	1.5	7.5	7.7
17	Malaysia	57	194	240.4	0.3	0.6	3.1	7.3
18	Iran	227	496	118.5	1.0	1.6	4.2	7.0
19	Ukraine	611	317	(48.1)	2.7	1.0	13.3	6.8
20	France	399	372	(6.8)	1.8	1.2	7.0	6.0
21	Venezuela	122	165	35.2	0.5	0.5	6.2	6.0
22	China	2459	6533	165.7	10.9	21.3	2.2	5.0
23	Mexico	357	471	31.9	1.6	1.5	4.3	4.5
24	Thailand	96	277	188.5	0.4	0.9	1.7	4.1
25	Algeria	79	140	77.2	0.4	0.5	3.1	4.1
26	Turkey	151	288	90.7	0.7	0.9	2.7	4.0
27	Egypt	76	185	143.4	0.3	0.6	1.3	2.3
28	Brazil	209	368	76.1	0.9	1.2	1.4	1.9
29	Indonesia	149	397	166.4	0.7	1.3	0.8	1.8
30	**India**	**690**	**1611**	**133.5**	**3.1**	**5.3**	**0.8**	**1.4**

Note: Countries are arranged according to per capita emission in 2007.
Source: *World Development Indicators 2011.*

252 : Energy Production and Use

Countries	Production Million Metric Tonnes of Oil Equivalent		Energy Use Million Metric Tonnes of Oil Equivalent		Per Capita Energy Use Per Capita Kg of Oil Equivalent	
	1990	2008	1990	2008	2001	2008
World	**8840.1**	**12357.7**	**8569.9**	**11899.4**	**1669**	**1835**
Bangladesh	10.8	23.4	12.7	27.9	110	175
Nepal	5.5	8.7	5.8	9.8	303	340
Sri Lanka	4.2	5.1	5.5	8.9	322	443
Philippines	15.7	23.3	27.5	41.1	440	455
Pakistan	34.3	63.3	43.0	82.8	398	499
Peru	10.6	12.3	9.7	14.7	447	510
India	**291.8**	**468.3**	**318.9**	**621.0**	**375**	**545**
Egypt	54.9	87.5	31.8	70.7	551	867
Indonesia	172.2	347.0	103.9	198.7	586	874
Brazil	104.2	228.1	140.2	248.5	938	1295
Turkey	25.8	29.0	52.8	98.5	941	1333
Thailand	26.5	63.9	42.0	107.2	742	1591
China	886.3	1993.3	863.0	2116.4	760	1598
Mexico	193.4	233.6	121.3	180.6	1457	1698
Chile	7.4	9.0	13.8	31.4	1049	1871
Argentina	48.4	82.9	46.1	76.4	1418	1915
Malaysia	48.8	93.1	22.0	72.7	1215	2693
South Africa	114.5	163.0	90.9	134.5	2581	2756
Italy	25.3	26.9	146.6	176.0	2584	2942
Spain	34.6	30.4	90.1	138.8	2320	3047
UK	208.0	166.7	205.9	208.5	3597	3395
Japan	75.2	88.7	439.3	495.8	3556	3883
Germany	186.2	134.1	351.4	335.3	4424	4083
France	111.9	136.6	223.9	266.5	3946	4279
Korea, Rep. of	22.6	44.7	93.1	226.9	2171	4669
Russia	1293.1	1253.9	879.2	686.8	5929	4838
Australia	157.5	302.1	86.2	130.1	5053	6071
Saudi Arabia	370.6	579.0	59.0	161.6	3631	6514
USA	1652.5	1706.1	1915.0	2283.7	7672	7503
Canada	273.8	407.4	208.7	266.8	7509	8008

Note: Countries arranged in ascending order of per capita use in 2008.
Energy production refers to forms of primary energy—crude oil, natural gas oil, oil from non-conventional sources—natural gas, solid fuel (coal, lignite, and other derived fuels) and combustible renewable and waste and primary electricity, all converted to oil equivalent.
Energy use refers to use of primary energy before transformation to other end-use fuels. It is computed as indigeneous production plus imports and stock changes minus exports and fuels supplied to ships and aircrafts engaged in international transport.
Combustible renewable and waste comprises solid and liquid biomass, biogas and industrial and municipal waste measured as percentage of total energy use.

Source: *World Development Indicators 2011.*

253 : Statistics on Traffic and Congestion

Countries	Motor Vehicles				Road Density
	Per 1000 People		Per km of Roads		
	1990	2008	1990	2008	2008
Argentina	181	314	27	na	8
Australia	530	687	11	18	11
Bangladesh	1	2	0	2	166
Brazil	88	198	8	18	21
Canada	605	605	20	14	14
Chile	81	172	13	36	na
China	5	37	4	13	39
Egypt	29	43	33	33	10
France	494	598	32	39	173
Germany	405	554	53	71	180
India	**4**	**15**	**2**	**4**	**129**
Indonesia	16	77	7	40	23
Italy	529	673	99	83	162
Jamaica	52	188	7	24	202
Japan	469	593	52	63	318
Korea, Rep. of	79	346	60	161	105
Malaysia	124	334	26	83	30
Mexico	119	264	41	77	19
New Zealand	524	733	19	33	35
Pakistan	6	11	4	8	33
Philippines	10	33	4	14	67
Russia	87	245	14	35	6
Saudi Arabia	165	na	19	20	11
South Africa	139	na	26	24	na
Spain	360	606	43	41	132
Sri Lanka	21	61	4	13	148
Thailand	50	na	8	na	35
Turkey	48	138	38	24	54
UK	400	526	64	77	172
USA	758	809	30	38	68

Note : na: not available.
Road Density refers to km of road per 100 sq km of land.

Source : *World Development Indicators 2011.*

254 : Real GDP: Per cent Growth

Country	Decadal Averages			Annual Growth		
	1981-1990	1991-2000	2001-2010	2008	2009	2010
Argentina	(1.1)	4.3	4.6	6.8	0.8	9.2
Australia	3.2	3.5	3.1	2.6	1.3	2.7
Bangladesh	3.7	4.9	5.8	6.0	5.8	6.0
Brazil	1.6	2.6	3.6	5.2	(0.6)	7.5
Canada	2.8	2.9	1.9	0.5	(2.5)	3.1
Chile	3.1	6.5	3.8	3.7	(1.7)	5.3
China	9.3	10.5	10.5	9.6	9.2	10.3
Egypt	5.2	4.4	4.9	7.2	4.7	5.1
France	2.4	2.0	1.2	0.1	(2.5)	1.5
Germany	2.3	2.1	0.9	0.7	(4.7)	3.5
India	**5.6**	**5.6**	**7.5**	**6.2**	**6.8**	**10.4**
Indonesia	5.5	4.2	5.2	6.0	4.6	6.1
Italy	2.4	1.6	0.3	(1.3)	(5.2)	1.3
Jamaica	3.2	0.7	0.8	(0.9)	(3.0)	(1.1)
Japan	4.6	1.2	0.7	(1.2)	(6.3)	3.9
Korea, Rep. of	9.7	6.6	4.1	2.3	0.2	6.1
Malaysia	6.1	7.2	4.6	4.7	(1.7)	7.2
Mexico	1.9	3.6	1.7	1.5	(6.1)	5.5
Nepal	4.8	5.0	4.0	6.1	4.9	4.6
New Zealand	1.8	2.9	2.3	(0.2)	(2.1)	1.5
Pakistan	6.2	4.0	4.7	1.6	3.4	4.8
Peru	(0.6)	4.0	5.7	9.8	0.9	8.8
Philippines	1.8	3.1	4.7	3.7	1.1	7.3
Russia	0.0	-2.1	4.9	5.2	(7.8)	4.0
Saudi Arabia	(0.4)	2.8	3.3	4.2	0.6	3.7
South Africa	1.5	1.8	3.5	3.6	(1.7)	2.8
Spain	3.0	2.9	2.1	0.9	(3.7)	(0.1)
Sri Lanka	4.2	5.2	5.3	6.0	3.8	9.1
Thailand	7.9	4.6	4.4	2.5	(2.3)	7.8
Turkey	5.2	3.8	3.9	0.7	-4.7	8.2
United Kingdom	2.8	2.5	1.4	-0.1	-4.9	1.3
United States	3.3	3.4	1.7	0.0	-2.6	2.8

Source : International Monetary Fund Data Base 2011.

255 : Per Capita GDP (At Current Prices)

(US $)

Country	1980	1990	2000	2009	2010
Argentina	--	2,119	7,732	28,519	35,604
Australia	9,846	24,416	35,724	56,867	60,456
Bangladesh	216	264	334	584	638
Brazil	1,372	3,464	3,751	8,360	10,816
Canada	10,988	21,089	23,653	39,683	46,215
Chile	2,493	2,409	4,944	9,485	11,828
China	205	341	946	3,739	4,382
Egypt	552	1,779	1,566	2,456	2,789
France	12,865	22,017	22,574	42,410	41,019
Germany	10,759	19,610	23,220	40,832	40,631
India	**263**	**378**	**460**	**1,058**	**1,265**
Indonesia	644	699	807	2,327	3,015
Italy	8,169	20,029	19,334	35,251	34,059
Jamaica	1,314	2,134	3,512	4,562	5,039
Japan	9,172	24,774	36,800	39,459	42,820
Korea, Rep. of	1,689	6,308	11,347	17,074	20,591
Malaysia	1,812	2,432	4,030	6,917	8,423
Mexico	3,353	3,458	6,859	8,203	9,566
Nepal	131	204	235	462	562
New Zealand	7,190	13,099	13,746	27,284	32,145
Pakistan	347	447	539	989	1,050
Peru	1,192	1,332	2,116	4,363	5,172
Philippines	672	718	987	1,748	2,007
Poland	1,591	1,625	4,454	11,299	12,300
Russia	n/a	n/a	1,775	8,614	10,437
Saudi Arabia	17,629	7,689	9,216	14,745	16,996
South Africa	2,764	3,039	2,986	5,758	7,158
Spain	6,005	13,408	14,464	32,030	30,639
Sri Lanka	301	511	915	2,074	2,435
Switzerland	17,383	35,490	34,786	63,536	67,246
Thailand	696	1,521	1,983	4,151	4,992
Turkey	2,235	3,860	4,245	8,711	10,399
United Kingdom	9,630	17,782	25,142	35,315	36,120
United States	12,249	23,198	35,252	45,934	47,284

Source : International Monetary Fund Data Base 2011.

256 : Structure of Output

Countries	GDP (US $ billion)		Average Annual Growth (%)		Value Added (as % of GDP) 2009		
	1990	2009	1990-2000	2000-2009	Agriculture	Industry	Services
World	**21785**	**58260**	**2.9**	**2.9**	**3**	**27**	**70**
China	355	4985	10.6	10.9	10	46	43
India	**317**	**1377**	**5.9**	**7.9**	**18**	**27**	**55**
Russia	517	1232	(4.7)	6.0	5	33	62
Bangladesh	30	89	4.8	5.9	19	29	53
Sri Lanka	8	42	5.3	5.5	13	30	58
Argentina	141	307	4.3	5.4	8	32	61
Indonesia	114	540	4.2	5.3	16	49	35
Pakistan	40	162	3.8	5.2	22	24	54
Malaysia	44	193	7.0	5.1	10	44	46
Turkey	151	615	3.8	4.9	9	26	65
Philippines	44	161	3.3	4.9	15	30	55
Egypt	43	188	4.4	4.9	14	37	49
Thailand	85	264	4.2	4.6	12	43	45
Korea, Rep. of	264	833	5.8	4.5	3	37	60
Chile	32	164	6.6	4.1	3	42	55
South Africa	112	285	2.1	4.1	3	31	66
Saudi Arabia	117	376	2.1	3.8	3	51	46
Nepal	0	13		3.7	34	16	50
Brazil	462	1594	2.0	3.6	6	25	69
Australia	319	925	4.0	3.3	3	29	68
Spain	521	1460	2.7	2.8	3	26	71
Mexico	263	875	3.1	2.2	4	35	61
Canada	574	1336	3.1	2.1			
UK	990	2175	2.7	2.0	1	21	78
USA	5758	14119	3.5	2.0	1	21	77
France	1239	2649	1.9	1.5	2	19	79
Japan	3018	5069	1.1	1.1	1	28	71
Germany	1707	3330	1.8	1.0	1	26	73
Italy	1133	2113	1.5	0.9	2	25	73

Note : Countries arranged in descending order of GDP growth in 2000-2008.
Source : *World Development Indicators 2011.*

257 : GDP based on Purchasing Power Parity Valuation of Country

Country	Gross Domestic Product (PPP) Current International $ in Billion			Per Capita GDP (PPP) Current International $		
	1990	2000	2010	1990	2000	2010
Argentina	182	338	642	5,599	9,193	15,854
Australia	305	527	882	17,776	27,364	39,699
Bangladesh	59	117	259	513	834	1,572
Brazil	782	1234	2172	5,335	7,204	11,239
Canada	542	888	1330	19,632	28,979	39,057
Chile	63	145	258	4,809	9,501	15,002
China	911	3014	10086	796	2,378	7,519
Egypt	132	248	498	2,561	3,910	6,354
France	1,028	1,535	2,145	18,128	25,995	34,077
Germany	1,435	2,162	2,940	18,190	26,345	36,033
India	**750**	**1582**	**4060**	**870**	**1,518**	**3,339**
Indonesia	277	501	1030	1,539	2,441	4,394
Italy	972	1397	1774	17,147	24,541	29,392
Jamaica	13	17	24	5,604	6,811	8,727
Japan	2,327	3,213	4,310	18,851	25,334	33,805
Korea, Rep. of	335	775	1459	7,825	16,495	29,836
Malaysia	88	213	414	4,841	9,169	14,670
Mexico	612	1065	1567	7,353	10,868	14,430
Nepal	10	19	36	505	791	1,271
New Zealand	46	76	118	13,632	19,659	26,966
Pakistan	135	244	465	1,248	1,777	2,791
Peru	70	128	276	3,241	5,067	9,330
Philippines	108	179	351	1,752	2,320	3,737
Russia	..	1,120	2,223	..	7,658	15,837
Saudi Arabia	220	353	622	14,488	17,253	23,826
South Africa	201	296	524	5,456	6,640	10,498
Spain	551	900	1369	14,193	22,349	29,742
Sri Lanka	25	51	107	1,543	2,770	5,220
Thailand	164	310	587	2,909	5,004	9,187
Turkey	291	513	961	5,556	8,169	13,464
UK	961	1516	2173	16,789	25,737	34,920
USA	5,801	9,951	14,658	23,198	35,252	47,284

Note: These data form the basis for the country weights used to generate the World Economic Outlook (WEO) country group composites for the domestic economies. However, the IMF is not a primary source for purchasing power parity (PPP) data. WEO weights have been created from primary sources and are used solely for the purpose of generating country group composites. For primary source information, refer to one of the following sources; Organisation for Economic Co-operation and Development, World Bank or the Penn World Tables.

Source: International Monetary Fund.

258 : Structure of Demand

% of GDP

Countries	Final Consumption Expenditure				Gross Capital Formation		Gross Domestic Savings	
	Household		Government					
	1990	2009	1990	2009	1990	2009	1990	2009
World	**60**	**62**	**17**	**19**	**23**	**19**	**22**	**19**
Argentina	77	59	3	15	14	21	13	23
Australia	59	57	19	17	23	28	19	21
Bangladesh	86	77	4	5	17	24	14	39
Brazil	59	62	19	22	20	17	19	15
Canada	56	59	23	22	21	21	18	18
Chile	61	60	10	13	25	19	24	22
China	46	35	14	13	36	48	40	54
Egypt	73	76	11	11	29	19	21	17
France	57	58	22	25	22	19	21	16
Germany	57	59	20	20	24	16	24	21
India	**66**	**56**	**12**	**12**	**24**	**36**	**22**	**35**
Indonesia	59	57	9	10	31	31	28	23
Italy	57	60	20	22	22	19	21	16
Jamaica	65	81	13	16	26	21	19	13
Japan	53	60	13	20	33	20	34	24
Korea, Rep. of	52	54	12	16	38	26	37	30
Malaysia	52	50	14	14	32	14	30	31
Mexico	70	67	8	12	23	22	20	22
New Zealand	61	60	19	20	20	18	17	16
Pakistan	74	80	15	8	19	19	23	22
Philippines	72	74	10	11	24	15	20	40
Russia	49	54	21	20	30	19	36	23
Saudi Arabia	47	38	29	25	15	26	18	32
South Africa	57	60	20	21	18	19	20	15
Spain	60	56	17	21	26	24	23	20
Sri Lanka	77	64	10	18	23	25	17	24
Thailand	57	54	9	13	41	22	33	30
Turkey	69	72	11	15	24	15	24	13
UK	63	65	20	23	20	14	16	12
USA	67	71	17	17	18	14	15	10

Source : *World Development Indicators 2011.*

259 : Agricultural Inputs: Land

	Land Area (thousand sq km)		Arable Land (hectares per 100 person)		Agricultural Land (% of land area)	
	2009	Share in %	1990	2008	1990	2008
World	**129562**	**100.0**	**22.2**	**20.7**	**10.1**	**11.8**
Russian Federation	16377	12.6	0.0	85.7	8.2	7.5
China	9328	7.2	10.9	8.2	14.1	13.1
United States	9147	7.1	74.4	56.0	20.5	18.9
Canada	9094	7.0	163.7	135.4	5.7	5.8
Brazil	8460	6.5	33.9	31.8	6.8	8.1
Australia	7682	5.9	280.7	205.4	6.2	5.7
India	**2973**	**2.3**	**19.2**	**13.9**	**57.0**	**57.0**
Argentina	2737	2.1	81.2	80.2	10.0	12.1
Spain	2376	1.8	39.5	27.4	40.4	34.6
Saudi Arabia	2000	1.5	20.9	13.9	1.7	1.8
Mexico	1944	1.5	29.2	23.3	13.5	14.2
Indonesia	1812	1.4	11.4	9.7	17.7	20.4
Peru	1280	1.0	16.1	12.7	3.0	3.5
South Africa	1215	0.9	38.2	29.7	11.8	12.7
Egypt, Arab Rep.	996	0.8	4.0	3.4	2.7	3.6
Pakistan	771	0.6	19.0	12.2	27.2	27.5
Turkey	770	0.6	43.9	29.2	35.9	31.8
Chile	744	0.6	21.2	7.5	4.1	2.3
France	548	0.4	31.7	29.3	35.1	35.3
Thailand	511	0.4	30.9	22.6	40.3	36.9
Japan	365	0.3	3.9	3.4	14.4	12.7
Germany	349	0.3	15.1	14.5	35.6	34.8
Malaysia	329	0.3	9.4	6.7	21.2	23.1
Philippines	298	0.2	8.8	5.9	33.2	34.6
Italy	294	0.2	15.9	11.9	40.7	33.2
United Kingdom	242	0.2	11.6	9.8	20.5	18.9
Nepal	143	0.1	12.0	8.2	16.5	17.2
Bangladesh	130	0.1	7.9	4.9	72.5	66.8
Korea, Rep. of	97	0.1	4.6	3.2	21.4	17.9
Sri Lanka	63	0.0	5.3	5.2	30.3	35.0

Note : Countries arranged according to their share in world land area in descending order.

Source : *World Development Indicators 2011.*

260 : Agricultural Inputs and Mechanisation

	Fertiliser Consumption (kg/hectare of arable land)	Land under Cereal Production (million hectares)		Tractors per 100 sq km of Arable Land	
	2008	1990	2009	1990	2008
World	**119**	**708.1**	**708.5**	**186**	**na**
India	**154**	**102.5**	**99.8**	**61**	**na**
China	468	93.6	88.6	67	277
United States	103	65.7	58.0	238	258
Russian Federation	16	59.5	41.8	98	30
Brazil	166	18.5	20.2	144	129
Australia	34	13.4	19.8	na	na
Indonesia	189	13.7	17.0	2	na
Canada	57	21.5	14.9	165	163
Pakistan	163	11.9	13.7	130	205
Thailand	131	10.5	12.3	33	na
Bangladesh	165	11.1	12.0	2	4
Turkey	89	13.6	12.0	280	489
Mexico	45	10.5	10.2	124	97
France	146	9.1	9.4	800	635
Argentina	39	9.0	8.0	100	na
Philippines	131	7.1	7.2	65	na
Germany	160	6.9	6.9	1309	646
Spain	107	7.6	6.0	483	824
Italy	156	4.4	3.5	1587	na
Nepal	8	3.0	3.4	22	123
South Africa	50	6.2	3.3	108	na
United Kingdom	208	3.7	3.2	761	na
Egypt, Arab Rep.	724	2.3	3.1	250	372
Japan	278	2.5	1.9	4493	4382
Peru	82	0.7	1.3	36	na
Korea, Rep. of	480	1.4	1.0	211	1633
Sri Lanka	284	0.9	1.0	na	na
Malaysia	930	0.7	0.7	153	na
Chile	589	0.8	0.6	128	426
Saudi Arabia	75	1.0	0.5	19	na

Note : na : not available.
Countries arranged in descending order of share in land under cereal production in descending order.

Source : *World Development Indicators.*

261 : Top Ten Rice/Paddy Producing Countries

(million tonnes)

Countries	2001 Production	2001 Share (%)	2001 Rank	2008 Production	2008 Share (%)	2008 Rank
World	**598.2**	**100.0**		**689.1**	**100.0**	
China	179.3	30.0	1	193.4	28.1	1
India	**139.9**	**23.4**	**2**	**148.8**	**21.6**	**2**
Indonesia	50.5	8.4	3	60.3	8.8	3
Bangladesh	36.3	6.1	4	46.7	6.8	4
Vietnam	32.1	5.4	5	38.7	5.6	5
Thailand	26.5	4.4	6	31.7	4.6	6
Mynamar	21.9	3.7	7	32.6	4.7	7
Philippines	13.0	2.2	8	16.8	2.4	8
Brazil	10.2	1.7	10	12.1	1.8	9
Japan	11.3	1.9	9	11.0	1.6	10

Source : Food and Agriculture Organization.

262 : Top Ten Wheat Producing Countries

(million tonnes)

Countries	2001 Production	2001 Share (%)	2001 Rank	2008 Production	2008 Share (%)	2008 Rank
World	**589.8**	**100.0**		**683.1**	**100.0**	
China	93.9	15.9	1	112.5	16.5	1
India	**69.7**	**11.8**	**2**	**78.6**	**11.5**	**2**
USA	53.0	9.0	3	68.0	10.0	3
Russia	47.0	8.0	5	63.8	9.3	4
France	31.5	5.3	4	39.0	5.7	5
Canada	20.6	3.5	9	28.6	4.2	6
Germany	22.8	3.9	7	26.0	3.8	7
Pakistan	19.0	3.2	10	21.0	3.1	8
Turkey	19.0	3.2	11	17.8	2.6	9
Argentina	15.4	2.6	12	8.5	1.2	10

Source : Food and Agriculture Organization.

263 : Top Five Cotton Producing Countries

(million tonnes)

	2001		2008	
Countries	Production	Rank	Production	Rank
China	5.3	1	7.5	1
India	**1.7**	**4**	**3.8**	**2**
USA	4.4	2	2.8	3
Pakistan	1.8	3	2.0	4
Brazil	0.9	7	1.3	5

Source : Food and Agriculture Organization.

264 : Top Five Groundnut Producing Countries

(million tonnes)

	2001		2008	
Countries	Production	Rank	Production	Rank
China	14.5	1	14.3	1
India	**7.0**	**2**	**7.2**	**2**
Nigeria	2.7	3	2.9	3
USA	1.9	4	2.3	4
Indonesia	1.2	5	1.3	5

Source : Food and Agriculture Organization.

265 : Top Five Sugarcane Producing Countries

(million tonnes)

	2001		2008	
Countries	Production	Rank	Production	Rank
Brazil	345.9	1	645.3	1
India	**296.0**	**2**	**348.2**	**2**
China	78.0	3	124.9	3
Thailand	49.6	4	73.5	4
Pakistan	43.6	6	63.9	5

Source : Food and Agriculture Organization.

266 : Revenue, Expenditure and Fiscal Balance

Countries	% of GDP					
	Revenue		Expenditure		Fiscal Balance	
	1995	2009	1995	2009	1995	2009
World	**na**	**24.3**	**na**	**31.1**	**na**	**-(7.1)**
Argentina	na		na		na	
Australia	na	24.6	na	26.6	na	(2.4)
Bangladesh	na	11.1	na	11.3	na	(1.7)
Brazil	26.9	23.1	32.9	25.6	(2.7)	(3.5)
Canada	19.8	17.4	23.8	19.2	(4.0)	(1.9)
Chile	na	20.1	na	22.6	na	(4.5)
China	5.4	11.1	na	na	na	na
Egypt	34.8	27.0	28.1	30.2	3.4	(6.6)
France	43.3	40.5	47.6	47.6	(4.1)	(7.3)
Germany	29.9	29.4	38.6	31.7	(8.3)	(2.2)
India	**12.3**	**11.9**	**14.4**	**16.2**	**(2.2)**	**(4.9)**
Indonesia	15.6	15.4	9.5	15.7	1.7	(1.7)
Italy	40.4	38.5	48.0	44.0	(7.5)	(4.9)
Jamaica	na	27.0	33.3	41.5	na	(15.9)
Japan	na	na	na	na	na	na
Korea, Rep. of	17.8	23.1	14.3	21.9	2.4	0.0
Malaysia	23.3	23.3	18.7	22.7	1.5	(6.4)
Mexico	15.3	na	15.0	na	(0.6)	na
New Zealand	na	36.1	na	32.1	na	3.1
Pakistan	17.2	14.0	19.1	16.8	(5.3)	(4.8)
Philippines	17.7	14.6	15.9	18.6	(0.8)	(3.9)
Russia	na	35.4	na	30.9	na	5.3
Saudi Arabia	na	na	na	na	na	na
South Africa	na	28.2	na	33.0	na	(4.9)
Spain	32.0	22.4	37.1	30.7	(5.8)	(8.6)
Sri Lanka	20.4	14.9	26.0	19.2	(7.6)	(6.6)
Thailand	na	18.6	na	19.6	na	(3.0)
Turkey	17.7	21.8	19.1	27.3	(1.8)	(5.5)
UK	35.2	35.9	40.4	46.4	(5.5)	(10.9)
USA	27.6	15.9	27.1	26.3	(1.2)	(10.4)

Note : na : not available.
Source : *World Development Indicators 2011.*

267 : Consumer Price Inflation

Countries	Average Annual Price Increase (%)			Annual Increase (%)				
	1981-1990	1991-2000	2001-2010	2006	2007	2008	2009	2010
World	16.0	12.2		3.6	3.9	5.9		
Argentina	787.0	22.2	9.7	10.9	8.8	8.6	6.3	10.5
Australia	3.4	2.0	1.9	1.7	2.2	3.2	0.4	1.7
Bangladesh	10.8	5.6	6.3	6.8	9.1	8.9	5.4	8.2
Brazil	613.8	560.7	6.7	4.2	3.6	5.7	4.9	5.0
Canada	6.0	2.0	2.0	2.0	2.1	2.4	0.3	1.8
Chile	20.5	9.5	3.3	3.4	4.4	8.7	1.7	1.5
China	7.2	7.5	2.2	1.5	4.8	5.9	-0.7	3.3
Egypt	17.6	9.0	8.0	4.2	11.0	11.7	16.2	11.7
France	6.4	1.8	1.9	1.9	1.6	3.2	0.1	1.7
Germany	2.6	2.3	1.6	1.8	2.3	2.8	0.2	1.2
India	**8.9**	**9.1**	**6.5**	**6.2**	**6.4**	**8.3**	**10.9**	**13.2**
Indonesia	4.6	14.0	8.5	13.1	6.0	9.8	4.8	5.1
Italy	9.9	3.7	2.2	2.2	2.0	3.5	0.8	1.6
Japan	2.1	0.8	-0.3	0.3	0.0	1.4	-1.4	-0.7
Korea, Rep. of	6.4	5.1	3.2	2.2	2.5	4.7	2.8	3.0
Mexico	69.1	18.7	4.7	3.6	4.0	5.1	5.3	4.2
Nepal	10.6	9.3	6.3	4.5	8.0	6.4	7.7	13.0
Pakistan	7.0	9.1	8.4	7.9	7.8	12.0	20.8	11.7
Philippines	13.7	8.7	5.2	6.2	2.8	9.3	3.2	3.8
Poland	117.5	27.3	2.8	1.0	2.5	4.2	3.5	2.6
Russia	0.0	197.1	12.6	9.7	9.0	14.1	11.7	6.9
South Africa	14.7	9.0	6.0	4.7	7.1	11.5	7.1	4.3
Spain	9.4	4.0	2.8	3.6	2.8	4.1	-0.2	2.0
Sri Lanka	12.4	9.7	11.0	10.0	15.8	22.6	3.4	5.9
Thailand	2.9	4.5	2.6	4.6	2.2	5.5	-0.8	3.3
Turkey	46.4	76.4	18.5	9.6	8.8	10.4	6.3	8.6
United Arab Emirates	4.2	3.6	5.5	9.3	11.1	12.3	1.6	0.9
United Kingdom	6.0	2.7	2.1	2.3	2.3	3.6	2.1	3.3
United States	4.7	2.8	2.4	3.2	2.9	3.8	-0.3	1.6

Source : IMF Data Base.

268 : Financial Development Index: 2008

Countries	Overall Index		Factors, Policies and Institutions					
	Score	Rank among 52 Countries	Institutional Environment		Business Environment		Financial Stability	
			Score	Rank	Score	Rank	Score	Rank
Argentina	3.04	47	3.35	45	3.92	39	2.92	50
Australia	4.98	11	5.94	13	5.24	14	5.13	21
Brazil	3.28	40	3.69	40	4.00	37	3.60	44
Canada	5.26	5	6.06	7	5.43	8	5.26	14
Chile	3.79	30	5.38	21	4.89	22	4.47	31
China	4.09	24	3.33	46	4.07	35	5.17	19
Egypt	3.32	37	4.07	35	3.91	40	3.41	47
France	5.25	6	5.83	16	5.20	15	5.17	20
Germany	5.28	3	6.08	6	5.41	10	5.77	6
India	**3.63**	**31**	**3.42**	**43**	**3.61**	**45**	**4.67**	**28**
Indonesia	3.31	38	4.46	29	3.46	49	3.65	43
Italy	4.38	22	4.66	26	4.63	29	4.82	24
Japan	5.28	4	5.88	14	5.17	16	5.71	8
Korea, Rep. of	4.55	19	5.08	23	5.42	9	4.42	32
Malaysia	4.48	20	5.14	22	4.80	23	5.18	18

contd...

...contd...

Countries	Overall Index		Factors, Policies and Institutions					
	Score	Rank among 52 Countries	Institutional Environment		Business Environment		Financial Stability	
			Score	Rank	Score	Rank	Score	Rank
Mexico	3.21	43	4.31	31	3.81	44	4.69	27
Pakistan	3.46	34	3.09	49	3.46	50	4.11	37
Philippines	3.03	48	3.60	41	3.50	48	3.32	48
Russia	3.40	36	3.10	48	4.08	34	4.41	33
Saudi Arabia	3.90	27	4.18	33	4.54	31	5.97	3
South Africa	4.00	25	4.58	27	4.03	36	4.72	26
Spain	4.90	12	5.62	19	4.80	24	5.00	22
Thailand	3.82	29	4.46	29	4.24	33	4.54	29
Turkey	3.30	39	3.36	44	4.38	32	2.73	52
UK	5.83	2	6.09	5	5.34	11	4.97	23
USA	5.85	1	5.98	12	5.32	12	5.51	10

Note: Financial Development Index captures the factors, policies and institutions that lead to effective financial intermediation and markets and deep and broad access to capital and financial services.

Source: The Financial Development Report 2008, World Economic Forum.

269 : Financial Development Index: 2008

	Financial Intermediation						Capital Availability Size, Depth and Access	
	Banks		Non-Banks		Financial Markets			
Countries	Score	Rank	Score	Rank	Score	Rank	Score	Rank
Argentina	2.85	46	2.48	22	2.18	37	3.54	46
Australia	4.12	21	4.26	6	4.58	8	5.60	14
Brazil	2.47	52	2.82	21	2.28	34	4.10	37
Canada	5.15	6	4.37	5	4.07	13	6.47	5
Chile	3.72	30	1.68	44	2.10	40	4.27	35
China	4.97	7	3.30	15	2.66	30	5.14	24
Egypt	3.40	34	1.75	41	2.15	38	4.58	31
France	4.55	14	5.29	3	5.07	4	5.66	11
Germany	4.85	9	4.12	7	4.87	7	5.84	9
India	**2.61**	**50**	**3.24**	**16**	**2.99**	**22**	**4.90**	**28**
Indonesia	4.60	13	1.58	46	1.70	46	3.72	42
Italy	4.41	16	3.35	14	3.83	15	4.97	25
Japan	4.92	8	4.50	4	5.03	5	5.72	10
Korea, Rep. of	4.81	11	3.62	11	3.15	20	5.33	20
Malaysia	5.72	2	1.93	35	2.93	23	5.65	12
Mexico	2.65	49	1.88	38	1.77	45	3.37	48
Pakistan	3.91	25	1.73	42	3.58	17	4.33	33
Philippines	2.96	42	1.78	40	1.97	42	4.07	38
Russia	2.87	45	3.71	10	2.08	41	3.56	45
Saudi Arabia	4.07	23	1.40	49	2.73	29	4.43	32
South Africa	4.09	22	2.42	23	2.83	28	5.30	21
Spain	4.84	10	3.77	9	3.86	14	6.38	6
Thailand	4.45	15	1.89	37	2.25	36	4.95	26
Turkey	3.32	37	2.19	28	3.07	21	4.04	39
UK	5.51	3	6.55	1	5.87	2	6.48	4
USA	5.80	1	6.05	2	6.15	1	6.15	8

Note : Financial Development Index captures the factors, policies and institutions that lead to effective financial intermediation and markets and deep and broad access to capital and financial services.

Source : The Financial Development Report 2008, World Economic Forum.

270 : Exports (billion US dollars)

Countries	Decadal Averages					
	1991-2000			2001-2010		
	US $ Bn	Growth (%)	Share (%)	US $ Bn	Growth (%)	Share (%)
World	**4878.9**	**6.5**	**100.0**	**10828.9**	**9.7**	**100.0**
Argentina	20.0	8.5	0.4	45.0	10.3	0.4
Australia	52.7	5.1	1.1	121.0	13.9	1.1
Bangladesh	3.1	11.5	0.1	8.6	11.9	0.1
Brazil	45.1	6.0	0.9	125.8	15.1	1.2
Canada	191.0	8.2	3.9	340.7	4.5	3.1
Chile	14.2	9.5	0.3	45.0	15.9	0.4
China	148.0	15.4	3.0	878.1	21.3	8.1
Egypt	3.5	2.4	0.1	13.9	20.8	0.1
France	266.9	3.7	5.5	447.5	6.3	4.1
Germany	483.4	3.3	9.9	1011.6	9.5	9.3
India	**29.4**	**9.3**	**0.6**	**117.8**	**18.7**	**1.1**
Indonesia	45.9	10.2	0.9	97.7	10.1	0.9
Italy	215.5	3.8	4.4	384.0	7.3	3.5
Jamaica	1.2	1.5	0.0	1.6	2.8	0.0
Japan	397.5	5.5	8.1	595.0	6.1	5.5
Korea, Rep. of	116.6	10.6	2.4	299.2	11.4	2.8
Malaysia	66.8	13.3	1.4	145.0	8.5	1.3
Mexico	90.8	15.4	1.9	223.0	6.9	2.1
New Zealand	12.2	3.9	0.3	22.2	9.2	0.2
Pakistan	8.0	5.2	0.2	15.4	9.5	0.1
Philippines	21.2	17.4	0.4	42.2	3.8	0.4
Russia	74.8	14.1	1.5	258.5	16.8	2.4
Saudi Arabia	52.2	8.4	1.1	162.3	20.4	1.5
South Africa	26.7	2.7	0.5	55.0	11.9	0.5
Spain	88.7	7.7	1.8	197.3	8.8	1.8
Sri Lanka	3.8	11.3	0.1	6.5	4.8	0.1
Thailand	49.5	12.1	1.0	122.8	11.7	1.1
Turkey	21.4	8.1	0.4	79.2	16.3	0.7
UK	236.8	4.5	4.9	365.9	4.5	3.4
USA	590.6	7.2	12.1	970.9	5.7	9.0

Note : Figures in brackets are average annual growth rate.

Source : International Financial Statistics Year Book, IMF & UNO, International Merchandise Trade Statistics.

271 : Imports

(billion US dollars)

Countries	Decadal Averages					
	1991-2000			2001-2010		
	US $ Bn	Growth (%)	Share (%)	US $ Bn	Growth (%)	Share (%)
World	**4996.5**	**6.6**	**100.0**	**11018.6**	**9.6**	**100.0**
Argentina	21.8	24.7	0.4	31.8	13.8	0.3
Australia	58.2	5.6	1.2	133.3	11.9	1.2
Bangladesh	5.9	9.4	0.1	15.3	12.9	0.1
Brazil	45.7	11.4	0.9	103.3	15.1	0.9
Canada	176.3	7.2	3.5	313.2	3.6	2.8
Chile	15.2	10.1	0.3	36.0	14.4	0.3
China	130.8	16.1	2.6	745.1	21.0	6.8
Egypt	11.9	1.1	0.2	26.3	17.4	0.2
France	264.1	3.3	5.3	496.6	7.5	4.5
Germany	433.3	4.0	8.7	823.7	8.8	7.5
India	**34.9**	**8.7**	**0.7**	**173.2**	**21.8**	**1.6**
Indonesia	35.0	7.9	0.7	76.8	14.8	0.7
Italy	199.0	3.3	4.0	393.6	8.4	3.6
Jamaica	2.6	6.2	0.1	4.8	6.2	0.0
Japan	298.2	5.5	6.0	524.4	7.5	4.8
Korea, Rep. of	115.3	10.8	2.3	280.7	11.7	2.5
Malaysia	62.3	12.3	1.2	118.6	8.5	1.1
Mexico	101.5	15.9	2.0	232.0	6.6	2.1
New Zealand	12.3	4.5	0.2	24.3	8.9	0.2
Pakistan	10.2	4.7	0.2	25.2	15.0	0.2
Philippines	27.2	11.8	0.5	47.7	5.5	0.4
Russia	51.2	5.3	1.0	133.9	25.7	1.2
Saudi Arabia	28.7	3.1	0.6	67.2	13.4	0.6
South Africa	26.1	5.5	0.5	57.8	13.6	0.5
Spain	115.3	6.3	2.3	280.3	8.8	2.5
Sri Lanka	5.0	9.1	0.1	9.5	9.2	0.1
Thailand	54.0	8.1	1.1	118.3	12.9	1.1
Turkey	36.5	11.5	0.7	121.5	15.7	1.1
UK	268.9	4.3	5.4	483.0	6.1	4.4
USA	811.0	9.4	16.2	1662.4	5.5	15.1

Note : Figures in brackets are average annual growth rate.

Source : International Financial Statistics Year Book, IMF & UNO, International Merchandise Trade Statistics.

272 : Foreign Trade: Annual Growth (%)

	Imports			Exports		
	2008	2009	2010	2008	2009	2010
World	**15.5**	**-23.1**	**20.6**	**15.8**	**-22.6**	**20.5**
Argentina	28.4	-31.9	22.9	26.5	-20.6	15.4
Australia	21.3	-17.5	21.9	32.7	-17.8	38.0
Bangladesh	30.2	-8.2	26.4	15.1	5.7	14.1
Brazil	44.0	-26.7	43.2	23.2	-22.7	32.0
Canada	7.2	-21.3	21.9	8.6	-30.6	22.9
Chile	31.3	-31.2	38.5	-1.8	-18.7	31.5
China	18.3	-11.3	38.9	17.3	-15.9	31.3
Egypt	80.2	-7.9	17.7	62.0	-12.1	14.6
France	13.2	-22.1	7.6	10.5	-22.0	9.5
Germany	12.4	-22.0	15.3	9.6	-22.8	13.4
India	**40.0**	**-19.9**	**25.8**	**29.7**	**-15.3**	**31.5**
Indonesia	36.9	-26.4	40.8	18.3	-14.3	31.9
Italy	10.5	-26.4	17.3	9.0	-25.4	10.0
Jamaica	21.0	-37.2	7.0	22.8	-48.1	0.9
Japan	23.1	-27.8	25.8	9.5	-25.7	32.6
Korea, Rep. of	22.0	-25.8	31.7	13.6	-14.3	29.0
Malaysia	12.0	-24.8	33.2	19.1	-24.9	26.2
Mexico	9.6	-24.5	28.6	7.3	-21.3	29.8
New Zealand	11.0	-26.4	16.8	13.9	-18.9	21.0
Pakistan	29.9	-25.2	19.4	13.9	-13.8	22.2
Philippines	4.8	-24.4	27.3	-2.1	-22.1	34.3
Russia	33.7	-37.3	37.2	32.9	-35.5	31.8
Saudi Arabia	27.6	-17.0	1.6	34.3	na	na
South Africa	18.8	-32.1	24.4	21.1	-25.9	30.6
Spain	9.0	-30.3	8.5	12.5	-20.5	11.5
Sri Lanka	23.5	-26.8	32.4	5.1	-12.9	17.2
Thailand	26.5	-24.5	36.9	14.3	-13.6	28.5
Turkey	18.8	-30.2	31.7	23.1	-22.6	11.6
UK	3.1	-24.3	15.7	7.7	-23.9	15.0
USA	7.4	-26.0	22.6	11.9	-18.8	20.9

Note : na : not available.

Source : International Financial Statistics Year Book, IMF & UNO, International Merchandise Trade Statistics.

273 : Indicator of Trade Openness

Country	Trade (Export+Import) (US $ billion)			Trade Openness (Trade as % to GDP)		
	1990	2000	2010	1990	2000	2010
Argentina	16.4	51.5	112.8	11.62	18.12	30.58
Australia	81.7	135.4	414.0	25.73	34.72	44.76
Bangladesh	5.3	13.2	40.3	17.34	28.06	40.24
Brazil	53.9	113.7	393.4	10.62	17.65	18.84
Canada	250.9	521.4	776.5	43.05	71.93	49.33
Chile	16.1	37.7	130.0	51.06	50.13	63.89
China	115.4	474.3	2973.0	29.58	39.58	50.57
Egypt	21.7	18.7	79.4	23.79	18.86	36.25
France	451.0	612.5	1118.9	36.12	45.94	43.71
Germany	756.3	1045.5	2339.4	48.88	54.86	70.68
India	**41.5**	**93.9**	**540.5**	**13.24**	**20.32**	**31.26**
Indonesia	47.5	108.5	289.9	37.79	65.55	41.03
Italy	352.5	477.9	934.1	31.04	43.42	45.53
Jamaica	3.1	4.6	6.5	60.95	51.05	32.64
Japan	522.9	858.7	1462.6	17.10	18.40	26.60
Korea, Rep. of	134.9	332.8	891.6	49.04	62.39	87.89
Malaysia	58.7	180.2	363.5	133.35	192.16	152.87
Mexico	84.3	349.1	599.6	32.07	55.51	57.67
New Zealand	18.9	27.2	59.6	42.78	51.94	47.06
Pakistan	13.0	19.9	59.2	26.88	26.86	33.86
Philippines	21.1	76.8	109.7	47.82	101.17	54.94
Russia	0.0	154.7	627.3	..	59.55	42.39
Saudi Arabia	68.5	107.8	97.1	58.65	57.12	25.83
South Africa	42.0	59.7	162.0	37.47	44.90	44.53
Spain	143.1	266.2	561.8	27.48	45.71	39.92
Sri Lanka	4.6	11.7	21.8	55.37	69.45	44.03
Thailand	56.1	131.0	380.0	65.52	106.71	119.17
Turkey	35.3	82.3	299.5	17.42	30.88	40.74
UK	409.7	616.0	971.7	40.25	41.60	43.26
USA	910.6	2041.2	3245.7	15.70	20.51	22.26

Note: Trade openness worked out by EPWRF.
Source: International Monetary Fund.

274 : Foreign Direct Investment: Inflow (million US dollar)

Countries	Inflow 1990		2000		2010	
World	**207455**	**(100.0)**	**1402680**	**(100.0)**	**1243671**	**(100.0)**
Argentina	1836	(0.9)	10418	(0.7)	6337	(0.5)
Australia	8479	(4.1)	15612	(1.1)	32472	(2.6)
Bangladesh	3	(0.0)	579	(0.0)	913	(0.1)
Brazil	989	(0.5)	32779	(2.3)	48438	(3.9)
Canada	7582	(3.7)	66795	(4.8)	23413	(1.9)
Chile	661	(0.3)	4860	(0.3)	15095	(1.2)
China	3487	(1.7)	40715	(2.9)	105735	(8.5)
Egypt	734	(0.4)	1235	(0.1)	6386	(0.5)
France	15614	(7.5)	43250	(3.1)	33905	(2.7)
Germany	2962	(1.4)	198277	(14.1)	46134	(3.7)
India	**237**	**(0.1)**	**3588**	**(0.3)**	**24640**	**(2.0)**
Indonesia	1092	(0.5)	-4495	-(0.3)	13304	(1.1)
Italy	6345	(3.1)	13375	(1.0)	9498	(0.8)
Jamaica	175	(0.1)	469	(0.0)	201	(0.0)
Japan	1806	(0.9)	8323	(0.6)	-1251	-(0.1)
Korea, Rep. of	759	(0.4)	9004	(0.6)	6873	(0.6)
Malaysia	2611	(1.3)	3788	(0.3)	9103	(0.7)
Mexico	2633	(1.3)	18110	(1.3)	18679	(1.5)
Nepal	6	(0.0)	0	(0.0)	39	(0.0)
New Zealand	1685	(0.8)	1347	(0.1)	561	(0.0)
Pakistan	278	(0.1)	309	(0.0)	2016	(0.2)
Philippines	550	(0.3)	2240	(0.2)	1713	(0.1)
Peru	41	(0.0)	810	(0.1)	7328	(0.6)
Russia	0	(0.0)	2714	(0.2)	41194	(3.3)
Saudi Arabia	312	(0.2)	183	(0.0)	28105	(2.3)
South Africa	-78	(0.0)	887	(0.1)	1553	(0.1)
Spain	13294	(6.4)	39575	(2.8)	24547	(2.0)
Sri Lanka	43	(0.0)	173	(0.0)	478	(0.0)
Turkey	684	(0.3)	982	(0.1)	90771	(7.3)
Thailand	2575	(1.2)	3410	(0.2)	5813	(0.5)
UK	30461	(14.7)	118764	(8.5)	45908	(3.7)
USA	48422	(23.3)	314007	(22.4)	228249	(18.4)

Note : Figures in brackets are percentages to total.

Source : *World Investment Report 2011*, UNCTAD.

275 : Foreign Direct Investment: Outflow (million US dollar)

Countries	Outflow					
	1990		2000		2010	
World	**241498**	**(100.0)**	**1232117**	**(100.0)**	**1323337**	**(100.0)**
Argentina	35	(0.0)	901	(0.1)	964	(0.1)
Australia	624	(0.3)	7221	(0.6)	26431	(2.0)
Bangladesh	1	(0.0)	2	(0.0)	15	(0.0)
Brazil	625	(0.3)	2282	(0.2)	11519	(0.9)
Canada	5237	(2.2)	44678	(3.6)	68585	(5.2)
Chile	8	(0.0)	3987	(0.3)	8744	(0.7)
China	830	(0.3)	916	(0.1)	68000	(5.1)
Egypt	12	(0.0)	51	(0.0)	1176	(0.1)
France	36233	(15.0)	177449	(14.4)	84112	(6.4)
Germany	24235	(10.0)	56557	(4.6)	104857	(7.9)
India	**6**	**(0.0)**	**514**	**(0.0)**	**14626**	**(1.1)**
Indonesia	-11	(0.0)	150	(0.0)	2664	(0.2)
Italy	7614	(3.2)	12316	(1.0)	21005	(1.6)
Jamaica	37	(0.0)	74	(0.0)	67	(0.0)
Japan	50775	(21.0)	31557	(2.6)	56263	(4.3)
Korea, Rep. of	1052	(0.4)	4233	(0.3)	19230	(1.5)
Malaysia	129	(0.1)	2026	(0.2)	13329	(1.0)
Mexico	223	(0.1)	363	(0.0)	14345	(1.1)
Nepal	0	(0.0)	0	(0.0)	0	(0.0)
New Zealand	2363	(1.0)	-1084	-(0.1)	589	(0.0)
Pakistan	2	(0.0)	11	(0.0)	46	(0.0)
Philippines	22	(0.0)	125	(0.0)	487	(0.0)
Peru	50	(0.0)	0	(0.0)	215	(0.0)
Russia	0	(0.0)	3177	(0.3)	51697	(3.9)
Saudi Arabia	-638	-(0.3)	1550	(0.1)	3907	(0.3)
South Africa	27	(0.0)	271	(0.0)	450	(0.0)
Spain	3349	(1.4)	58213	(4.7)	21598	(1.6)
Sri Lanka	1	(0.0)	2	(0.0)	46	(0.0)
Turkey	-16	(0.0)	870	(0.1)	1780	(0.1)
Thailand	154	(0.1)	-20	(0.0)	5122	(0.4)
UK	17948	(7.4)	233371	(18.9)	11020	(0.8)
USA	30982	(12.8)	142626	(11.6)	328905	(24.9)

Note : Figures in brackets are percentages to total.
Source : *World Investment Report 2011*, UNCTAD.

276 : External Sector Sustainability (Current Account Balance as Per cent to GDP)

Country	Decadal Average (%) 1981-1990	1991-2000	2001-2010	2008	2009	2010
Argentina	(1.6)	(3.1)	2.7	1.3	1.8	0.9
Australia	(4.5)	(3.8)	(4.5)	(4.5)	(4.2)	(2.6)
Bangladesh	(3.3)	(1.2)	0.8	1.9	3.3	1.4
Brazil	(2.1)	(2.0)	(0.6)	(1.7)	(1.5)	(2.3)
Canada	(2.3)	(1.3)	0.6	0.4	(2.9)	(3.1)
Chile	(6.4)	(2.4)	1.1	(1.9)	1.6	1.9
China	(0.0)	(1.5)	5.8	9.6	6.0	5.2
Egypt	(4.1)	(1.2)	1.1	0.5	(2.3)	(2.0)
France	(0.6)	1.3	(0.4)	(1.9)	(1.9)	(2.1)
Germany	(2.4)	(1.1)	4.5	6.7	5.0	5.3
India	**(1.9)**	**(1.1)**	**(0.8)**	**(2.0)**	**(2.8)**	**(3.2)**
Indonesia	(3.0)	(0.3)	2.1	0.0	2.6	0.9
Italy	(1.3)	0.7	(1.8)	(2.9)	(2.1)	(3.5)
Jamaica	9.1	3.3	10.5	17.8	10.9	8.1
Japan	2.3	2.5	3.4	3.2	2.8	3.6
Korea, Rep. of	0.9	1.0	2.3	0.3	3.9	2.8
Malaysia	(3.0)	(0.6)	13.3	17.5	16.5	11.8
Mexico	(0.7)	(3.2)	(1.1)	(1.5)	(0.7)	(0.5)
Nepal	(6.6)	(2.3)	2.5	2.7	4.2	(2.7)
New Zealand	(5.2)	(4.6)	(5.3)	(8.7)	(2.9)	(2.2)
Pakistan	(2.5)	(3.1)	(1.5)	(8.5)	(5.7)	(2.3)
Peru	(4.7)	(5.5)	(0.5)	(4.2)	0.2	(1.5)
Philippines	(1.7)	(3.1)	2.3	2.2	5.8	4.5
Russia	0.0	4.3	7.9	6.2	4.1	4.9
Saudi Arabia	(6.1)	(5.9)	16.8	27.8	6.1	8.7
South Africa	0.6	(0.2)	(3.3)	(7.1)	(4.1)	(2.8)
Spain	(1.0)	(1.8)	(6.2)	(9.7)	(5.5)	(4.5)
Sri Lanka	(8.5)	(4.8)	(3.2)	(9.8)	(0.5)	(3.5)
Thailand	(4.1)	(1.1)	3.0	0.8	8.3	4.6
Turkey	(1.0)	(1.1)	(3.6)	(5.7)	(2.3)	(6.5)
United Kingdom	(1.3)	(1.4)	(2.2)	(1.6)	(1.7)	(2.5)
United States	(1.9)	(1.8)	(4.6)	(4.7)	(2.7)	(3.2)

Note : Current Account Balance is the balance on current transactions excluding exceptional financing. It includes all transactions other than those in capital and financial items. Major classification are goods and services, income and current transfers.

Source : *World Investment Report 2011*, UNCTAD.

277 : Reserves Excluding Gold: Import Ratio—Number of Months

	1990	2000	2006	2007	2008	2009
Argentina	5.7	6.3	7.3	8.4	6.9	9.4
Bangladesh	1.9	1.8	2.6	3.0	2.6	5.0
Brazil	2.7	4.2	6.7	10.9	8.5	13.2
Chile	7.1	6.9	3.5	2.6	3.1	4.7
China	8.5	7.4	14.5	17.0	18.2	25
Colombia	6.1	6.1	4.9	5.3	5.0	6.1
Egypt	2.7	6.9	7.4	7.0	6.0	7.4
India	**2.0**	**6.1**	**8.9**	**11.2**	**7.9**	**10.5**
Indonesia	3.1	5.3	4.6	5.3	3.8	6.1
Jamaica	0.7	2.5	3.4	2.3	1.9	3.4
Kazakhstan	na	2.4	5.2	3.4	3.3	5.2
Malaysia	3.6	3.3	6.2	6.7	5.6	7.5
Mexico	1.9	2.0	3.0	3.2	3.2	4.3
Pakistan	1.1	1.7	4.0	4.4	2.0	4.2
Peru	3.8	8.8	7.8	9.8	8.4	11.5
Philippines	1.5	3.5	4.2	5.6	6.0	8.7
Russia	na	4.6	13.6	16.0	10.7	16.0
Romania	1.7	2.8	6.0	5.8	4.8	8.5
South Africa	na	2.4	3.2	3.4	3.3	5.2
Sri Lanka	1.7	1.6	2.8	3.1	1.9	4.7
Thailand	4.4	5.1	5.1	5.9	6.1	9.8
Turkey	3.2	4.2	4.8	4.8	3.9	5.5
Ukraine	na	0.9	4.8	5.1	3.5	5
Venezuela	11.9	7.4	9	6.5	7.7	7.8

Note : na : not available.
Source : *Global Development Finance 2011.*

278 : External Debt and Sustainability Indicator

	Stock of External Debt (US$ bn)			External Debt to National Income (%)		
	1990	2000	2009	1990	2000	2009
Argentina	62.2	140.9	120.2	46.0	50.9	40.1
Bangladesh	12.3	15.5	23.8	39.9	31.8	24.0
Brazil	119.7	241.6	276.9	26.6	38.5	17.9
China	55.3	145.7	428.4	15.4	12.3	8.7
Chile	19.2	37.3	71.6	64.5	51.5	46.7
Colombia	17.2	33.9	52.2	45.1	37.0	23.6
Egypt	33.0	29.0	33.3	78.5	28.8	17.6
India	**85.7**	**100.2**	**237.7**	**27.3**	**22.0**	**18.2**
Indonesia	69.9	143.4	157.5	64.0	95.4	30.2
Jamaica	4.8	4.7	11.0	114.5	54.5	77.8
Kazakhstan	na	12.4	109.9	na	84.5	113.0
Malaysia	15.3	41.9	66.4	36.4	48.6	35.8
Mexico	104.4	150.9	192.0	41.1	26.6	22.3
Nepal	1.6	2.9	3.7	44.7	52.0	28.7
Pakistan	20.6	32.7	53.7	49.3	44.8	31.3
Peru	20.0	28.6	29.6	78.6	55.2	24.8
Philippines	30.6	58.3	62.9	69.4	72.3	39.2
Russia	58.7	160.0	381.3	11.4	63.2	31.9
Romania	1.1	11.2	117.5	3.0	30.4	71.6
South Africa	na	24.9	42.1	na	19.2	15.1
Sri Lanka	5.9	9.1	17.2	73.5	56.8	41.5
Thailand	28.1	79.7	58.8	33.3	66.0	23.3
Turkey	49.4	116.6	251.4	23.5	44.4	41.2
Ukraine	na	12.2	93.2	na	40.2	83.8
Venezuela	33.2	42.3	54.5	71.7	30.2	16.7

Note : na : not available.
Data for India pertains to financial year and not calender year.

Source : *Global Development Finance 2011.*

279 : Short-Term Debt Indicators

	Short-Term Debt to Total Debt (%)			Short-Term Debt to Reserves (%)		
	1990	2000	2009	1990	2000	2009
Argentina	16.9	20.1	16.2	168.8	112.5	40.6
Bangladesh	1.3	2.2	8.1	23.6	22.0	18.7
Brazil	19.8	12.8	14.4	257.8	93.8	16.7
China	16.8	9.0	56.1	27.0	7.6	9.8
Chile	17.6	16.5	24.4	49.9	41.0	69.1
Colombia	8.4	8.5	7.9	29.5	31.9	16.4
Egypt	13.5	14.2	7.7	123.0	29.8	7.3
India	**10.0**	**3.5**	**18.1**	**151.6**	**8.4**	**15.1**
Indonesia	15.9	15.1	11.8	128.6	73.9	28.2
Jamaica	7.2	16.9	9.6	206.0	75.2	50.7
Kazakhstan	na	3.1	7.9	na	18.2	37.4
Malaysia	12.5	10.9	35.7	17.9	16.0	24.5
Mexico	15.4	12.5	12.2	157.4	53.2	23.4
Nepal	1.5	1.0	1.2	6.8	2.9	na
Pakistan	15.5	4.6	2.7	304.5	72.8	10.8
Peru	26.7	13.7	16.0	281.9	45.3	14.2
Philippines	14.5	9.4	6.4	217.4	36.5	9.1
Russia	20.1	9.8	8.0	na	56.5	7.0
Romania	82.7	6.8	17.9	66.2	22.5	45.9
South Africa	na	38.4	31.5	na	124.0	33.5
Sri Lanka	6.9	7.5	10.9	90.6	60.6	39.0
Thailand	29.6	18.7	47.5	58.4	45.6	20.1
Turkey	19.2	24.8	15.8	124.6	123.0	53.0
Ukraine	na	3.7	21.3	na	30.3	75.0
Venezuela	6.0	19.4	29.4	15.7	51.5	46.6

Note: na : not available.
Source: *Global Development Finance 2011.*

280 : Solvency Indicators

	Debt Service Ratio			Interest Service Ratio		
	1990	2000	2009	1990	2000	2009
Argentina	37.0	69.4	17.3	16.3	28.8	4.8
Bangladesh	34.5	10.5	5.6	9.2	2.7	1.3
Brazil	22.5	95.1	23.4	6.2	25.1	7.5
China	11.7	9.3	2.9	5.4	2.5	0.5
Chile	25.9	24.8	22.6	16.7	9.0	2.5
Colombia	43.1	30.3	22.4	18.8	13.1	7.4
Egypt	28.6	9.8	6.4	12.3	3.9	1.9
India	**34.9**	**17.5**	**5.9**	**20.5**	**6.7**	**2.0**
Indonesia	33.5	22.7	18.4	13.4	10.1	3.3
Jamaica	28.4	18.6	33.9	11.2	6.9	17.5
Kazakhstan	na	32.2	80.2	na	7.4	8.0
Malaysia	12.6	5.6	5.2	3.4	2.0	1.1
Mexico	21.7	31.5	16.0	14.0	7.6	4.1
Nepal	15.2	7.5	10.4	6.3	2.3	2.0
Pakistan	27.4	27.9	15.0	12.0	9.6	4.4
Peru	11.0	27.8	11.8	5.7	15.5	4.2
Philippines	27.6	16.0	18.5	13.6	6.8	6.6
Russia	na	9.9	17.7	na	4.7	4.8
Romania	0.3	20.1	31.4	0.2	5.6	6.1
South Africa	na	9.8	4.3	na	3.2	1.9
Sri Lanka	16.1	12.1	15.6	7.1	3.8	3.9
Thailand	16.9	16.3	6.8	6.5	5.6	0.9
Turkey	33.8	38.9	41.6	15.5	12.9	7.8
Ukraine	na	18.6	36.2	na	3.6	6.7
Venezuela	23.3	16.8	6.4	15.1	7.8	5.1

Note: na : not available.

Source: *Global Development Finance 2011.*

281 : Real Effective Exchange Rates (Base Year 2005=1000)

	1990	2000	2008	2009	2010
Australia	98.67	80.32	103.42	100.64	115.16
Brazil	149.25	99.77	128.08	128.44	146.90
Canada	112.80	82.29	100.63	96.57	104.95
Chile	89.60	110.73	101.65	100.28	105.72
China, P.R.: Mainland	117.59	108.54	115.29	119.21	118.68
Euro Area	106.44	82.66	104.44	105.80	96.78
Austria	100.15	95.02	100.70	101.48	98.75
Belgium	101.97	91.67	103.85	104.07	100.73
France	105.17	92.66	101.66	101.86	98.75
Germany	102.30	94.32	101.53	102.29	97.32
Greece	85.60	88.07	105.40	106.89	106.73
Italy	115.28	90.18	101.97	103.19	99.40
Netherlands	95.61	88.81	100.73	102.77	99.00
Portugal	82.45	90.35	102.68	102.15	99.94
Spain	107.78	88.82	106.09	106.20	103.69
India*	**na**	**na**	**108.52**	**97.80**	**94.74**
Japan	97.84	126.19	90.07	101.49	102.72
Malaysia	127.79	105.68	106.12	103.14	108.79
Mexico	83.15	104.69	97.51	85.37	92.72
New Zealand	87.95	72.42	92.02	86.65	94.92
Pakistan	125.38	106.60	97.74	98.40	103.38
Philippines	110.22	108.64	124.48	121.33	126.79
Russia	n.a.	66.66	123.74	115.23	125.94
Saudi Arabia	124.91	121.98	95.90	103.48	104.83
Singapore	102.93	108.90	107.64	107.68	111.37
South Africa	116.34	93.29	80.41	87.64	101.23
United Kingdom	89.69	98.65	92.14	80.77	83.64
United States	95.66	107.79	91.01	95.12	91.41

Note : Real Effective Exchange Rate is the index of the trade weighted average nominal exchange rate, adjusted for changes in the consumer price index. A rise in the index indicates a loss of competitiveness.
* : REER data is with base year 2004-05=100 and is on a financial year basis.

Source : IMF.